Gender and Human Rights Politics in Japan

Global Norms and Domestic Networks

JENNIFER CHAN-TIBERGHIEN

Gender and Human Rights Politics in Japan

Global Norms and Domestic Networks

STANFORD UNIVERSITY PRESS 2004

Stanford, California

Stanford University Press
Stanford, California

Library of Congress Cataloging-in-Publication Data

Chan-Tiberghien, Jennifer
Gender and human rights politics in Japan : global norms and domestic networks / Jennifer Chan-Tiberghien.
p. cm.
Includes bibliographical references and index.
ISBN 0-8047-5022-X (cloth : alk. paper)
1. Women's rights—Japan. 2. Children's rights—Japan. 3. Human rights advocacy—Japan. I. Title.
HQ1236.5.J3C53 2004
305.3'0952 dc22 2004006281

Printed in the United States of America
Original Printing 2004
Last figure below indicates year of this printing:
13 12 11 10 09 08 07 06 05 04

Typeset at Stanford University Press in 10/13 Minion

TO MY MOTHER

—who taught me how to embrace life gracefully—

AND IN MEMORY OF MATSUI YAYORI

—who inspired much of this project.

Acknowledgments

As so many other things in life, this project was rather unintended. I lived in Japan between 1991 and 1994 and worked in the private sector as a financial controller. I thought that the triple discrimination that I experienced there—due to my age, sex, and race—had vaccinated me against a country that I thought was rather uninteresting. I never imagined that I would return to Japan in 1999 as a researcher and would discover a whole new world—the civil society of Japan.

I want to thank, first and foremost, all the members of the Japanese nongovernmental groups that granted me interviews. I had the privilege of meeting Matsui Yayori, the chairperson of Violence against Women in War-Net Japan and founding director of the Asia-Japan Women's Resource Center, and joining her group for both the historic International Symposium on Chinese Comfort Women held in Shanghai in April 2000 and the Women's International War Crimes Tribunal on Japan's Military Sexual Slavery held in Tokyo in December 2000 before her untimely death in December 2002. She leaves behind a flame for all of us who care deeply about women's issues in Japan and Asia. I also want to thank Nakahara Michiko, Nishino Rumiko, and Kim Puja of VAWW-Net Japan; Takahashi Kikue of the Japan Anti-Prostitution Association; Hayashi Yoko of the Japan Civil Liberties Union; Ikeda Eriko of Video-Juku; Katsuki Kyoko of No! Sexual Harassment; and Otani Mikiko of the Japan Federation of Bar Associations, not only for their time and insights, but also for their contacts in the fields of human rights and women's rights.

Only toward the end of my one-year stay in Japan did I realize my blindness to race caused by looking through the lens of gender. I want to thank members of IMADR (International Movement against Discrimination and Racism)—Mushakoji Kinhide, Hanochi Seiko, Kumamoto Risa, Fujioka Mieko, Onoyama Ryo, and Morihara Hideki—for introducing me to the complexities of the minority movements in Japan. I especially want to thank Nakamura Hayato for his continuous help with Japanese documents and Hara Yuriko for arranging my accreditation to attend the Second World Congress against Commercial Sexual Exploitation of Children in Yokohama in 2001 and for her continuous support for my research. Three other academics/activists have also been generous in helping me to understand the racial scenes in Japan: Uemura Hideaki, founding director of the Citizen Diplomatic Center; Kikuzato Yasuko, founding director of the Okinawa Citizen Information Center; and Inaba Nanako of the Solidarity Network with Migrant Workers/Japan. I owe a great deal to Uemura san, in particular, for arranging my accreditation to attend the World Conference against Racism while he led the nongovernmental organizational coalition Durban 2001 Japan to South Africa. I also want to thank Shulamith Koenig, founding director of People's Decade for Human Rights Education, for arranging my accreditation to attend the Beijing-Plus-Five Conference in June 2000.

My fieldwork in Japan would not have been possible without the help of Kawashima Yoko, who arranged my affiliation with the Institute for Gender Studies at Ochanomizu Women's University. I am indebted to Hara Hiroko, director of the institute at the time, for her various introductions as well as institutional support. Six members of parliament—Domoto Akiko, Fukushima Mizuho, Kawahashi Yukiko, Moriyama Mayumi, Owaki Masako, and Shimizu Sumiko—also generously offered their time and insights. I want to thank in particular the legislative aide to Fukushima Mizuho, Saito Fumie, for kindly inviting me to the expert hearings at the Diet and for continuing to provide ample information on gender politics in Japan. I would also like to thank Akamatsu Kyoko, former minister of education; Yasuda Takahiko, director of the Office for Crime Victims of the National Policy Agency; Onishi Tamae, former director of the Office for Gender Equality; and Shimomichi Koji, deputy manager of the Family Assistance Division of the Ministry of Health and Welfare for their kind assistance.

The leap from business to academia was a big one, and it would not have happened without the guidance of my dissertation committee members. In 1996, when I searched left and right for a home department, it was my advisor, Francisco Ramirez, in the Stanford University School of Education, who generously accepted a simple idea—that nongovernmental organizations were pioneers in the field of human rights education—at a time when most human rights work was done either at law schools or departments of political science. Throughout these years, my advisor has never ceased to care, intellectually and otherwise. The simple idea grew into a master's thesis, a doctoral dissertation that won the Gail Kelly Award for Outstanding Dissertation in Comparative and International Education, and then this book. I am indebted to both his wisdom and humor. I also owe John Meyer in the Stanford Department of Sociology a great intellectual debt. I had a rather "neorealist" and "neoliberal" business training prior to Stanford. John Meyer introduced me to the wonderland of cultural constructivism. Despite his new emeritus status and his love for birds, he continues to provide the best and most timely feedback and support for my research. Two other committee members have also influenced the conceptualization of this project. Karen Mundy, who is now the Canada Research Chair in Global Governance and Comparative Education at OISE, University of Toronto, introduced me to the field of politics of education and global governance. Her own intellectual rigor has truly been an inspiring model. Dan Okimoto, director emeritus of the Asia-Pacific Research Center and professor in the Department of Political Science at Stanford University, introduced me to the field of Japanese politics and continues to guide me through its jungle.

Many friends and colleagues at Stanford University provided their warm support throughout my graduate career. I want to thank Christine Min Wotipka, Lynn Murphy, Paula Razquin, Nancy Kendall, and Keiko Inoue in the International Comparative Education program of the Stanford University School of Education; Falu Bakrania, Shelley Correll, Pauline Lee, Patricia Jane Pender, Celine Parreñas Shimizu, and Miriam Iris Ticktin at the Institute on Research on Women and Gender; colleagues at the comparative systems workshop, especially Colette Chabbott and Kiyoteru Tsutsui; and, finally, members of the Gender Forum of the Center for East Asian Studies, especially Helen Young and Connie Chin.

Several friends—Kim Warren, Peter Ninnes, Uemura Hideaki, and Lynn Murphy—courageously read through parts of the manuscript and gave me the motivation to continue writing. I am grateful for the funding support of the Institute of International Studies, Institute on Research on Women and Gender, and School of Education at Stanford University, and for the postdoctoral fellowship offered by the Department of Political Science, as well as the institutional support of the Centre for Research in Women's Studies and Gender Relations at the University of British Columbia. I would especially like to thank Barbara Arneil for her mentorship during my postdoctoral research.

Max Cameron and Peter Dauvergne of the Department of Political Science at the University of British Columbia extended their helping hands in the early stages of the manuscript preparation. Muriel Bell, Carmen Borbon-Wu, John Feneron, and Sharron Wood of Stanford University Press were most diligent and professional in their editorial assistance. Following common practice, all Japanese individuals' names in the main text are written surname first.

Parts of this manuscript appeared originally in my "The Rise of a Women's Human Rights Epistemic Network in the 1990s: Global Norms, Gender Politics and Civil Society," in Errol P. Mendes and Anik Lalonde-Roussy, eds., *Bridging the Global Divide on Human Rights: A Canada-China Dialogue* (Aldershot, Hants.: Ashgate Publishing, 2003). I thank Ashgate Publishing for granting permission to reproduce the material here.

Finally, I want to thank Yves, with whom this exciting journey all started. The past fifteen years were filled with one adventure after another: attending business school together, working in Japan, deciding to quit business, taking off for a sixteen-month backpacking trip around Asia, returning to graduate school, suffering from the same cultural and theoretical shock, witnessing the miraculous birth of our first baby, returning to Japan to do fieldwork with our four-month-old, finding a job, writing, defending our dissertations, and graduating together. It was he who gave me a call one afternoon in Tokyo in 1993, proposed dinner, and suggested a grand three-step plan: taking a world trip, getting a Ph.D. at Stanford, and teaching at the University of British Columbia, Vancouver. It is no less than a miracle that we did the first, accomplished the second, and, against all odds, both landed jobs at the beautiful University of British Columbia. As an adage says, good news comes in a bundle. We were blessed with the arrival of our second cherubin, Paul, in June 2002. As this book goes to press, I feel that I can finally explain to Claire and Paul, in a more tangible way, what this third "baby" is all about.

Vancouver
September 2003

Contents

1 Redefining Gender and Race in Japan: An Introduction 1

2 Constructing Japanese State Identity and Interests 12

3 Global Norms Concerning Women's, Children's, and Minority Rights 20

4 Policy, Institutional, and Legal Changes Concerning Women's and Children's Human Rights in Japan 39

5 Grassroots Mobilization: The Pill, Sexual Harassment, Military Sexual Slavery, Domestic Violence, and Child Prostitution 53

6 Human Rights Education in Japan 68

7 Japanese Nongovernmental Mobilization at the World Conference against Racism 95

8 Domestic Mobilization of Global Human Rights Norms: Issue Reframing, Advocacy Education, and Leverage Politics 119

9 Conclusions: Reconstructing Japanese Political Culture in the Age of Globalization 137

Appendixes

A. Interviewees, 155. B. Human Rights Symposia, Seminars, and Training Workshops Attended, September 1999 to December 2001, 159

Notes 163

References 189

Index 201

Tables

2.1 Constructing Japanese State Identity and Interests 18

3.1 The Absence of Women's Rights in Human Rights Treaties 22

4.1 Violence against Women and Children as a Legitimate Policy Concern in Japan 43

4.2 Policy, Institutional, and Legal Changes Concerning Women's and Children's Human Rights since the Mid-1990s 52

6.1 Explosion of Discourse on Women's Human Rights in Japan in the 1990s, by Issue 75

6.2 Embedded Knowledge: Global Human Rights Norms Redefining Local Education in Japan 86

6.3 Policy and Legal Stipulations on Human Rights Education in Japan 87

6.4 Japanese State Actors as Educators of Global Human Rights Norms: Some Examples 88

7.1 Mentioning of Racial Minorities in International Human Rights Instruments and Conferences by the Japanese Government, 1980–2001 117

7.2 Redefining Racism in Japan: Domestic Mobilization of Global Frames 118

8.1 Domestic Mobilization of Global Norms Redefining Women's and Children's Human Rights in Japan 135

Figures

1.1 Explosion of Discourse on Violence against Women in Japan 4
4.1 Number of Sexual Harassment Cases in Japan, 1994–98 45
5.1 Expansion of Children's Nongovernmental Groups in Japan, 1946–97 65
6.1 Redefining Human Rights Education in Japan: Global Norms and Local Education 73

Gender and Human Rights Politics in Japan

Global Norms and Domestic Networks

CHAPTER ONE

Redefining Gender and Race in Japan

An Introduction

> A gender-equal society is a graceful society that respects the individual, and is based on the idea of establishing human rights. Without the establishment of human rights, it would be impossible to create a society where women are free from discrimination and violence, where women can have independence in any field of society, and where women can be proud of themselves and are respected as individual beings. . . . Violence against women infringes upon their human rights and fundamental freedoms. It is not a problem for women as individuals alone: it constitutes a critical social and structural problem that drives them down to more subordinate positions than men.
>
> Vision of Gender Equality: Creating New Values for the 21st Century, 1996

> The kind of [Japanese] society I aim to create through the six reforms in preparation for the coming twenty-first century is one in which each and every citizen has a dream and objectives for the future and is able to fully display their creativity and spirit of challenge. This society that generates values to be shared with people throughout the world, when viewed from the perspective of men and women, is essentially a gender-equal society. The realization of this kind of society is the urgent demand of these times in which we grapple with rapid changes taking place in the socioeconomic environment—the aging population, the low birth rate, and the maturation and internationalization of the economy—in our quest for a prosperous and vigorous nation. Realization of this goal will be the key to Japan's future. For that reason, it is my belief that building a gender-equal society can be considered a form of social reform and that gender equality will be one of the pillars of "reform and creation" in every field of society.
>
> Address of Prime Minister Hashimoto Ryutaro to the Council for Gender Equality, 1997

The 1990s have often been described as a "lost decade" for Japan in terms of its economy, yet it was also the most significant decade for the advancement of the human rights of women and children in Japan. In 1996, in a comprehensive policy document called the "Vision of Gender Equality," the Japanese government espoused "women's human rights" as the goal of a gender-equal society. In 1997, for the first time in Japanese history, Prime Minister Hashimoto Ryutaro proclaimed "gender equality" to be a main pillar of societal and political reform. Between 1997 and 2001, eight legal changes concerning women's human rights and children's human rights took place. In 1997, the Equal Employment Opportunity Law was revised, legally requiring sexual harassment prevention at the workplace. In 1999, thirty-eight years after the government first established a panel to study the issue, the birth control pill was finally legalized. That same year, the first Basic Law on Gender Equality was enacted, mandating measures for gender equality at both the national and local levels. The Child Prostitution and Pornography Prohibition Law was also passed, outlawing child prostitution, pornography, and trafficking not only within Japan, but also by Japanese nationals overseas. In 2000, the Anti-Stalking Law and Child Abuse Prevention Law were passed. The Law to Promote Human Rights Education was also passed, mandating human rights education measures at both national and local levels. In 2001, the Domestic Violence Prevention Law was passed unanimously. In addition to these legal changes, two other bills have been tabled for Diet discussions. In March 2000, the opposition Democratic Party succeeded in submitting a bill on the issue of comfort women, the Promotion of Resolution for Issues concerning Victims of Wartime Sexual Coercion. Though it was not passed, the bill was resubmitted twice by three opposition parties the following year. In April 2002, the Upper House also started deliberations on a bill drafted by the Justice Ministry dealing with human rights discrimination based on race and sexual orientation, abuses by public authorities, and disclosure of information. If passed by the Diet, the new law would provide for the creation of a committee, supposedly independent of the Justice Ministry, comprised of five members, all named by the prime minister. The panel would be authorized to summon those involved in rights violations and conduct on-the-spot investigations.

Emphasized in these new policy and legal documents is not just the principle of women's and children's human rights, but also Japan's contribution to the global community and cooperation with nongovernmental organizations (NGOs). The drastic change of consciousness about women's and children's human rights as global issues has occurred not only at the governmental level. The mobilization of nongovernmental organizations around issues of women's and children's human rights has spread nationwide since the late 1980s. Established women's groups reframe their traditional agenda in terms of women's human rights. New groups and networks such as the Domestic Violence Survey Research Group (1992), National Shelter Network (1996), Violence against Women in War-Net Japan (1997), Campus Sexual Harassment Network (1997), and the Lawyers Network against Violence Against Women (1998) were formed. Feminist counseling, assertiveness training, and consciousness-raising activities, all of which emphasize self-respect (*jiko sonchō*) and self-assertion (*jiko hyōgen*)[1]—qualities not traditionally encouraged in women in Japan—have been gaining popularity. Men's groups such as Men's Lib Tokyo created batterer prevention programs and included violence against women as part of their consciousness-raising activities. The number of NGOs focused on children's rights has also increased dramatically in the past decade; the Federation for the Protection of Children's Human Rights Japan (Kodomo no Jinken Ren), for example, an organization formed in 1986, has expanded into a network of sixty NGOs. The number of books, journal articles, news reports, and government publications concerning women's rights exploded in the 1990s, especially after 1995 (Fig. 1.1).

Meanwhile, there has been minimal political or legislative change in minority rights in Japan. The Japanese government continues to deny that the Burakumin are a caste minority within Japan. The Ainu people have been recognized as an ethnic minority, protected by the 1997 Ainu Culture Promotion Law, but they are far from being considered the indigenous people of northern Japan with territorial rights. The Okinawans are treated neither as an ethnic minority nor as indigenous people of the Ryūkyū Islands.[2] The majority of Zainichi Koreans, many of whom were born in Japan, remain as "special permanent residents" who require reentry permits and who have no access to welfare benefits that are restricted to Japanese nationals. Unlike in other industrialized countries, migrant workers in Japan are denied national insurance or public assistance and are barred from local ballots.

How do we explain this drastic difference between the recognition of women's and children's human rights on the one hand and the continual denial of minority rights on the other? In a country not known for a strong human rights tradition or policy,[3] significant representation of women in politics, a well-developed women's movement, or speedy political change, why has the Japanese government suddenly taken elaborate measures to affirm the human rights of women and children? The paradigmatic changes are particularly puz-

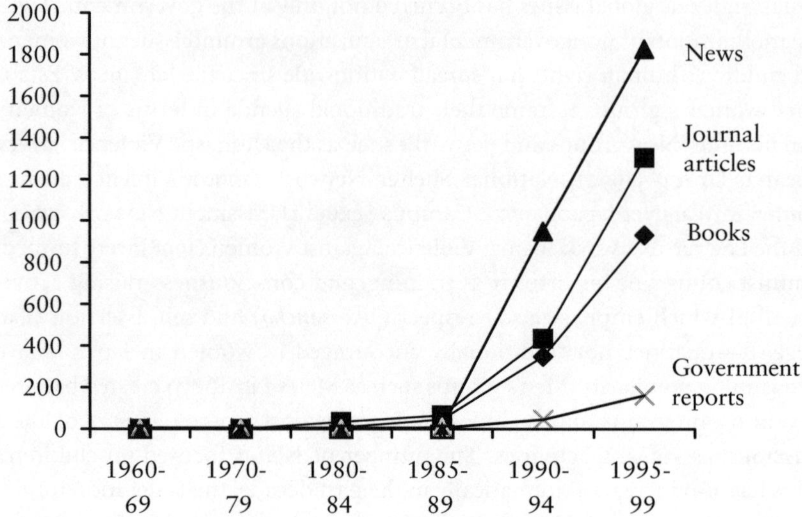

FIG. 1.1. Explosion of discourse on violence against women in Japan. Source: National Women's Education Center Database (as of November 1999). Findings under six separate keyword searches: "sexual violence," "sexual harassment," "domestic violence / family violence," "comfort women," "prostitution," and "reproductive rights / health."

zling at a time of continuous political crisis and protracted economic stagnation, when one might expect these social issues to be relegated to the margins. And why, despite a similar emergence of NGOs advocating minority rights, has the situation of the Burakumin, Ainu, Okinawans, Koreans, and migrant workers remained relatively constant?

Argument: Domestic Mobilization of Global Norms

It has often been argued that Japan is politically, economically, and culturally unique. Predominant conceptions of the Japanese state—emphasizing bureaucratic dominance, party politics, and interest groups—largely ignore the impact of globalization on Japan. This book departs from these predominant domestic explanations and places Japan within a global context. I use a constructivist approach within the field of international relations and argue that Japan is an *embedded network state*. Instead of looking at the traditional Liberal Democratic Party (LDP)–bureaucracy–interest group alignments, this study focuses on Japanese NGO networks that are embedded in the global human rights community. I focus on three mechanisms of norm diffusion: first, the reframing of issues at world conferences; second, local advocacy education; and third, leverage politics through alliance with target domestic politicians.[4] The ability of Japanese women's and children's groups to mobilize around specific frames on violence against women and children, to educate people about those new human rights norms, and to ally with target politicians explains the swift legal changes concerning women and children. The absence of specific global frames on minority rights until the World Conference against Racism, Racial Discrimination, Xenophobia, and Related Intolerance (WCAR) in 2001 and the lack of leverage politics account for the limited progress in minority rights protection in Japan.

Although most research on norm diffusion has focused on the impact of legally binding conventions, this study focuses instead on world conferences. Written at a time when mega-conference fatigue and realpolitik cast doubt on these costly enterprises, this study aims to show the potential of global discourses when followed up domestically. The diffusion of global human rights norms in domestic contexts is more than just a legal and political matter through the ratification of conventions and translation of those norms into national laws and policies. It is essentially an educational process. I use the concept of the "epistemic network"[5] to emphasize the knowledge production and dissemination functions of NGO networks. In particular, in countries like Japan, where public opinion is rarely expressed in the form of protests, human rights and feminist education is used as a political strategy.

This study traces the impact of discourses flowing from four world conferences in the 1990s—the 1993 World Conference on Human Rights in Vienna, the 1994 International Conference on Population and Development (ICPD) in Cairo, the 1995 Fourth World Conference on Women (FWCW) in Beijing, and the 1996 First World Congress against Commercial Sexual Exploitation of Children in Stockholm (CSEC)—on the redefinition of five issues of sexuality in Japan: the pill, sexual harassment, military sexual slavery, domestic violence, and child prostitution. These formerly separate and marginalized issues, casually known as "a problem of morality," "unpleasant sexual experiences," "comfort women," "marital disputes," and "assisted entertainment," respectively, were suddenly reconceptualized as human rights violations. The participation of the Japanese government in these conferences itself might have led to little change had Japanese NGO networks not mobilized around the newly available discourses of "women's human rights" and "children's human rights." In contrast, the absence of a mega–world forum and global frames on caste discrimination, indigenous peoples' rights, reparation for colonization and slavery, and migrants' rights until the WCAR in 2001 mean that lobbying for an anti-discrimination law has only just begun in Japan.

Beyond Universalism versus Cultural Relativism

The broader significance of this project lies in the implications of political and cultural translation of rights in a non-Western country. It touches on general but important questions: How Western is Japan? How Western is Japanese feminism? What is Japanese feminism? Who is authorized to speak on its behalf? What is the state of civil society in Japan?[6] Though it is beyond the scope of this book to address all these issues satisfactorily, this study of Japanese grassroots mobilization of global norms represents an attempt to go beyond the dichotomy of universalism versus cultural relativism, and "global/Western" versus "local/indigenous" feminisms. As Chow argues, "Japan did not stand outside the West. Even in its particularism, Japan was already implicated in the ubiquitous West, so that neither historically nor geopolitically could Japan be seen as the outside of the West."[7] The discourse of violence against women as a violation of women's human rights is global in that it emerges out of women's common experiences worldwide, but it is also local in that it manifests itself in the specific historical and sociopolitical conditions of Japan.

By looking at five issue areas that span more than fifty years of postwar Japan, this study critically analyzes issues of representation within the Japanese women's movement. In the cartography of global feminism, Japanese feminism does not fit neatly into the West or first world versus third world feminisms divide, and Japanese feminists are often seen as the silent/silenced Other. Yet, they are also the silencing Other in reproducing ethnic, racial, and sexual minorities on Japan's soil as well as within its regional boundaries. The case of "comfort women" and the mobilization of Japanese minority women in the Durban conference demonstrate that the Japanese women's movement is far from being homogenous and that only an intersectional approach to gender, race, and other social relations will help us understand the nature of discrimination in Japan.[8] Finally, embedding Japanese society and politics in global human rights norms gives us an opportunity to revisit several core notions in Japanese political culture: group orientation, harmony or nonlegalism, hierarchical social organization, and homogeneity or national citizenship. Instead of assuming that traditional Japanese culture is at odds with the individualistic and legalistic orientation of international human rights standards, the analysis in this book discusses how Japanese women's, children's, and minority groups, and in turn Japanese state actors, grapple with the rise of the individual, the new salience of the law in solving conflicts, the emergence of horizontal networks of cooperation, and the practice of postnational citizenship.

Methodology

Studies of globalization have forced us to reexamine the boundaries of the international system, state, and substate. Traditional theoretical approaches to nation-states and international relations are divided into micro and macro levels. Debates on economic and political globalization, for example, have largely been framed by this traditional split in levels of analysis about state convergence *or* divergence. This study ties in all three levels of the international system, state, and substate. It looks at the substate mobilization of global norms, and in turn its impact on the Japanese state. Japan is an intriguing case for investigation. On the one hand, it is known to be susceptible to *gaiatsu* (foreign pressure), even if this has mostly happened in trade and economics. On the other, a strong civilization and a relatively intact prewar conservative political apparatus mean that change does not come easily. Although there have been some studies on the impact of global norms, few have linked gender, children, and race.

This book focuses on five issues of sexuality: the pill, sexual harassment, military sexual slavery, domestic violence, and child prostitution. Contrary to women's rights to equal education, employment, and political participation, which are extensions of established rights of men to women qua abstract individuals, these five issues concern women's struggles for rights qua women in the "contested private domains."[9] More than the issue of equal employment opportunity, which is, at least in discourse, publicly recognized and legally guaranteed in Japan, these five cases represent particularly difficult cases for reforms. These five issues also allow interesting cross-temporal and cross-issue comparisons. The cases of comfort women, the pill, and domestic violence show how local mobilization since the 1970s was largely ineffective until new global frames became available in the 1990s. The issues of child prostitution (viewed from both the perspectives of the women's human rights movement and the children's human rights movement) on the one hand and comfort women on the other demonstrate how the "strength" of global norms might differ depending on the crucial alliance between NGOs and target politicians. The former was the easiest while the latter the most difficult to mobilize among the five cases within Japan.

Below I briefly introduce these five issues.

1. *The pill.* Next to prostitution, the pill has the longest history of mobilization by women in Japan. The pill was announced at a world congress of the International Family Planning Association in Tokyo in 1955. Japanese women had to wait for almost four decades, however, between the government's establish-

ment of its first panel on the pill in 1961 and its final legalization in 1999. Local mobilization since the 1970s had been marginalized and ineffective until the pill was redefined as an issue of women's reproductive rights at the 1994 World Conference on Population and Development in Cairo.

2. *Sexual harassment.* Although U.S. court cases and local mobilization in Japan since the late 1980s attracted public attention, sexual harassment was largely seen as an issue of sexual discrimination rather than violence until the Fourth World Conference on Women in Beijing in 1995. The Equal Employment Opportunity Law was finally revised in 1997 to mandate sexual harassment prevention in the workplace. Further, administrative guidance by the Ministry of Education was put in place to prevent sexual harassment in schools.

3. *Military sexual slavery.* The issue of comfort women—Asian women drafted to serve Japanese soldiers stationed throughout Asia during World War II—was raised neither in the postwar Tokyo Tribunal nor in the bilateral treaties between Japan and various Asian governments. It was also ignored in both the Korean resident and mainstream women's movements in Japan until women's groups in Korea brought up the issue in the late 1980s. The Japanese government consistently denied its responsibility until a Japanese historian published some evidence of the government's culpability in 1992. The government publicly expressed remorse but refused legal responsibility. Korean women's groups then brought the issue to the United Nations, which resulted in a recommendation in 1994. That year, the Japanese government finally set up a private Asian Women's Fund. Despite subsequent UN reports in 1996 and 1998 and an international conference in 2000 defining the Japanese "comfort system" as sexual slavery, there has been little legal progress on the issue. Contrary to the other four issues, which have primarily focused on Japanese women and girls, the comfort women issue links gender to racial politics. It has also bitterly divided the Japanese women's movement between the "nationalists" ("the Japanese government has already apologized enough") and the "globalists" ("sexual slavery is a crime"). It places Japanese women in a "victimizer" status, as many were an active part of the war machinery.[10] Among the five issues, it is also the only one that became part of a larger Asian women's human rights movement, based on what Mackie calls the "mutually imbricated histories of women in the region."[11]

4. *Domestic violence.* In the early 1990s, a Japanese ambassador to the UN, when asked about domestic violence in Japan, answered, "the problem did not exist in Japan."[12] As late as 1999, a Japanese consul in Canada, when arrested for domestic violence, told a news reporter that it is normal to beat one's wife. He claimed that it was a question of cultural difference, and nothing serious.[13] The

battered women's movement in the United States in the 1970s and 1980s had minimal impact on Japan. Local NGO mobilization in the early 1990s also proved to be marginalized. The term "domestic violence" did not even exist in Japanese. The Fourth World Conference on Women in Beijing squarely established domestic violence as a public issue worthy of state attention. In 2001, the Domestic Violence Prevention Law was finally passed. In contrast to the issue of sexual harassment, which concerns public workplaces, mobilization on domestic violence proved to be difficult because of the traditional *ie* (family) institution. The response of the Japanese government to domestic violence also shows its bias toward addressing violence against *Japanese* women, rather than violence against women *in Japan*. Illegal immigrant women in Japan have consistently been denied most welfare and medical services.

5. *Child prostitution.* Finally, the issue of child prostitution was chosen for three reasons. First, in contrast to the Vienna, Cairo, and Beijing conferences, the 1996 First World Congress against Commercial Sexual Exploitation of Children in Stockholm was largely an NGO-led effort. Although "*enjo kōsai,*" or assisted entertainment, attracted considerable media attention in the early 1990s, the Japanese government did not see any need for action, even after it signed the Convention of the Rights of the Child in 1994. The First World Congress against CSEC redefined child prostitution and pornography as a violation of children's human rights. The Child Prostitution and Pornography Prohibition Law was passed in 1999. Second, the swift legal change stands in stark contrast to the issue of trafficking in women, both because of the race dimension (Japanese children versus non-Japanese women), and because of the distinction between voluntary and forced prostitution, used even in the Beijing Platform for Action. Third, the inclusion of child prostitution and pornography as an example of violence against girls also represents an attempt to engender mainstream children's rights discourse in Japan when most literature on Japanese children focuses primarily on educational issues.

TO PROVIDE a contrast to these five cases of relatively successful change, I then discuss the limited impact of global norms regarding minority rights on five minority movements within Japan. The ratification of the broad International Convention on the Elimination of All Forms of Racial Discrimination (ICERD) by Japan in 1995 did little to change the legal recognition and protection of the Burakumin, Ainu, Okinawans, Koreans, and migrant workers. The lack of a specific UN convention on indigenous peoples' rights and on migrant rights (the 1990 International Convention on the Protection of the Rights of All

Migrant Workers and Members of Their Families finally came into force in July 2003) on the one hand and the absence of global human rights frames around caste and reparation for colonization and slavery until the Durban racism conference on the other not only render local NGO mobilization "illegitimate," but also make alliance with key politicians difficult.

Findings of this study are based on three sources: first, nearly one hundred interviews with diverse human rights groups, Diet members, ministry officials, academics, and the media in Japan (Appendix A); second, a textual analysis of reports by the Japanese government to the Human Rights Committee, the Committee on the Elimination of All Forms of Discrimination against Women (CEDAW), and the CERD committees, and by NGOs , as well as the preparatory and official outcome documents of all six world conferences in Vienna (1993), Cairo (1994), Beijing (1995), Stockholm (1996), New York (2000), and Durban (2001); and third, participant observation in forty-four international, regional, and national conferences and training workshops concerning human rights in Japan, including the Beijing-Plus-Five Conference on Women in New York in June 2000, the Women's International War Crimes Tribunal on Japan's Military Sexual Slavery in December 2002, the World Conference against Racism in Durban in September 2001, and the Second World Congress against Commercial Sexual Exploitation of Children in Yokohama in December 2001 (Appendix B). Before I continue, however, let me state clearly two caveats. First, it is not my contention that constructivism replaces predominant bureaucratic, political party, and interest group explanations in the understanding of Japanese politics. Rather, the institutionalization of human rights norms at the global level and the change in power balance between NGOs and the traditional "triumvirate" in the 1990s within Japan provide an opening for constructivist interpretations of the Japanese state. Second, the purpose of this book is to explain discursive and legal change concerning women's and children's human rights rather than to demonstrate that the new discourses and laws have actually improved gender relations or children's rights. Though there have been some arrests in cases of sexual harassment, domestic violence, and child prostitution (both within Japan and in Asia), it will be the scope of a separate study to follow up on the actual impact of these laws.

Organization of the Book

Eight chapters follow. Chapter 2 contrasts predominant domestic political and social movement approaches with a constructivist interpretation of the Japanese state. Chapter 3 contextualizes the changes in Japan by outlining a genealogy of the global movement for women's, children's, and minority rights within the United Nations. Chapter 4 then analyzes the extensive policy, institutional, and legal changes concerning women's and children's human rights in Japan. Chapter 5 discusses the grassroots mobilization on each of the five issues, and chapter 6 focuses on the educational processes when Japanese nongovernmental organizations appropriate global discourses of women's and children's human rights locally. Chapter 7 then provides a contrasting case of minority rights through a discussion of three important changes in racial scenes in Japan since the early 1990s, and then Japanese NGO mobilization at the World Conference against Racism in 2001. Chapter 8 provides an explanatory framework for the changes, focusing on three mechanisms of norm diffusion: issue reframing at world conferences, local advocacy education, and leverage politics. Finally, chapter 9 concludes by discussing the implications of this study on the engendering of global governance, the connections between transnational social movements and grassroots education, and the reconstruction of Japanese political culture in the era of globalization.

CHAPTER TWO

Constructing Japanese State Identity and Interests

> How dare we continue to write about Japan as a unity? How can we decide what is Japanese and what is alien? . . . The foreign is quite capable of being imported and "remade in Japan." And this is not only true in Japan, but of any modern nation-state.
>
> D. P. Martinez, ed., *The Worlds of Japanese Popular Culture*

This chapter first critiques conventional domestic approaches to political change in Japan and then reexamines the Japanese state from a constructivist perspective. I argue that Japan is an "embedded network state," that is, it is embedded in global human rights norms that are mobilized by domestic networks made up of nongovernmental organizations, academics, and sympathetic politicians.

Predominant Domestic Approaches

A central concern in most studies of the Japanese state has been to account for Japan's extraordinary economic success. Many different models have emerged that focus primarily on the dominance of three institutions: the bureaucracy, political parties, and interest groups. One early strand of strong Japanese state theories emphasizes the power of the Japanese bureaucracy relative to all other institutions. According to this explanation, the elite bureaucracy, largely intact from the Meiji era, is the prime political actor in Japan. Policy outcomes can be explained by examining bureaucratic interests, power, and strategy. Political parties and leaders only rubber-stamp plans made by bureaucrats, who are either motivated by their own particularistic interest or by a larger sense of national interest. The classic formulation of this bureaucratic dominance model is Johnson's analysis of the Japanese "developmental" state.[1] He argues that the cooperative relations between the state bureaucracy and private businesses account for the extraordinary success of the postwar Japanese economy. The bureaucratic dominance model has been applied beyond economic issues. Upham, for example, argues that most of the postwar social conflicts in Japan, including those related to the environment, Buraku liberation, sex discrimination, and industrial policy, have been managed through "bureaucratic informalism," that is, informal bureaucratic mediation, rather than through legal settlements.

> Litigation as idealized in the rule-centered model, on the other hand, would not only bypass the current power structure but would destroy it whenever, as is frequently the case in Japan, the formal norms of the legal system were substantially at variance with those of the elite. . . . The identification of litigation as a threat to the political and social status quo is implicit in all writing on Japanese law and society, and recent scholarship argues persuasively that self-interest has led the Japanese elite to take deliberate steps to discourage litigation. . . . Given these limitations, the bureaucrats do retain a surprising degree of control over the pace and course, if not the substance, of social change in Japan, and one of its major instruments for such control is the manipulation of the legal framework within which social change and its harbinger, social conflict, occur.[2]

A second strand of strong Japanese state theories focuses on party politics. According to this explanation, political parties, factions, and leaders are the primary actors in Japanese politics. Policy changes are a result of shifting interests and power among parties. Ultimately, all key policy decisions occur through votes in the Japanese parliament, the Diet. Some argue that elections are essential events through which voters may have a strong impact on policy or reform outcomes, while others emphasize instead the ability of party leaders to shape outcomes. In particular, many have noted the strength of Japan's one-party rule until 1993. The durability of the Liberal Democratic Party (LDP) could be attributed to its competence on economic issues, political clientism, adaptation strategies, and fragmented opposition.[3] Curtis, for example, argues that politicians represent the core in the "logic of Japanese politics."

> The conceptual starting point for this analysis is that the voter is an object of political action by those who make politics their profession. This places voters in a reactive posture vis-à-vis politicians who hold public office. It is politicians who act and voters who react, not the other way round. Accordingly, politicians are at the center of the analysis in this book. They are there because politicians have become the focal point of modern democratic politics. This is as true in Japan as in every other mass-media-saturated, technologically advanced, affluent country in which political leaders are chosen through open and fair elections. This book then is an interpretative essay about contemporary Japanese politics that focuses on politicians and the institutions within which they operate.[4]

Kohno, in his analysis of Japan's postwar party politics, also argues that political actors in Japan, as in any democratic state, are self-seeking and competitive, and respond rationally to incentives and public pressure. Interest-based interactions between these actors consequently resulted in the topographic changes in Japan's political structure observed throughout the postwar period.[5]

In contrast to the bureaucratic dominance and party dominance models, a third theory is that the Japanese state is weak, penetrated, and often paralyzed by the gridlock of strong interest groups. According to this view, both bureaucratic and party behaviors are heavily influenced by interest group politics, and policy changes are often a result of competition among interest groups. Calder, for example, argues that LDP politicians in power need the support of crucial interest groups to stabilize their precarious position and that the politicians are ready to develop clientelist relationships with them. Hence, the major policy changes have been a result of the LDP's co-optation of interest groups and the expansion of its circles of compensation.[6] The Japanese state is neither strong nor monolithic. Politicians and the bureaucracy need powerful interest groups to survive. According to this view, Japanese women's groups can be conceived as one of the interest groups that have expanded in the context of increasing "structural fragmentation" in a negotiated polity, fostered by sustained postwar economic growth.[7]

In the late 1980s, some Japan scholars started to formulate hybrid models of the three predominant explanations. In his analysis of the rapid growth in targeted industries in postwar Japan, Okimoto argues that the strength of the Japanese state derives from its network characteristics rather than the particular dominance of the bureaucracy, the parties, or interest groups. Because of a densely knit network of formal and informal relationships between the Ministry of International Trade and Industry (MITI), the LDP, and the private sector, MITI was able to form a consensual industrial policy that promoted competition and efficiency. He maintains that "the convergence of public and private interests and the extensive network of ties binding the two sectors together" enable the Japanese state to exercise its power.[8] Van Wolferen, in his attempt to explain the "Japan problem"—that is, Japan's sluggish behavior in international relations despite its power—argues that the enigma of Japanese power lies in a balance of power between the bureaucracy, the Liberal Democratic Party, and business interests groups, or what he calls "the Triumvirate."[9]

All of these conceptions of the Japanese state focus on domestic institutions. Japan's political economy, its success and then its failure, remains the core object of analysis. Although some have looked at grassroots social movements in Japan, especially those related to the environment, they generally focus on localized struggles and argue for the limited impact of social movements on politics. McKean, in her analysis of environmental protests in Japan, focuses on local problems such as garbage disposal and factory construction and argues that citizen activism has an impact on local politics.[10] Similarly, Broadbent argues that three domestic factors—the natural intensity (amount of pollution), the social intensity (impact on the community), and the societal perception—shape environmental policy.[11] Finally, in their classic analysis of the protracted grassroots opposition to the Narita airport, Apter and Sawa argue that the extrainstitutional protests have largely failed to generate institutional reforms.

> In Japan institutional opposition is both present and constitutionally provided for along with appropriate channels and instruments for its expression. However, there are serious constraints at work which are relatively absent in most other democracies. We have described some of these; the lack of effective local government and the powerlessness of opposition parties in the face of the LDP's long dominance are two factors that help to explain why extra-institutional protest in Japan has been so bitter and violent for such a long time. But there is a more important factor. Even today, and especially in the ranks of the civil service, there is a distrust of opposition of all kinds, even institutional. Mediation, yes; opposition, no.[12]

As many authors have attempted to render Japanese women more visible in the Japanese political culture, there has been a proliferation of studies on Japanese women since the 1980s. However, as LeBlanc points out, "Japanese women are frequently studied, but their political life is not."[13] In works that do look at the Japanese women's movement, few go beyond "housewife feminism," or, in Lerner's words, "housewife-feeder-breeder" images.[14] LeBlanc, for example, in her analysis of the political participation of women in nonparty grassroots organizations, makes an eloquent defense of "*shufu pawā*" (housewife power) without mentioning a new form of political participation of Japanese women—housewives and politicians alike—in world conferences and their mobilization of global norms within Japan. In sum, predominant conceptions of the Japanese state would have us believe that external influences are unlikely to produce political change in Japan, that citizen movements are likely to be neutralized and co-opted by the Japanese state, and that women and gender relations are largely irrelevant in Japanese political life.

Another approach to political change focuses on the impact of contentious collective action on states. In the past few decades, the focus of social movement theorists has shifted from resource mobilization, political process, and framing, to political opportunities.[15] Most of these approaches, however, remain at the level of the nation-state. As McAdam, Tarrow, and Tilly argue,

> As Western parliamentary regimes arose during the nineteenth century, a special variety of social movement—the *national* social movement—formed, generalized, and rapidly became a standard fixture of national political struggles. . . . [N]ational social movement

came to involve associations, symbolic displays, publications, meetings, marches, demonstrations, petitions, lobbying, and threats to intervene directly in formal political life (Tilly 1995b; Tarrow 1994). It still does today.[16]

By focusing uniquely on domestic cultural repertoires and political opportunities, social movement theorists have until recently largely ignored the plausible influence of international factors, or the interaction of international and domestic forces, in creating new opportunity structures for new social movements. McAdam, Tarrow, and Tilly, for example, voice reservations about the strong version of the transnational social movement thesis. They argue that movements do not depend on interest or opportunity alone, but build on indigenous social networks, networks of people linked together more by interpersonal bonds than by formal organizations. In their opinion, "advocates of the 'strong' globalization thesis will have to show that transnational (and inevitably long-distance) activist networks have the same effects as the face-to-face networks and resulting collective identities that have been at the basis of the national social movement."[17]

A Constructivist Approach: Embedding Japan in Global Human Rights Norms

In contrast to these domestic political and social movement approaches, I use a constructivist argument to show how Japan's interests and identity are shaped by global human rights norms. One strand of constructivism under the name of "world culture / society" emerges out of sociology. Meyer et al. argue that properties of institutions and nation-states are determined by the larger world society, made up of international organizations, NGOs, professional associations, and "epistemic communities."[18] These groups are carriers of international norms, providing the definition, discourse, and models for global organization around principles of individualism, universalism, progress, and world citizenship.[19] Despite the Western origins of these principles, they are global in the sense that they are reified as globally legitimate even if their specific contents might be contested. Models built around these principles help nation-states to construct modern national identity.

A second, less expansive strand of constructivism coming out of the international relations tradition focuses on shared ideas in the international structure that shape state identity and interests.[20] As John Ruggie puts it,

> Constructivists hold the view that the building blocks of international reality are ideational as well as material; that ideational factors have normative as well as instru-

> mental dimensions; that they express not only individual but also collective intentionally; and that the meaning and significance of ideational factors are not independent of time and place. . . . [A]t the level of individual actors constructivism seeks, first of all, to problematize the identities and interests of states, to show that and how they are socially constructed.[21]

A transnational advocacy network approach, for example, focuses on "relevant actors working internationally on an issue, who are bound together by shared values, a common discourse, and dense exchanges of information and services."[22] It engages in information politics, symbolic politics, leverage politics, and accountability politics.[23] A common weakness of both strands of constructivism, however, is their lack of clarity on what actually happens on the ground. As Finnemore critiques,

> Norms of international society may create similar structures and push both people and states toward similar behavior, but the body of international norms is not completely congruent. Certainly, it is not congruent enough to produce homogeneity or equifinality. Tensions and contradictions among the norms leave room for different solutions and different arrangements, each of which makes legitimacy claims based on the same norms. The compromises arrived at may be contingent on local circumstances and personalities and are likely to reflect the local norms and customs with which international norms have had to compromise.[24]

Several scholars posit that the degree of international institutionalization on a particular issue area and domestic structures are both important in determining the impact of transnational actors on domestic policy. Risse-Kappen (1995), for example, argues,

> Almost nobody denies that transnational relations exist; their presence is well established. But despite more than twenty years of controversy about the subject, we still have a poor understanding of their impact on state policies and international relations. Transnational relations do not seem to have the same effects across states. . . . The main question to be asked in this volume is therefore: under what domestic and international circumstances do transnational coalitions and actors who attempt to change policy outcomes in a specific issue-area succeed or fail to achieve their goals? . . . This book argues, in short, that the impact of transnational actors and coalitions on state policies is likely to vary according to: 1) differences in domestic structures, i.e., the normative and organizational arrangements which form the "state," structure society, and link the two in the polity, and 2) degrees of international institutionalization, i.e., the extent to which the specific issue-area is regulated by bilateral agreements, multilateral regimes, and/or international organizations.[25]

In the case of Japan, several studies have looked at the interactions between international norms and domestic institutions. Schreurs argues, in the case of

TABLE 2.1
Constructing Japanese State Identity and Interests

Models	Explanatory variables
Bureaucratic dominance	Bureaucracy
Party politics	Politicians and political institutions
Interest groups	Business and other interest groups
Network state / triumvirate	Bureaucracy–LDP–Business
Embedded network state	Global norms and domestic epistemic networks

the environment, "international pressures were not very effective in promoting policy change, however, until those pressures were successfully linked, positively or negatively, to the interests of key domestic policy actors."[26] In the case of immigrant rights, on the other hand, Gurowitz argues that activists play an important role in bringing about changes. As she explains,

> But norms do not diffuse automatically to states. First, most of the international norms invoked by pro-immigrant activists had existed for a number of years prior to their having an impact in Japan (for example, the international covenants were adopted in 1966). Furthermore, the changes in immigrant rights that took place internationally and across Europe occurred during the early 1970s, a decade before most of the changes occurred in Japan. We therefore need to account for why international norms had an impact when they did. Rather than happening by some automatic diffusion, ratification was fought for by activists, and only after that were there substantial gains for Korean rights. Japan's low ratification rate is one indication that norms do not automatically proliferate to governments. Had the government not been pushed to ratify, it is reasonable to assume that it would not have done so and that the norms embedded in these international documents would not have worked their way into the courts.[27]

I follow a similar line of analysis by combining the global and the local. Instead of focusing on *either* policy actors *or* activists, however, this study argues that *network* mobilization of global human rights norms by NGOs, academics, and sympathetic politicians explains the recent dramatic changes concerning women's and children's rights. I borrow from Okimoto's concept of a "network state." Okimoto argues that the strength of the Japanese state derives from its network characteristics rather than the particular dominance of the bureaucracy, political parties, or interest groups.[28] However, instead of the traditional LDP–bureaucracy–interest group networks, this research focuses on the rise of a new type of "epistemic human rights network" made up of globally linked human rights advocacy NGOs, academics, and politicians. Table 2.1 contrasts this constructivist view with predominant conceptions. For NGOs to be effective, they need to engage not only in issue reframing at world conferences but also in local advocacy education and leverage politics through alliance with domestic politicians. In sum, I propose a new conceptualization of Japan as an embedded network state, embedded in global norms that are mobilized by domestic epistemic networks.

CHAPTER THREE

Global Norms Concerning Women's, Children's, and Minority Rights

> Dr. Sadik, who will retire at the end of the year, has presided over a social revolution. . . . The United Nations itself is now in new territory, supporting the concept that women should have the right to make their own decisions about bearing children, and that they should have access to education and health services, a range of family planning tools and, as a last resort, safe abortions. . . . "The most difficult issues of behavior or practices like rape, incest, female genital mutilation, the idea of female reproductive rights, all these concepts we would never have been able to discuss just a few years ago," Dr. Sadik said. That sexual violence, the sex trade, AIDS and other issues like the need to provide adolescents with information and services to promote safe sex can be talked about openly in the United Nations and government offices "is an indication of massive, massive change in thinking," she said.
>
> "Working for Women's Sexual Rights," *New York Times*, Oct. 2, 2000

This chapter discusses the emergence of global norms concerning women's, children's, and minority rights. Until women's human rights became an issue within the UN in the early 1990s, women's rights and human rights had traditionally been treated separately. I focus on the process that led to the major turning point in 1993, when women proclaimed "women's rights are human rights" at the World Conference on Human Rights. Since then, norms concerning women's human rights have become further institutionalized through a series of mechanisms, including a convention and a declaration on violence against women, special rapporteurs, and three optional protocols dealing with sexual exploitation of children, trafficking of women and children, and an individual complaint procedure. The women's human rights movement also exerted an influence on the global campaign against commercial sexual exploitation of children. The affirmation of women's and children's human rights, however, did not go unchallenged. I briefly describe a backlash movement in evidence since the mid-1990s. I conclude by contrasting the global movements for women's and children's human rights with the development of minority rights within the United Nations.

A Global Epistemic Network for Women's Human Rights

International women's networking and organizing are not new. As many scholars have argued, the international women's movement was already in place at the turn of the last century.[1] As Rupp argues, "The first international women's congress, the Congrès international de droit des femmes, convened in Paris in 1878, in connection with the World Exposition. All of this activity laid the groundwork for the founding of international women's organizations, which institutionalized and perpetuated the muscle to work on behalf of women on the international stage."[2] Feminists from different regions of the world already used the transnational arena for their mobilization. Miller writes,

> The evidence suggests that the transnational arena held a particular appeal for Latin American feminists. There are a number of reasons for this: First, within their national communities, they were disenfranchised; and as elsewhere, the national social and political arenas were characterized by androcracy. Second, Latin American female intellectuals were particularly alienated from politics as practiced within their countries, excluded from leadership positions not only by the status quo but by forces of opposition. By the 1920s and 1930s, the international forums seemed to offer activist women the opportunity to effect reform through the passage of resolutions that would oblige signatory governments to raise the issues within their domestic arena.[3]

At the turn of the twentieth century, various international women's movements already existed on diverse issues, including abolitionism, socialism, peace, temperance, labor, and moral reform. Issues of violence against women were already on the agenda of some nongovernmental groups. The World's Woman's Christian Temperance Union (1891) and the International Bureau for the Suppression of Traffic in Women and Children (1899), for example, took up the issues of prostitution and traffic in women. The International Council for Women Peace Committee had already raised the issue of rape in war in 1913.[4] However, two major differences distinguish this turn-of-the-century internationalism from the transnational movements that have developed since the 1980s. First, the number and diversity of women participants at the earlier international conferences differed significantly from those at conferences in the 1990s. International women activists at the turn of the century were primarily bourgeois European-Americans. Although issues of representation remain in

TABLE 3.1

The Absence of Women's Rights in Human Rights Treaties

	Major human rights treaty bodies				
	Human Rights Committee	Committee on Economic and Social Rights	Committee on the Elimination of Racial Discrimination	Committee against Torture	Committee on the Rights of the Child
Gender provisions in treaty	Articles 3, 4, 23, 25, 26	None	None	None	Articles 2, 18, 24
Female committee members (%)	17 (3/8)	11 (2/18)	11 (2/18)	10 (1/10)	70 (7/10)
Gender-specific reporting requirements	None	None	None	None	None

Source: "Violence Against Women: A Report," World Organization Against Torture, 1999.

today's global feminist organizing, there is no doubt that the base has significantly broadened in the past decades.[5] Second, although some issues of violence against women were addressed at the turn of the twentieth century, they were mostly seen as issues of public health or morality. There was not the same kind of global consensus as was observed in the 1990s that violence against women is a violation of women's basic human rights.

Within the UN system, human rights and women's rights were treated separately because of both structural and conceptual differences.[6] The Commission on Human Rights and various treaty-based committees had pursued a variety of rights issues except those of women, which had been dealt with by the much weaker and marginalized Commission on the Status of Women. At the treaty level, almost all mainstream human rights declarations and conventions contained only gender-neutral provisions (Table 3.1). On the one hand, although human rights experts had assumed that there was no gender difference with regard to the right to bodily integrity, the right to work, the right to freedom from racial discrimination, the right to protection from torture, and the right to education for a child, in fact women were more likely to be victims of violence, to be harassed at work, to suffer double discrimination as minority women, to be subject to gender-based torture, and to face additional barriers in education. On the other hand, the Commission on the Status of Women, since its establishment in 1947, had focused primarily on extending the acquired rights of men to women, including the right to education, nondiscrimination at work, and political participation, leaving out the rights of women qua women. This equality / equal opportunity approach had been dominant from the first world conference on women in Mexico in 1975 through the Nairobi conference in

1985, and it was the guiding principle behind the Convention on the Elimination of Discrimination Against Women (CEDAW), which contained no specific provision on gender-based violence.[7]

Mobilization around issues of violence against women had remained mostly local until the 1980s and did not receive serious attention at the UN until the late 1980s. In 1980, influenced by their domestic women's movements, delegates from the United States, Canada, and Austria introduced resolutions on domestic violence at the Commission on the Status of Women, but they had no support from the governments of the Southern and Eastern blocs.[8] When female genital mutilation was first discussed at the intergovernmental level at the Copenhagen conference in 1980, the North-South divide prevented feminists from coming to a consensus on the issue.[9] Although the term "violence against women" first appeared in the platform adopted in Copenhagen, it remained framed as a health issue and was narrowly defined.[10] However, the two conferences became an opportunity for many women's organizations to learn about the existence and the potential of the UN.

The Copenhagen encounter kicked off a process of local research, education, and conferencing. Few of the women's groups knew how the agenda-setting process worked, how they could gain access to governments, how to present their information, or how to lobby.[11] Upon returning to their countries, these women's groups started to form national, regional, and international networks such as ISIS International and the Latin American Committee for the Defense of Women's Rights (CLADEM). They organized international, regional, and local study groups and conferences on issues of violence against women, on female genital mutilation, for example, in 1982, and on global trafficking in 1983. By 1985, violence against women was included in the Nairobi Forward-Looking Strategies as an impediment to peace, and member states were urged to establish national machinery to deal with violence against women in family and society.[12]

After the Nairobi conference, violence against women became an object of study within UN agencies and international organizations. In 1986, the Division for the Advancement of Women (DAW), the secretariat of the Commission on the Status of Women (CSW), organized a meeting of nongovernmental experts, Violence within the Family with Special Emphasis on Women, which culminated in the first resolution by CSW on violence against women, Efforts to Eradicate Violence against Women within the Family and Society, in 1988. In 1991 CSW convened another expert meeting, Violence against Women in All Its Forms, focusing on three issues: the strengthening of the general recommendations of CEDAW, the appointment of a special rapporteur, and a declaration on violence against women. In 1992, the issue of "women's human rights" was included in the meeting of an Expert Group on Women in Development of the OECD (Organization for Economic Cooperation and Development).[13]

Meanwhile, research and training activities by international NGOs intensified. In 1990, in preparation for the Vienna World Conference on Human Rights, Charlotte Bunch, the director of the Center for Women's Global Leadership, a U.S.-based international nongovernmental group, brought together leaders of women's rights networks for a training workshop. It soon became clear to the participants that violence against women was a concern to all of them and that they wanted to link it to human rights. In 1991, the center convened its first Global Leadership Institute that focused on women, violence, and human rights, and, after that workshop, the center started the first global campaign on violence against women, called Sixteen Days of Activism (waged between the International Day Against Violence Against Women, November 25, and Human Rights Day, December 10). They also initiated a petition—which received more than half a million signatures—urging governments to recognize gender violence as a violation of human rights at the Vienna conference. The Global Campaign for Women's Human Rights, involving ninety NGOs, was launched.[14] Women's groups organized to prepare NGO papers at satellite meetings at the grassroots level prior to each official regional "prepcom" (preparatory committee) for the Vienna conference. As a researcher notes, "as it turned out, this seemingly cumbersome process offered excellent opportunities to the women's movement, which had developed extensive regional and international networks during the three world conferences on women and which was experienced at international coordination on the issue of women's rights as human rights."[15] In particular, the satellite conference, La Nuestra, organized by Inter-American Institute for Human Rights in San Jose, Costa Rica, resulted in a nineteen-point recommendation, which included the recognition of violence against women as a human rights violation, the appointment of a special rapporteur on gender violence, and the call for an optional protocol for CEDAW to allow for individual complaints.

By the Rio Conference on Environment and Development in 1992, women were organized enough to generate a gender-sensitive lobbying document, "Women's Action Agenda 21," based on the official conference document drafts.[16] In 1993, women's groups "seized" the Vienna World Conference on Human Rights. The nineteen-point recommendation drafted at La Nuestra was adopted by the women's NGO caucus. The thirty-three testimonies by women about their experiences of violence in the parallel NGO Global Tribunal on Violations of Women's Human Rights captured media attention. Although NGOs were excluded from the official drafting process, UNIFEM organized a daily women's caucus, attended by NGOs, government delegates, and UN staff members. In the final Vienna Declaration and Platform for Action, gender-based violence was for the first time defined at the intergovernmental level as a human rights issue.

> The human rights of women and of the girl-child are an inalienable, integral and indivisible part of universal human rights. The full and equal participation of women in political, civil economic, social and cultural life, at the national, regional and international levels, and the eradication of all forms of discrimination on grounds of sex are priority objectives of the international community. Gender-based violence and all forms of sexual harassment and exploitation, including those resulting from cultural prejudice and international trafficking, are incompatible with the dignity and worth of the human person, and must be eliminated. This can be achieved by legal measures and through national action and international cooperation in such fields as economic and social development, education, safe maternity and health care, and social support. The human rights of women should form an integral part of the United Nations human rights activities, including the promotion of all human rights instruments relating to women. The World Conference on Human Rights urges governments, institutions, intergovernmental and non-governmental organizations to intensify their efforts for the protection and promotion of human rights of women and the girl-child. (Vienna Declaration and Platform for Action, 1993, paragraph 18)

What emerged in the process leading to Vienna was a network of women's human rights activists and experts, made up of local, regional, and international NGOs, academics (feminist legal scholars, sociologists, biologists, and educators), professionals (lawyers, doctors, counselors, therapists, and journalists), and intergovernmental organization (IGO) staff members. A crucial factor enabling this development was the formation of the Women's Caucus. As Chen puts it, "introduced at the 1992 Conference on Environment and Development, it became a fixture at subsequent UN conferences, coordinating lobbying efforts among women's NGOs while also disseminating information."[17]

After 1993, the women's human rights community dramatically expanded. Many established groups, such as Amnesty International, Human Rights Watch, and Women in Law and Development in Africa, added women's human rights to their programs. New national, regional, and global networks proliferated. By the late 1990s, global networks with overlapping memberships had emerged on all the major issues of violence against women: female genital mutilation, domestic violence, honor killings, sexual abuse of children, trafficking and prostitution, reproductive rights, violence against women in war, violence against minority women, and violence against migrant women. But this global women's human rights epistemic network has not restricted itself only to the women's cause. As early as the 1980s women's activists were already mobilizing around other issues, such as environment.[18] By the early 1990s, a decade of cross-mobilizations came to fruition in the final outcome documents of the 1992 Rio Conference on Environment and Development and the 1993 Vienna World Conference on Human Rights.[19] Thus what has emerged since is a community of feminist activists concerned not only with issues related to women, but also with the environment, development, human rights, population, human settlements, indigenous peoples, and children.

Above all, a great number of UN agencies have jumped on the bandwagon in the crusade for women's human rights. Since the 1994 Cairo conference, United Nations Population Fund (UNFPA) has consistently linked violence against women to population and development. In 1998, six UN agencies—the United Nations Development Fund for Women (UNIFEM), the UN Development Program (UNDP), the UNFPA, the United Nation's Fund for Children (UNICEF), the UN Commission for Trade and Development (UNCTAD), and the UN High Commission on Refugees (UNHCR)—launched a global campaign and organized a videoconference on violence against women. On International Women's Day in 2000, UNICEF launched a global campaign against "honor killings." In late 2001, the World Health Organization issued the first World Report on Violence and Health. From a nonissue a mere decade ago, then a marginalized issue dealt with by the Commission on the Status of Women and the Commission on Human Rights until 1993, "women's human rights" has become incorporated to various extents in various UN bodies and agencies.[20]

Since 1993, state actors have also joined this global women's human rights community. In 1993, for example, Australia created a National Committee on Violence against Women, and in 1994 Malaysia passed the Domestic Violence Act and initiated domestic violence awareness campaigns. In 1999, four French ministries—employment, justice, the interior, and defense—signed an interministerial circular calling for a strengthening of policies concerning domestic violence, and in 2000 they initiated the first national survey on violence against women in France. Women's human rights has become a new category for research and training at the global as well as at the local level. Old statistics are reexamined and new ones collected. Research centers are created and programs funded by international foundations. Study groups, expert meetings, and regional conferences continue. Community education and training programs spread. Manuals, guidelines, and cross-national comparisons are published. By the Beijing-Plus-Five Conference in June 2000, intergovernmental organizations, states, and NGOs were ready to show their latest studies, data, and publications.[21] In short, within the span of just a few years, a whole new body of knowledge concerning women's human rights has emerged worldwide.

Institutionalization of Global Norms on Women's Human Rights

"Women's rights are human rights" represented a major conceptual and organizational breakthrough in the global as well as local women's movements. Since the 1993 Vienna conference, the Inter-American Convention on the Prevention, Punishment, and Eradication of Violence against Women (1994) and the UN Declaration on the Elimination of Violence against Women (1994) were adopted. A special rapporteur on violence against women was also appointed in 1994. In 2000, the Optional Protocol to CEDAW, allowing an individual complaint procedure, if ratified by member states, was to further strengthen UN mechanisms on women's human rights.

Above all, women's human rights became a rallying point for women activists at all the major world conferences after 1993. At the 1994 Cairo Conference on Population and Development, women introduced the issue of violence as a form of control of women's health and sexuality and as a clear obstacle to women's right to self-determination in matters related to their reproduction.[22] As a journalist reported,

> "Cairo represented a fundamental paradigm shift in the way the population field perceives the problem and, most important, the solution," said Adrienne Germain, president of the International Women's Health Coalition in New York, which assists women's health groups in the third world. "It put women's health and rights at the center of the agenda, recognizing that in so doing, demographic ends would also be served."[23]

In the subsequent Programme of Action, "reproductive health" was defined as a women's human rights issue:

> Reproductive health is a state of complete physical, mental, and social well-being and not merely the absence of diseases or infirmity, in all matters relating to the reproductive system and to its functions and processes. Reproductive health therefore implies that people are able to have a satisfying and safe sex life and that they have the capability to reproduce and the freedom to decide if, when and how often to do so. Implicit in this last condition are the right of men and women to be informed and to have access to safe, effective, affordable and acceptable methods of family planning of their choice, as well as other methods of their choice for regulation of fertility which are not against the law, and the right of access to appropriate health-care services that will enable women to go safely through pregnancy and childbirth and provide couples with the best chance of having a healthy infant. In line with the above definition of reproductive health, reproductive health care is defined as the constellation of methods, techniques and services that contribute to reproductive health and well-being by preventing and solving reproductive health problems. It also includes sexual health, the purpose of which is the en-

hancement of life and personal relations, and not merely counseling and care related to reproduction and sexually transmitted diseases. (1994 Programme of Action of the International Conference on Population)

Further, at the 1995 World Summit for Social Development in Copenhagen, violence against women was linked to poverty, unemployment, and social disintegration, and it was seen as an impediment to the full participation of women in society. As the director of UNIFEM, Noeleen Heyzer, noted at the summit,

Violence against women is pervasive not just in war or refugee camps but on the street, in the workplace, and in the home. Domestic violence not only causes physical suffering but disrupts women's lives and blocks their individual growth and participation in society. . . . One cannot ignore another kind of violence against women—from which the first derives—the violence of economic systems that do not value the contributions women make.[24]

In the Copenhagen Declaration and Programme of Action, an entire commitment was devoted to the protection and promotion of women's human rights. During the subsequent 1995 Fourth World Conference on Women in Beijing, all forms of violence against women were redefined as legitimate public and international human rights issues in the final Platform for Action:

The term "violence against women" means any act of gender-based violence that results in, or is likely to result in, physical, sexual or psychological harm or suffering to women, including threats of such acts, coercion or arbitrary deprivation of liberty, whether occurring in public or private life. Accordingly, violence against women encompasses but is not limited to the following:

a) Physical, sexual and psychological violence occurring in the family, including battering, sexual abuse of female children in the household, dowry-related violence, marital rape, female genital mutilation and other traditional practices harmful to women, non-spousal violence and violence related to exploitation;

b) Physical, sexual and psychological violence occurring within the general community, including rape, sexual abuse, sexual harassment and intimidation at work, in educational institutions and elsewhere, trafficking in women and forced prostitution.

c) Physical, sexual and psychological violence perpetrated or condoned by the State, wherever it occurs.

Other acts of violence include violation of the human rights of women in situations of armed conflict, in particular murder, systematic rape, sexual slavery and forced pregnancy. Acts of violence against women also include forced sterilization and forced abortion, coercive/forced use of contraceptives, female infanticide and prenatal sex selection. (1995 Beijing Platform for Action)

Two further developments after the historic Beijing conference advanced women's human rights at the international level. In 1998, 120 states signed the

Rome Statute for the creation of a permanent International Criminal Court (ICC). Despite the initial skepticism of some of the judges of the International Criminal Tribunal for the Former Yugoslavia (ICTY) and the International Criminal Tribunal for Rwanda (ICTR) about sexual assault prosecutions,[25] the ICC Statute contains the most elaborate international legal definitions of sex crimes to date. The London Charter creating the International Military Tribunal for Nuremberg made no mention of the offense of rape, although the Tokyo War Crimes Tribunal did charge rape as an offense based on the 1907 Hague Convention provisions relating to "family honor." Though rape was specifically prohibited under the Geneva Conventions of 1949 and the Additional Protocols of 1977,[26] it was not until the ICTY and ICTR statutes in 1993 and 1995, respectively, that rape was listed among the crimes against humanity. The jurisprudence of both tribunals further recognizes rape and other sexual and gender violence as among the most serious breaches of the laws and customs of war.[27] The statute of the permanent ICC takes these developments further by specifically prohibiting rape, sexual slavery, enforced prostitution, forced pregnancy, enforced sterilization, persecution based on gender, enslavement, trafficking, and other forms of sexual violence.[28]

> Article 7(1). Crimes against humanity . . .
>
> (g) Rape, sexual slavery, enforced prostitution, forced pregnancy, enforced sterilization, or any other form of sexual violence of comparable gravity; . . .
>
> Article 8(2)(b). War crimes in international armed conflict . . .
>
> (xxii) Committing rape, sexual slavery, enforced prostitution, forced pregnancy, as defined in article 7, paragraph 2 (f), enforced sterilization, or any other form of sexual violence also constituting a grave breach of the Geneva Conventions; . . .
>
> Article 8(2)(e). War crimes in non-international armed conflict . . .
>
> (vi) Committing rape, sexual slavery, enforced prostitution, forced pregnancy, as defined in article 7, paragraph 2 (f), enforced sterilization, or any other form of sexual violence also constituting a serious violation of Article 3 common to the four Geneva Conventions.

Negotiations held since the Rome treaty conference have also made it explicit that rape and other sexual violence can constitute acts of genocide under Article 6 of the ICC Statute. In addition to the substantive jurisdiction on crimes of sexual violence, the ICC statute is equally historic in integrating gender in its procedures as well as in its structure, including a "fair representation of female and male judges" (seven out of eighteen judges are women in the first round of appointments in 2003) and the appointment of legal advisors on sexual and gender violence. In April 2002, the statute finally acquired the sixty state signatures necessary to formally establish the ICC, which occurred in July 2002.

One last instrument that has furthered women's human rights is the Protocol to Prevent, Suppress and Punish Trafficking in Persons, Especially Women and Children, supplementing the United Nations Convention against Transnational Organized Crime passed by the UN Millennium General Assembly in December 2000. The protocol stipulates the responsibility of states to "prevent and combat" trafficking, defined as the "recruitment, transportation, transfer, harboring or receipt of persons" by improper means, such as force, abduction, fraud, or coercion, for an improper purpose such as forced or coerced labor, servitude slavery, or sexual exploitation. It also requires states to "protect and assist" trafficked persons.[29]

Institutionalization of Global Norms on Children's Human Rights

Although the Convention on the Rights of the Child (adopted by the UN in 1990 and ratified by most states) has specific provisions on sexual abuse, prostitution, and trafficking, few children's rights groups focused on sexuality issues before the 1990s. By the mid-1990s, the children's rights movement was able to build on the feminist global campaign combating violence against women. In each of the conference and outcome documents concerning women's human rights, the human rights of the girl child were emphasized. Paragraph 7.3 of the Cairo Programme of Action (1994) recognizes that "full attention should be given to the promotion of mutually respectful and equitable gender relations and particularly to meeting the educational and service needs of adolescents to enable them to deal in a positive and responsible way with their sexuality." Paragraph 269 of the Beijing Platform for Action affirms that:

> Sexual violence and sexually transmitted diseases, including HIV/AIDS, have a devastating effect on children's health, and girls are more vulnerable than boys to the consequences of unprotected and premature sexual relations. Girls often face pressures to engage in sexual activity. Due to such factors as their youth, social pressures, lack of protective laws, or failure to enforce laws, girls are more vulnerable to all kinds of violence, particularly sexual violence, including rape, sexual abuse, sexual exploitation, trafficking, possibly the sale of organs and tissues, and forced labor.

In 1996, two international NGOs (End Child Prostitution in Asian Tourism [ECPAT] and the NGO Group for the Convention on the Rights of the Child), UNICEF, and the Swedish government jointly organized the First World Congress against Commercial Sexual Exploitation of Children in Stockholm. One hundred and twenty-two governments at the conference endorsed the Declaration and Agenda for Action, which since then has provided the framework for the implementation of the specific articles of the Convention on the Rights of the Child (CRC). The Declaration and Agenda for Action reaffirms that:

> The commercial sexual exploitation of children is a fundamental violation of children's rights. It comprises sexual abuse by the adult and remuneration in cash or kind to the child or a third person or persons. The child is treated as a sexual object and as a commercial object. The commercial sexual exploitation of children constitutes a form of coercion and violence against children, and amounts to forced labor and a contemporary form of slavery.

In 2000, the UN adopted the Optional Protocol on Sexual Exploitation of Children to the Convention on the Rights of the Child. Further, at the follow-up Second World Congress against Commercial Sexual Exploitation of Children in Yokohama in December 2001, representatives of states, intergovernmental organizations, and NGOs, as well as the private sector, reiterated their commitment to:

> Reinforce their efforts against commercial sexual exploitation of children, in particular by addressing root causes that put children at risk of exploitation, such as poverty, inequality, discrimination, persecution, violence, armed conflicts, HIV/AIDS, dysfunctioning families, the demand factor, criminality, and violations of the rights of the child, through comprehensive measures, including improved educational access for children, especially girls, anti-poverty programmes, social support measures, public awareness-raising, physical and psychological recovery and social reintegration of child victims, and action in accordance with the relevant international instruments, while not criminalizing or penalizing the child victims.[30]

Human Rights Research, Training, and Information Dissemination

Each of the international instruments mentioned above also emphasizes the need for increased information, research, and training on women's and children's human rights. Though the promotion of human rights has been seen as key in the creation of a new world order since the dawn of postwar international cooperation, human rights education has at best been marginalized on the agendas of international organizations. Despite its official mandate of human rights education in the UNESCO charter, ideological conflicts between the "intellectuals" and the "functionalists" soon made it clear that education for peace and human rights would give way to more technical educational planning and literacy programs.[31] Postwar human rights education efforts had been sporadic, focusing largely on intergovernmental participation.[32]

It was not until the early 1990s that a renewed impetus for human rights education emerged, driven largely by nongovernmental organizations participating in the 1993 Vienna World Conference on Human Rights. Human rights education advocates managed to put human rights education back into the core of the UN's human rights mission:

> The World Conference on Human Rights reaffirms that States are duty-bound . . . to ensure that education is aimed at strengthening the respect of human rights and fundamental freedoms. . . . Education on human rights and the dissemination of proper information, both theoretical and practical, play an important role in the promotion and respect of human rights with regard to all individuals without distinction of any kind such as race, sex, language or religion, and this should be integrated in the education policies at the national as well as international levels. (Vienna Declaration and Platform for Action, 1993)

This affirmation was further elaborated in the declaration by the General Assembly for the UN Decade for Human Rights Education (1995–2004) in 1994:

> Convinced that human rights education should involve more than the provision of information and should constitute a comprehensive life-long process by which people at all levels in development and in all strata of society learn respect for the dignity of others and the means and methods of ensuring that respect in all societies . . .
>
> Believing that human rights education constitutes an important vehicle for the elimination of gender-based discrimination and ensuring equal opportunities through the promotion and protection of the human rights of women . . .
>
> [The General Assembly] Calls upon international, regional and national non-governmental organizations, in particular those concerned with women, labor, development and the environment, as well as all other social justice groups, human rights advocates, educators, religious organizations and the media, to increase their involvement in formal and non-formal education in human rights and to cooperate with the Centre for Human Rights in implementing the United Nations Decade for Human Rights Education. (General Assembly resolution 1994/184)

The subsequent Plan of Action for the Decade, which focuses on stimulating and supporting national and local initiatives under the coordination of the High Commissioner for Human Rights, became the most comprehensive international document on human rights education in UN history. Not only the various human rights commissions and committees but all UN agencies are urged to take action in human rights education, training, and public information.[33] Governments are encouraged to set up a national committee for human rights education and formulate national plans of action.[34] Nongovernmental organizations are seen as important, legitimate partners in the comprehensive efforts. Education on women's human rights is particularly emphasized.

Backlash

The affirmation of women's and children's human rights at these world conferences did not go unchallenged, however. Since the Cairo conference in 1994, the presence of antifeminist right-wing groups at the UN has actually intensified. As a feminist scholar writes, "On an international level, the counter-movement was disorganized but came together on the Beijing plan of action and attacked what it considered 'radical feminist' ideas."[35] A grand imam circulated a statement asserting:

> The Beijing Conference is only one stage in a connected series aiming at innovating new ways of life. Contravening religious values and destroying well-established customs and traditions without considering that these values, restrictions, and traditions have protected many nations from collapsing into the dungeon of sexual promiscuity, the disorders of psychological troubles or slipping into the quagmire of moral decay and disintegration [*sic*].[36]

As Morgan notes:

> At the UN conferences prior to Beijing, the Vatican, Roman Catholic–dominated countries, and fundamentalist Muslim governments had raised objections, especially about reproductive rights and issues of sexuality. In Beijing, these same forces contested parts of the official Platform for Action during the five regional preparatory conferences. This resistance took the form of bracketing the parts of the Platform the countermovement found objectionable, thus reserving them for discussion at the conference rather than agreeing on language ahead of time. This resulted in almost 40 percent of the text enclosed in what came to be called the Holy Brackets.[37]

These right-wing groups organized parallel workshops and conferences such as "The Vital Role of Women in the 21st Century" and "Family as the Cornerstone of Society," by REAL Women of Canada; "Educating Women to Control Their Fertility by a Natural Cost-Free Method," by the World Organization of the Ovulation Method Billings (Australia, Canada, Ireland, and the United States) at the Beijing Conference in 1995; and "Church, Synagogue, Mosque: Solutions for the Modern Family," by the Catholic Family and Human Rights Institute, in collaboration with the Organization of Islamic Conference, the governments of Argentina and Nicaragua, and others in 1999.[38]

By the Beijing-Plus-Five conference in June 2000, these right-wing groups had succeeded in getting governments (the Vatican, Roman Catholic–dominated countries, and some Muslim countries) to block sections in the final document that touched on women's sexual and reproductive rights. Although the final draft of the outcome document retained most of the Beijing wording and spirit, conservative religious groups had managed to stall the negotiation process. At the follow-up to the First World Conference on Children in 1990, the UN General Assembly Special Session on Children in May 2002, attended by 180 states and 400 youth delegates, negotiations on the final agreement, entitled "A World Fit For Children," nearly collapsed over issues of children's reproductive health, including birth control and sex education. The United States, the Vatican, and Islamic countries had refused to sign the agreement unless it stated that abstinence is the only acceptable approach to AIDS and sex education in UN-supported aid programs.[39] Twenty-one specific goals were finally agreed upon at the eleventh hour, with elusive language on child rights and reproductive health.[40]

Development of Minority Rights within the United Nations

Ironically, the International Convention on the Elimination of All Forms of Racial Discrimination (ICERD) was adopted much earlier (in 1965) than CEDAW (1979) and CRC (1989). Article 1 of ICERD prohibits any "distinction, exclusion, restriction or preference based on race, color, descent, or national or ethnic origin." Further, Article 27 of the 1966 International Covenant on Civil and Political Rights (ICCPR) states, "In those States in which ethnic, religious or linguistic minorities exist, persons belonging to such minorities should not be denied the rights, in community with the other members of their group, to enjoy their own culture, to profess and practice their own religion, or to use their own language." The problem, however, is twofold. On the one hand, both of these provisions are so broad that individual minority groups still need specific human rights instruments to delineate their rights. On the other, interpretation of the scope of these two articles is so varied that states often engage in arm twisting with CERD members. As Wolfrum notes, ICERD's approach to "race" has always been a general one:

> CERD [the Committee] has so far not made an attempt to further specify what is meant by the notion of race as referred to in Article 1, para. 1, of the Convention. . . . In general, it was felt that there was no need to do so since the terms of reference in Article 1, para.1, of the Convention are broad enough to cover all situations the Convention attempts to eliminate.[41]

The issue of caste, for example, came up when the CERD Committee examined the Indian government's periodic report in 1996. Although CERD members argued that because one became a member of a caste by birth it was a matter of descent and therefore fell under Article 1 of ICERD, India denied that the caste system fell under the jurisdiction of CERD.[42]

How Article 1 of ICERD and Article 27 of ICCPR translate into the protection of indigenous peoples continues to be hotly debated. Despite tremendous local and international mobilization since the early 1980s, indigenous peoples have yet to fight for their rights within the framework of a UN convention. Several other issue areas have also traditionally been outside the jurisdiction of ICERD. There is no specific provision within ICERD, for example, for migrant workers and their families, even though most would fall within the scope of Article 1. The 1990 International Convention on the Protection of the Rights of All Migrant Workers and Members of Their Families finally came into force in 2003, but few states have ratified it. Further, though paragraph 2 of Article 1 of ICERD specifically stresses the lack of a distinction between citizens and noncitizens, CERD has yet to react effectively against xenophobic phenomena.[43] The issue of reparation for colonization and slavery, covered neither in ICERD nor in any other UN convention, also resurfaced in the 1990s. Finally, the invisibility of minority women across a spectrum of UN treaties exposes the linearity in which human rights instruments are set up to treat different aspects of discrimination separately.[44] In contrast to other mainstream human rights instruments, ICERD makes no specific mention of nondiscrimination based on sex. The CERD Committee has traditionally completely ignored gender in its committee composition, treaty interpretation, and reporting procedures, and has operated in almost total isolation from the CEDAW Committee.[45] As Michael Banton, chairman of the CERD Committee, expressed in 1996, directives regarding amendment of reporting guidelines to encourage the integration of gender into state parties reports were "fundamentally misconceived." According to him, the purpose of the committee was to deal with cases of racism, and it was CEDAW's job to deal with women.[46] Only in 2000, in preparation for WCAR, did CERD issue a General Recommendation (XXV), entitled "Gender-Related Dimensions of Racial Discrimination," in which:

> The Committee notes that racial discrimination does not always affect women and men equally or in the same way. There are circumstances in which racial discrimination only or primarily affects women, or affects women in a different way, or to a different degree than men. . . . Accordingly, the Committee, when examining forms of racial discrimination, intends to enhance its efforts to integrate gender perspectives, incorporate gender analysis, and encourage the use of gender-inclusive language in its sectional working methods.

In November 2000, the Office of High Commissioner for Human Rights, the Division for the Advancement of Women, and UNIFEM organized the Expert Group Meeting on Race and Gender in Zagreb, Croatia. Reflecting on the fact that "neither the gender aspects of racial discrimination nor the racial aspects of gender discrimination are fully comprehended within human rights discourses," and building on the "growing recognition that race and gender discrimination are not mutually exclusive phenomena," Kimberlé Crenshaw, a professor of law at Columbia University, proposes an intersectional conceptual as well as methodological framework. She explains,

> Intersectionality is a conceptualization of the problem that attempts to capture both the structural and dynamic consequences of the interaction between two or more axes of subordination. It specifically addresses the manner in which racism, patriarchy, class oppression and other discriminatory systems create background inequalities that structure the relative positions of women, races, ethnicities, classes, and the like . . .
>
> Intersectional subordination by its very nature is often obscured because it tends to happen to those who are marginal even within subordinate groups and because the existing paradigms for assessing discriminatory behavior do not consistently anticipate this form of discrimination. . . . Recognizing and accommodating this problem requires that intersectional protocols place primary focus on contextual analysis. Attention to intersectional discrimination thus calls for an analytical strategy that values a bottom-up analysis. Beginning with questions about how women live their lives, the analysis can build upward, accounting for the various influences that shape the lives and life changes of marginalized women.[47]

In 2001, the Committee on the Status of Women finally issued its Agreed Conclusions on Gender and All Forms of Discrimination, in Particular Racism, Racial Discrimination, Xenophobia, and Related Intolerance. It urges the UN and governments as well as civil society to:

> Examine the intersection of multiple forms of discrimination including the root causes from a gender perspective with special emphasis on gender-based racial discrimination in order to develop and implement strategies, policies and programmes aimed at elimination of all forms of discrimination against women, and to increase the role women play in the design, implementation and monitoring of gender-sensitive anti-racist policies.

The World Conference against Racism, Racial Discrimination, Xenophobia, and Related Intolerance, held in Durban, South Africa, in 2001, represented the first world conference at which a wide spectrum of minority issues was raised. The two previous world conferences to combat racism and racial discrimination, in 1978 and 1983, were largely consumed by struggles against apartheid. The five official themes of WCAR were: 1) Sources, causes, forms, and contemporary manifestations of racism, racial discrimination, xenophobia, and related intolerance; 2) Victims of racism, racial discrimination, xenophobia, and related intolerance; 3) Measures of prevention, education, and protection at the national, regional, and international levels; 4) Provision of effective remedies, recourse, redress, compensatory, and other measures; and 5) Strategies to achieve full and effective equality, including international cooperation and enhancement of the United Nations and other international mechanisms. As it turned out, the most contentious exercise was actually the fundamental task of defining race and racism. The statement of Turkey best summarizes the position of the "status-quo states," which prefer a narrow, unchanging definition of grounds of racism: "it is not the subject of this conference to strengthen the capacity of CERD."[48] Although "women" and "gender" are relatively visible in the outcome document (contained in thirty-five and sixteen paragraphs, respectively), the now familiar footnote, which reads "For the purpose of this Declaration and Programme of Action, it was understood that the term 'gender' refers to the two sexes, male and female, within the context of society. The term 'gender' does not indicate any meaning different from the above," reminds us that the issue of sexual orientation continues to be policed tightly, notably by many Asian, African, and Islamic states and the Holy See.[49] One country from the OIC (Organization of Islamic Countries) protested the frequent use of the term "gender-sensitive" in the outcome document, arguing that it "made no sense in Arabic."[50] OAU (Organization of African Unity) states were adamantly against adding "disability"as a cause of racism, arguing that doing so would "dilute" the conference. But the expression "multiple forms of discrimination" does find its way into ten paragraphs, while the term "intersectionality" appears for the first time in a UN human rights document under "other victims."[51] Although there were major setbacks for the global movements concerning caste (excluded at eleventh hour from the final outcome document), indigenous peoples' rights (circumscribed by national sovereignty), reparation for colonization and slavery (no compensation despite the fact that they constitute crimes against humanity), and migrant workers (undocumented migrant workers excluded), WCAR did become the first world conference in which these issues were substantially raised within UN settings. I shall further discuss the outcomes of WCAR with respect to minority rights in Japan in chapter 7.

IT IS ONE THING to assert that there is an emergent body of global norms concerning women's and children's human rights, and it is yet another to demonstrate that they actually matter and impact states. As Stienstra argues, "despite the successes, it is difficult to measure the impact that various achievements for women at the international level have had at national levels."[52] On the one hand, governments seemed to have done little to fulfill their pledges. On the other, as Elshtain notes, "the significance of international documents is not that governments will automatically implement them but that national and local groups can use them to hold their governments accountable. In this sense, what appears as universal standards can be adapted and used in local contexts to further specific emancipatory agendas."[53] I will now turn to the policy, institutional, and legal changes concerning women's and children's human rights norms in Japan since the mid-1990s.

CHAPTER FOUR

Policy, Institutional, and Legal Changes Concerning Women's and Children's Human Rights in Japan

On December 13, 1999, a court awarded the largest sum to date—$110,000—in a sexual harassment case in Japan to a 21-year-old female student who was molested by the Osaka governor during his campaign. Women's groups, offended by the governor's comments about "such a small thing as sexual harassment," mounted a letter campaign to press for criminal charges. "An unprecedented number of complaints poured in from the public. . . . We felt a great deal of pressure as a result of the letters," a senior prosecutor told a news conference.[1] A mere week later, the extremely popular comedian-turned-politician was forced to resign, to be replaced by the first woman governor in Japan's history. "This indictment must be considered a major step forward for women's rights in Japan," said an Upper House member. "In the past, sexual harassment and rape victims typically ended up being treated like the accused." In March 2000, the former governor apologized to the victim during his trial for indecent assault. This infamous case occurred two months after the vice-minister for defense, Nishimura Shingo, was forced to resign in October 1999, partly because of his comments comparing nuclear deterrence to rape laws.[2]

About a decade ago, terms such as sexual harassment, domestic violence, sexual slavery, and sexual exploitation did not exist in Japanese. Sex and violence, and especially sexual violence, were largely taboo and remained absent from debate within both academia and public policy. Since the late 1980s, however, there has been an explosion of discursive and institutional changes concerning women's human rights. In 1989, the phrase "*seku hara*," the abridged translation of "sexual harassment," was selected by a magazine as one of the most popular phrases of the year. Sexual harassment trials throughout the 1990s were the subject of intense media attention and even managed, as the above examples show, to end the careers of popular politicians. In 1992, after almost fifty years of silence, the Japanese government finally admitted its involvement in establishing comfort women stations during World War II and made its first public apology during the Japan-Korea summit meeting. This confession then kicked off in 1993 a process of research, witness hearings, and public statements on a problem that had long been regarded by the Japanese government as concluded by bilateral treaties. In 1996, the term "domestic violence" first appeared in a public policy paper, the "Vision of Gender Equality: Creating New Values for the 21st Century," drafted by the Council on Gender Equality within the Prime Minister's Office. Between 1997 and 2001, eight important legal changes regarding women and children took place: requiring sexual harassment prevention at workplaces; legalizing the pill; mandating provisions on gender equality at state and local levels; banning child prostitution and pornography; banning child abuse; banning stalking; promoting human rights education; and, finally, outlawing domestic violence. Further, in 2001, three opposition parties submitted a united bill, the Promotion of Resolution for Issues Concerning Victims of Wartime Sexual Coercion. Though it still had not been passed as of 2003, this bill represents a significant breakthrough on the issue of "comfort women" in Japan. This chapter discusses the policy, institutional, and legal changes concerning violence against women and children in Japan since the mid-1990s.

Violence against women is certainly not new in Japan, and women's groups have consistently fought against it. The oldest nongovernmental women's group in Japan, the Christian Temperance Women Union, created in the nineteenth century, campaigned against alcoholism and, in conjunction, domestic violence. In 1919, two feminist pioneers, Hiratsuka Raicho and Ichikawa Fusae, created the Shin Fujin Kyōkai (New Women Association). In addition to fighting for the right of women to vote, the organization also launched a campaign to prohibit the marriage of men infected with sexually transmitted diseases. But their most difficult and protracted battle was to abolish the four-hundred-year-old public prostitution system.

Japan has been called a prostitution culture.[3] Prostitution was officially sanctioned by the Tokugawa government, and it continued to flourish after World War II, as daughters of poor families were sent to the cities. The Japanese government actually spent 100 million yen to create sex-related "comfort" facilities for the occupation forces.[4] Although licensed prostitution was banned by the Allied powers in 1946 to limit the spread of sexually transmitted diseases, "special eating and drinking districts" were allowed. Successive attempts by female Diet members and a network of thirty-three women's groups to pass a law to prohibit prostitution failed so pitifully that women's groups described it as a "*nanzan*" (difficult delivery).[5] In spite of the Anti-Prostitution Law passed in 1956, the prostitution industry—including nude studios and Turkish baths in the 1960s, Asian sex tours[6] in the 1970s; "*Japayuki san*" (women migrant workers from Asia and other regions ending up in the "entertainment" businesses) in the 1980s; and "*enjo kōsai*" (child prostitution) and child pornography in the 1990s—has actually flourished under the Japanese economic miracle.[7] The multi-billion-dollar "ejaculation businesses" (*shasei sangyō*)[8] are legal and regulated by the government through the Regulatory Law on Adult Entertainment Businesses.

What is new, however, are the definition, scope, and political legitimization of discussion concerning violence against women and children as a human rights issue. Before the early 1990s, the term "violence against women" did not exist in Japanese. Campaigns against sexual violence focused mostly on anti-prostitution efforts. Even then, many Japanese women, including feminists, were reluctant to be involved in the liberation of fellow Asian women involved in the sex trade outside or within Japan.[9] Prostitution was rarely treated as a human rights issue. Since the Anti-Prostitution Law was passed in 1956, there had been no policies concerning sexual violence implemented for almost forty years. Although the issues of sexual harassment, comfort women, domestic violence, and the sexual exploitation of children have surfaced successively in Japanese society since the late 1980s, it was not until 1996 that the Japanese government finally formally incorporated the issue of violence against women (*josei ni tai suru bōryoku*) under the rubric of "women's human rights" (*josei no jinken*) in its policy paper. Since then, "violence against women" has become a legitimate topic for media coverage, national and local surveys,[10] and public symposia and seminars,[11] as well as bureaucratic and legislative interventions.

The World Conference of the International Year of the Woman in 1975 played an irreversible role in introducing the question of the "status of women" in Japan.[12] The first "national machinery," made up of the Headquarters for the Planning and Promotion of Policies Relating to Women, the Office for Women's Affairs, and the Advisory Council to the Prime Minister on Women's Affairs, was created in 1975. Since then, the Japanese government has elaborated national plans of action in 1977, 1981, 1987, 1990, and 1996. The term "violence against women" (*josei ni tai suru bōryoku*) first appeared in a Japanese government report, the 1993 Status and Policy Concerning Women (Josei no Genjō to Seisaku), an annual review of the national plan of action initiated soon after the International Year of the Woman in 1975. However, violence against women appeared under the heading "International Peace and Cooperation" as a foreign, rather than domestic, issue. In 1994, when the Japanese government prepared its report for the Beijing Conference, violence against women was treated in a separate chapter, even though the focus was still on peace.[13] Only in 1996 was violence against women defined for the first time as a human rights violation in a broad policy paper known as the "Vision of Gender Equality."

> Violence against women infringes upon their human rights and fundamental freedoms. It is not a problem for women as individuals alone: it constitutes a critical social and structural problem that drives them down to more subordinate positions than men. . . . Violence against women is not limited to physical harm. According to Article 1 of the Declaration on the Elimination of Violence Against Women adopted at the United Nations General Assembly in 1993, the term "violence against women" means any act of gender-based violence that results in, or is likely to result in, physical, sexual or psychological harm or suffering to women, including threats of such acts, coercion or arbitrary deprivation of liberty, whether occurring in public or in private life. In order to abolish violence against women, it is first necessary for each and every member of society to clearly recognize the definition of this term. . . . In recent years, however, there has been a strong awareness of violence against women in the international community. In the 4th World Conference on Women held in Beijing last year, this problem was pointed out as one of the critical areas of concern, and effective efforts to abolish it were urged. In Japan, violence against women is being increasingly revealed due to initiatives by NGOs and such. Efforts are required to abolish violence against not only Japanese but also foreign women, based upon reflections on the problem of the so-called comfort women, whose honor and dignity have long since been seriously damaged. ("Vision of Gender Equality," part II, 4(1), 1996)

The "Vision of Gender Equality," the most comprehensive document concerning gender relations in Japan to date, marks a drastic departure from all previous policy papers concerning women in Japan. It introduces for the first time the term "gender equality" to replace the traditional concept of "the status of women." It links human rights to women's rights. It defines "violence against women" and includes sexual crimes against children. It incorporates reproductive rights as an issue of violence against women. Finally, it emphasizes the need to strengthen cooperation among the state, local public bodies, and NGOs. The document largely set the tone not only for the subsequent National Plan of Action for the Promotion of a Gender-Equal Society by Year 2000 in 1996, which contains fuller provisions on violence against women, but also for the first Basic Law for a Gender-Equal Society (1999), which requires all local governments to implement measures promoting equal gender participation and gender equality.

In 1997, the Council for Gender Equality, the national machinery on the status of women in Japan, established the Subcommittee on Violence against

TABLE 4.1

Violence against Women and Children as a Legitimate Policy Concern in Japan

	Policy papers			
	Status and Policy Concerning Women	National Report for the Fourth World Conference on Women	Vision of Gender Equality	Report by the Council for Gender Equality to the Prime Minister
Year	1990	1994	1996	1999
Policy objective	Status of women	Status of women	Gender equality	Gender equality
How covered as VAW	Nonissue	International peace	Human rights	Human rights
Definition of violence against women	None	None	UN Declaration on VAW	UN Declaration on VAW
Scope	None	Sex crimes Prostitution Sexual harassment Violence at home	Sex crimes Prostitution Sexual harassment Violence at home Child prostitution Comfort women	Sex crimes Prostitution Sexual harassment "DV" Reproductive rights
Action measures	None	Legislation Prevention Police training Inclusion of women in the police and judiciary	Legislation Prevention Relief services Training of state personnel	Survey Coordination of institutions Education Batterers counseling

Women. By 1999, when the subcommittee delivered its first report on violence against women to the prime minister, there was comprehensive coverage not only on sex crimes and prostitution, but also on sexual harassment, domestic violence, and reproductive rights. Despite conscious efforts by the government to avoid foreign terminology, the term "DV" (domestic violence) was used for the first time in a Japanese policy document. "Violence against women" was defined according to the 1994 UN Declaration on Violence against Women. The report also outlined five action items, including the creation of a national survey, the improvement of coordination among ministries, establishment of education and outreach, development of a prevention policy, and the creation of a batterer rehabilitation policy. In late 1999, the first national survey on domestic violence was carried out. In a sample of 3,405 people, 1,773 of whom were women, 4.6 percent of women acknowledged that they had experienced life-threatening violence from their current or former spouse or partners. In sum, between 1990 and 1996 "violence against women" was drastically redefined; originally considered a nonissue, it was redefined as an issue of international cooperation in 1994, and finally considered a top policy concern in 1996. Table 4.1 shows the swift changes in the definition and scope of "violence against women" in four policy documents from 1990 to 1999: the "Status and Policy Concerning Women" (Fujin no Genjō to Seisaku) in 1990, the National Report of the Government of Japan for the Fourth World Conference on Women in 1994, the Vision of Gender Equality: Creating New Values for the 21st Century in 1996, and the Report by the Council for Gender Equality to the Prime Minister: Towards a Society without Violence against Women in 1999.

Institutional Changes

MINISTRY OF LABOR

Besides these policy changes, ministries as well as local governments have created a new body of "administrative guidance" (informal rules) concerning women's human rights since the latter part of the 1990s. The Ministry of Labor has taken on sexual harassment prevention as an integral part of their mandate. When the Equal Employment Opportunity Law (EEOL) was passed in 1985 as a result of Japan's ratification of CEDAW, some sort of grievance council was created to handle work-related complaints, including sexual harassment at work. However, the fact that both the employer and employee needed to agree before an investigation could be initiated meant that most complaints were rarely investigated. In 1993, the Ministry of Labor created a research group on sexual harassment and published the first government study on sexual harassment in Japan, "Women Employment Management and the Communication Gap." Twenty-five percent of the one thousand female respondents reported having experienced some form of sexual harassment. In 1994, the Ministry of Labor published two pamphlets on sexual harassment and distributed 180,000 copies to companies throughout Japan. In 1997, the EEOL was revised, mandating sexual harassment prevention in the workplace. Since then, the Ministry of Labor has designated sexual harassment counselors and sexual harassment prevention advisors, issued guidelines and prevention manuals for employers, and organized basic and advanced courses on sexual harassment prevention for companies.[14] The number of cases of sexual harassment reported by the Bureau of Women in the Ministry of Labor jumped from 850 in 1994 to 968 in 1995, 1,615 in 1996, 2,534 in 1997, and 7,019 in 1998 (Fig. 4.1).[15]

By 2000, it was estimated that about a third of all private companies had put in place some kind of sexual harassment policy.[16] For example, *Nikkei Shimbun*, the Japanese financial newspaper, had instituted sexual harassment training for managers as well as for new employees. They also produced sexual harassment training videos that have been used by other corporations. As the general manager of its Legal Affairs Office put it,

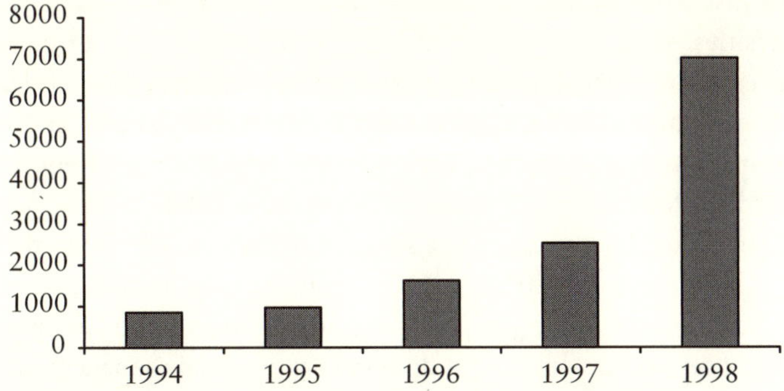

FIG. 4.1. Number of sexual harassment cases in Japan, 1994–98. Source: Ministry of Labor. Figures quoted in Kuninobu 2000.

We see it as a company strategy. It's better than the lawsuits if we didn't do anything to prevent harassment. We see sexual harassment training as part of our human rights education programs. I have done some training myself, but I also invite sexual harassment counselors from within or outside the government. Since the law took effect, we have included sexual harassment in our employment rules, and I know that most newspapers such as *Asahi* and *Yomiuri* have put in place sexual harassment policies. Many companies have purchased the sexual harassment prevention training videos that we produced.[17]

Dentsu, another giant Japanese corporation in the communications market, has also created a consultation section and treats sexual harassment seriously as part of risk management. As the company's sexual harassment counselor explains,

We published a whole book called *Company Ethics and Human Rights* in March 1999, which was distributed to all employees in order to explain clearly that sexual harassment is a human rights violation. We started with training for the management and then organized a lecture for all employees in March 1999 with a total of one thousand participants. Now we are planning our next training session for temporary workers who have been traditionally left out in this kind of training.[18]

In addition to the Ministry of Labor, the Personnel Authority has also set up sexual harassment guidelines for civil servants. In 1997, its first survey on sexual harassment among civil servants found that 70 percent of 2,500 women in the sample had experienced some form of sexual harassment.[19] In 1999, the Personnel Authority passed the so-called Rule 10–10, which mandates that heads of all ministries and agencies are responsible for the prevention of sexual harassment. Perhaps the most dramatic change concerns sexual harassment prevention in universities and schools. For almost an entire decade, between 1988 and 1998, sexual harassment was believed to be a problem only at the workplace. In

1998, the Ministry of Education conducted its first survey on 587 public and private universities. Only 6.6 percent of the institutions had put in place some kind of investigative mechanism for sexual harassment; 2.4 percent had conducted school-wide surveys; 8.2 percent had prevention programs; and 18.7 had consultation or counseling services for students who had experienced sexual harassment.[20] In March 1999, however, the Ministry of Education, too, issued guidelines on sexual harassment for all school personnel. Although the wording is not as strong as that in the Ministry of Labor guidelines or the Personnel Authority Rule 10–10 (Article 3 requires all school personnel to "pay attention" not to commit sexual harassment), it does mandate school management of sexual harassment prevention and resolution. By April 2000, one year after the guidelines took effect, it is estimated that about 70 to 80 percent of central and local government institutions[21] and a majority of universities had put into place some kind of sexual harassment policy.[22]

MINISTRY OF HEALTH AND WELFARE

Although the Ministry of Labor has taken a proactive stand on the issue of sexual harassment, the Ministry of Health and Welfare has found itself in a rather embarrassing position since violence against women became a political concern in the late 1990s. The major issue was that, until 1999, there was simply no policy or structure regarding battered women in Japan. The existing system of counseling and shelters for women, mandated by the 1956 Anti-Prostitution Law, is restricted to prostitutes or would-be prostitutes. There are forty-seven counseling centers in Japan (one center per prefecture), which can also serve as emergency shelters if needed,[23] and there are fifty-two "shelters" (*fujin hōgō shisetsu*, "women protection facilities"). In 1998, there were only 659 women counselors (most of whom were part-timers) and 634 staff members in the fifty-two shelters for the entire country. In the Tokyo metropolitan area, there were only two public shelters, with fewer than fifty rooms for a population of twelve million people. Since 1975, public women's centers have also provided some kind of counseling services, but they have neither the legal mandate nor the resources to address domestic violence. As one women's center counselor explained, "Eighty percent of our cases fall under domestic violence broadly defined. Often they come because of the violence. When no violence is involved, they do not come. But we used to call it a drug problem, a lack of family harmony, or a mental problem. The word 'domestic violence' appeared less than ten years ago."[24] A different kind of shelter, the *boshiryō*, or "mother-child apartment," was originally created after the war for widows, but its use was extended to single mothers in 1983. The *boshiryō* can in theory be used by battered women, but only if they are legally divorced.[25] Above all, it was designed for the protection of children.[26] In fact, this women-equals-mothers approach typifies the overall approach of the Ministry of Health and Welfare toward "women protection" (*fujin hōgō*). As the deputy manager of the Women's Assistance Unit admits, "Assistance for women is covered by two different services within the ministry. The Women's Assistance Unit under the Family Assistance Section of the Social Protection Bureau is a tiny structure within family assistance, and the other, the main organ, under the Child Family Bureau (Jidokatei Kyokku), protects mothers from the point of view of children."[27] It became increasingly clear that prostitutes account for only a minute portion of the counseling and shelter services. Data from 1998 show that prostitutes accounted for only 0.2 percent of those using the counseling centers, whereas victims of domestic violence represented 11.4 percent, the third largest category after those dealing with divorce and poverty.[28] In 1993, the Ministry of Health and Welfare extended the use of the current counseling and shelter facilities from prostitutes to women in distress in general. In 1999, it issued a special notice to local governments, officially extending use of the facilities to battered women.[29]

NATIONAL POLICE AGENCY

Meanwhile, the National Police Agency (NPA) has also stepped up its efforts in combating sex crimes more broadly defined. Until 1999, sex crimes had been narrowly conceived as rape and sexual assaults. Official statistics show a steady decline in reported rapes, from 5,161 in 1970 to 2,610 in 1980, 1,548 in 1990, and 1,500 in 1995. Of these cases, fewer than half were brought to court.[30] Similarly, the first nationwide survey conducted by the Office for Gender Equality on domestic violence found that 38 percent of the women who had suffered from domestic violence did not seek help from anybody. As the deputy director of the First Criminal Investigation Division of the NPA explained in front of an international audience in 1997,

> Japanese police have regarded sex crimes as especially serious crimes, to be investigated in the same manner as murder, robbery, arson, and abduction, since about ten years ago. We must admit, however, that we have not made enough effort to develop techniques to investigate sex crimes whereby victims are taken into consideration, to train detectives specializing in sex crimes, or to improve the system so that victims may report to the police more easily.[31]

A major reason for underreporting is the lack of sensitivity of the police, who often refuse to intervene, especially in the case of "family disputes." The near absence of female police officers until recently has also made the experience of reporting a sex crime often a harassing one. In 1997, female police officers made up only 3.4 percent (7,800) of the total police force and 1.3 percent of all detectives.[32] According to one shelter activist, "the police are the worst among all the government agencies [victims of sex crimes] have to deal with. Many of the women actually went to the police but were blamed instead, told that 'it's because you are bad' or 'it's because you don't *gaman*.'"[33] In 1996, the NPA devised its first general policy on sex crimes as part of the Basic Policy Concerning the Measures for Victims of Crime. It spelled out eleven measures:

(1) Designation of a special assistant for sex crime investigation who heads the sex crimes investigation squad (of which at least one officer is female) in the criminal investigation department of each prefectural police headquarters

(2) Recruitment and training of female police officers and detectives

(3) Information leaflets for sex crime victims

(4) Designation of a victim liaison officer

(5) Development of a sexual offenses evidence collection kit and substitute clothes for victims of sex crimes

(6) Special interview facilities for victims of sex crimes

(7) Hot lines for victims of sex crimes, operated by trained female police officers with counseling skills

(8) Education on sex crimes

(9) Creation of the "Sex Crimes Investigative Techniques Manual"

(10) Special training for special assistants for sex crime investigation

(11) In-house counseling services

By 1999 most of the eleven new measures had been initiated to some extent, although it remains unclear how they are enforced at the local levels. In 1999, the NPA also categorized domestic violence as a sex crime and began to formulate a specific policy on domestic violence.[34] In May 2000, the Ministry of Justice also submitted a proposal to examine the elimination of the time limit to report rape, currently set at six months.

MINISTRY OF EDUCATION

Perhaps the most unexpected change came from the Japanese Ministry of Education, which is notorious for its conservatism. For decades, "women's education" (*fujin kyoiku*) has meant ghettoized nonformal education for adult women in women's centers (*fujin kaikan*). Started before the war and expanded in the 1950s and 1960s,[35] women's education was further formalized in the 1970s under UNESCO's concept of women's education as lifelong education. After the first world conference on women in 1975, "women's education" in Japan did undergo a significant shift in approach and content. The first public National

Women's Education Center (NWEC) was established in 1977. In 1978, every city with a population of more than 300,000 was required to have a local women's center. There was a change, and not just in name, from "*fujin mondai*" (married women's problem), "*fujin kyoiku*" (women's education) in "*fujin kaikan*" (married women's centers) to "*josei mondai*" (women's problem), "*joseigaku kyoiku*" (women's studies) in "*josei sentā*" (women's centers).[36] The number of legitimate topics on women, by women, and for women has also greatly expanded. Whereas "*fujin kyoiku*" has primarily referred to the teaching of cooking, flower arrangement, the tea ceremony, and similar pursuits, *joseigaku kyoiku / josei kōza* (women's studies lectures) in the 1980s emphasized a critical examination of sex role division. The 1990s signaled the "second stage," with a new focus on sexuality, human rights, and empowerment. Arguably, yet a third phase has been unfolding since the second half of the 1990s, with the introduction of the concepts of gender and women's human rights in women's studies.[37] In 1998, the Women's Education Division within the Lifelong Learning Bureau in the Ministry of Education was renamed the Gender Equality Education Division. A gender-equal approach, or gender mainstreaming, has become a goal in the Japanese education system.[38] The number of workshops organized by the National Women's Education Center, the women's education arm of the Ministry of Education, on violence against women jumped from zero in 1996 to ten (out of a total of ninety-six workshops) in 1999, becoming the leading theme in its women's studies activities.[39] In April 2000, the Ministry of Education further sent out a memo to universities and other educational facilities and institutions, urging for their cooperation in organizing the annual Elimination of Violence Against Women Week, formerly known as the Purification of Social Moral Environment Campaign.[40]

LOCAL GOVERNMENTS

If central government ministries have just begun to move on the issue of violence against women, local governments have been more proactive. The decentralization movement in the 1990s has without doubt strengthened local governments. According to a survey conducted by a nongovernmental group, Femin Net, in November 1999, of thirty-one ward governments within the Tokyo metropolitan area, nine have conducted surveys on violence against women; twenty-two have organized sexual harassment training for their staff members and eleven have conducted violence against women training for their staff members; and fourteen have held seminars on the subject of violence against women for the general public. The Tokyo metropolitan government has played a particularly significant role in raising public awareness of domestic violence. In 1997 it carried out the first public survey on domestic violence in Japan. That more than a third of the respondents reported experiencing domestic violence sent shock waves throughout Japan. In 1999, the Tokyo government held the first public symposium on domestic violence and also published a training manual for related institutions. Similarly, the Sapporo city government has become known for their efforts in combating violence against women. Like the Tokyo metropolitan government, the Sapporo city government has created a unit within the women's planning section to deal with violence against women, and the government has carried out surveys and symposia. Others, such as the Yokohama city government, have also begun to create a network to coordinate the related institutions on violence against women.[41] In particular, local women's centers (numbering a few hundred throughout Japan) have, without exception, integrated the theme of violence against women into their counseling and outreach activities. Some larger centers, such as Forum Yokohama, have launched five-year projects addressing domestic violence. Forum Yokohama also started the three-year DV Mondai Kenkyū Project (Domestic Violence Research Project) after 1995 and completed five surveys. Since 1998, the group has thrice held a women's human rights lecture series.[42] The Dawn Center of Osaka has also chosen violence against women as its primary theme and created a special telephone counseling system, support groups, seminars, and surveys. As its pamphlet states,

> Gender-based violence has just begun to be addressed by Japanese women. Violence against women is a serious violation of women's human rights, which impairs the dignity of women and their right to be independent human beings. This is deeply rooted in the inaccurate view of gender consciousness in society. Dawn Center chose violence against women as an important theme to tackle as women and men work together to create a new society for the twenty-first century.[43]

Legal Changes

Perhaps the most drastic changes of all were the legal changes concerning women's and children's human rights in Japan in the 1990s. In a country notorious for the absence of legal reforms, the eight legal changes enacted between 1997 and 2001 listed above represent a puzzle. First, the Equal Employment Opportunity Law was revised in 1997. Employers now have a legal responsibility (*hairyō gimu*) to prevent sexual harassment in the workplace. Employers are now prohibited from (*kinshi*) discriminating against women in recruitment and promotion rather than simply "required to avoid" (*doryoku gimu*) it, as they were previously. Similarly, the government is now required to take measures to promote affirmative action for women. Finally, now one party, either the employer or the employee, can initiate an investigation of a labor dispute without the agreement of the other, and the name of the company will be disclosed if sanctions are applied.[44] Second, a low-dose contraceptive pill was finally legalized in 1999. Third, the first comprehensive Basic Law for a Gender-Equal Society was also passed that same year, mandating gender equality measures at both national and local levels.[45] Article 3 of the law reads, "Formation of a gender-equal society shall be promoted based on respect for the human rights of women and men, including: respect for the dignity of men and women as individuals; no gender-based discriminatory treatment of women or men; and the securing of opportunities for men and women to exercise their abilities as individuals."[46]

Fourth, the Child Prostitution and Pornography Prohibition Law was passed in 1999. Sexual intercourse and similar acts performed by adults with children under the age of eighteen though offers or promises of compensation to the child, whether in Japan or overseas, are prohibited. The production, distribution, and sales of child pornography, and the trafficking of children for the purpose of prostitution or pornography, are equally prohibited.

Fifth, the Child Abuse Prevention Law, whereby child abuse, including sexual abuse, was for the first time legally defined, was passed in May 2000. The law establishes the legal responsibility of medical and educational officials to investigate child abuse cases at an early stage, requires that police officers conduct investigations of suspected abuse, provides for the temporary injunction of parental access to their children, and requires that abusive parents receive counseling. In April 2000, the Tokyo metropolitan government became the first local government in Japan to establish an administrative section to deal exclusively with child abuse. Sixth, at the same time the Child Abuse Prevention Law was enacted, the Anti-Stalking Law was also passed in May 2000. The National Police Agency is to establish an anti-stalking task force in each of the forty-seven prefectural police headquarters by the end of March 2002. The task forces can issue binding verbal cautions to suspected stalkers. In December 2000, the Law on the Promotion of Human Rights Education, of which women's human rights is a central part, was passed. Finally, in March 2001, the Domestic Violence Prevention Law was also passed. If a court concludes that a victim of domestic violence is living in fear of being seriously injured by a spouse or partner, the law can ban the spouse from approaching the victim's home and office for six months, or order the spouse or partner to leave his/her home for two weeks. Table 4.2 summarizes the policy, institutional, and legal changes concerning women's and children's human rights.

In sum, the 1990s marked an exceptional decade for the advancement of women's and children's human rights in Japan. Violence against women, first a

TABLE 4.2

Policy, Institutional, and Legal Changes Concerning Women's and Children's Human Rights since the Mid-1990s

I) Policy Changes
- Vision of Gender Equality (1996): violence against women as a violation of women's human rights
- Plan for a Gender-Equal Society (1996): violence against women as a violation of women's human rights
- "Towards a Society without Violence against Women" Report to the Prime Minister (1999)

II) Institutional Changes
- Council for Gender Equality, Prime Minister's Office: Elimination of Violence against Women Week (1999)
- Ministry of Labor: sexual harassment prevention guidelines and manual (1999)
- Personnel Authority: sexual harassment prevention guidelines and manual (1999)
- Ministry of Education: sexual harassment prevention guidelines (1999), Gender Equality Education Unit (1988)
- Ministry of Health and Welfare: counseling and shelter services for battered women (1999)
- National Police Agency: eleven new measures for victims of sex crimes, including domestic violence and stalking (1996)

III) Legal Changes
- Revised Equal Employment Opportunity Law (1997)
- Legalization of the pill (1999)
- Basic Law for a Gender-Equal Society (1999)
- Child Prostitution and Pornography Prohibition Law (1999)
- Child Abuse Prevention Law (2000)
- Anti-Stalking Law (2000)
- Law on the Promotion of Human Rights Education (2000)
- Domestic Violence Prevention Law (2001)

nonissue and then a concern related to international cooperation, dealt with mainly by the Ministry of Foreign Affairs, was transformed into a domestic policy concern within a few short years between 1995 and 1999. In December 1995, the Japanese government actually submitted a resolution, the Role of the United Nations Development Fund for Women in Eliminating Violence against Women, to the Third Committee of the UN General Assembly and financially backed up the initiative. It was to convey "the government's intention to cooperate toward the strengthening of UN activities in this area."[47] Perhaps the Japanese government little expected the sweeping changes it had to make to incorporate "violence against women" on its *own* soil. The following chapter proceeds to discuss mobilization around five specific issue areas—the pill, sexual harassment, military sexual slavery, domestic violence, and child prostitution—at the grassroots level.

Grassroots Mobilization

The Pill, Sexual Harassment, Military Sexual Slavery, Domestic Violence, and Child Prostitution

> To speak is to fight. . . . Great joy is had in the endless invention of turns of phrase, of words and meanings, the process behind the evolution of language on the level of parole. But undoubtedly even this pleasure depends on a feeling of success won at the expense of an adversary—at least one adversary, and a formidable one: the accepted language, or connotation.
>
> Jean Francois Lyotard, *The Postmodern Condition*

Unraveling sexual violence in Japan has been a formidable fight. Until ten years ago, there was no term for, no information or data on, violence against women in Japan. Global norms on violence against women might provide the readily available discourse, definition, and blueprint for action, but they are hard to apply if the problem is said not to exist. This chapter is about how women in Japan spoke out on violence against women before the Japanese government took action in the late 1990s. I discuss how each of the five issues—the pill, sexual harassment, military sexual slavery, domestic violence, and child prostitution—has successively emerged as a topic of concern in Japan.

The Pill

The birth control movement in the United States and Europe has a long history, dating back to the early twentieth century and the indefatigable crusader Margaret Sanger. It might seem puzzling to the foreign reader why the pill remained such an issue in Japan in the 1990s. Although most industrialized countries legalized the pill in the 1960s and made the low-dose pill available in the 1970s, Japan was one of the few industrialized countries in the world where the pill was illegal until 1999. As Norgren describes,

Japan's pill ban is highly unusual: among countries where birth control is legal, Japan is one of only two or three countries where the pill has not been approved. Japan's policy on the pill stands in particular contrast to policy in other advanced industrial democracies, where tens of millions of women have been using the pill, legally, for the last 35 years. An average of 30 percent of contraceptors in the United States and Western Europe are pill users, and the pill is either the first or second most commonly used contraceptive method. In Japan, on the other hand, the primary method of contraception is the condom: as of 1994, 78 per cent of Japanese contraceptors relied on condoms, 7 per cent had been surgically sterilized, 3.7 per cent used IUDs, and 0.6 per cent used oral contraceptives. These figures have varied little in the postwar period.[1]

Why did Japanese women have to wait almost three decades longer for access to the pill, something that most of their Western counterparts took for granted as a basic right? As early as 1961, the Japanese Ministry of Health and Welfare set up the Oral Contraception Committee to look into the pill, but the approval process was abruptly stopped because of concerns about side effects. The unofficial story, although, is that the wife of Prime Minister Sato Eisaku was opposed to the pill because of fears that it would prompt sexual immorality.[2] Despite a declaration by the World Health Organization about the safety and reliability of the pill in 1967, the Japanese government continued its ban on the pill. In 1972, as part of the women's liberation movement in Japan, the Women's Coalition for Abortion Rights and Contraceptive Pills, commonly known as the Chūpiren, was formed. They wore pink helmets, stormed into the National Convention on Family Planning and Maternal and Child Health in Tokyo, and frequently demonstrated. But their impact was at best limited, if not adverse. The media was not friendly to the group, and the women's movement was split about the pill.[3] In 1974, the issue was brought to the Diet. Prime Minister Tanaka Kakuei reiterated that, for reasons of safety, the government would not approve the pill. Doctors, however, would have the discretion to dispense the pill for medical purposes. From that time until the pill was finally legalized in 1999, some 200,000 Japanese women used the pill to regulate hormonal or menstrual irregularities.[4]

In 1985, an important shift occurred. The Japan Society of Obstetrics and Gynecology and the Japan Association of Obstetrics and Gynecology for Maternal Protection, both of which until then had opposed the pill, sought permission to conduct clinical tests on the low-dose pill. The pill was tested on about five thousand Japanese women, and by 1990 the pill was deemed safe for approval. However, by this time two new concerns, AIDS and the "population crisis," had arisen. After repeatedly denying the existence of AIDS within Japan, the Ministry of Health and Welfare finally gave the first official definition of

AIDS, and the Minister of Health and Welfare had to apologize for its denial in 1993. At the same time, Japan recorded the lowest birth rate in the world, which caused a population decline, a labor shortage, the aging of the population, and a panic about the potential decline of the nation. The pill issue was once again shelved for larger public health and population reasons. In 1994, a nongovernmental network, Japan's Network for Women and Health, was formed, in part to lobby for the pill. In 1998, when approval of the pill seemed imminent, Japanese environmentalists raised yet a new objection: estrogen contained in the pill was considered an endocrine-disrupter, and hence a pollutant. Meanwhile, the Ministry of Health and Welfare approved the new drug for male impotence, Viagra, within less than six months in January 1999. When criticized both domestically and internationally, the Central Pharmaceutical Affairs Council within the Ministry of Health and Welfare responded that "Viagra is used for treating impotence, which is an illness, whereas the pill is used by healthy women; therefore, we need to be more prudent about the pill."[5] These comments inspired a new round of protests and petitions. Finally, the pill was approved in June 1999.

Sexual Harassment

Nude calendars, sexual innuendo, and explicit sexual demands were all part of office life for Japanese women. Until the Equal Employment Opportunity Law was passed in 1985, women were often relegated to a separate track and referred to as "office flowers." In addition to serving tea, wiping desks, and making photocopies, they were often expected to entertain clients or "be part of the group" when colleagues went to after-hours karaoke bars. Attending year-end parties or annual company trips to hot springs where many male colleagues got drunk and turned wild were de facto job duties.

In February 1988, a women's group called Action Women's Group introduced the sexual harassment guidelines of the International Confederation of Trade Unions. In June, the Labor Counseling Digest of the Tokyo metropolitan government started to record "sexual harassment" as a new counseling category. But it was the publication of the translation of an American handbook, "Stopping Sexual Harassment" by the Santama Group Concerned with Work and Sexual Discrimination, in October 1988 that changed Japanese office life. "Now that they were armed with the clearly defined term and concept of 'sexual harassment,' these women were able to see for the first time exactly what the mixture of displeasure, humiliation, frustrated anger, and fear of losing their jobs had been."[6] The publication struck such a chord with Japanese readers that it set off an avalanche of hot lines, study groups, surveys, and publications, as well as court cases. In October 1989, the Second Tokyo Lawyers Association started a telephone hot line addressing sexual harassment. The Network to Study Sexual Harassment in the Workplace published "Testimony on Sexual Harassment." "Sexual harassment" quickly became one of the most popular phrases of 1989.

The following year nongovernmental efforts continued while local governments and business federations started to respond to the issue. The Japan Pacific Information Network launched a national sexual harassment campaign. *Nikkei Woman* magazine spearheaded a survey of 1,300 businesswomen and -men. Of those who encountered sexual harassment, 48 percent "ignored it," 19 percent "silently put up with it," 17.2 percent "protested and asked that it be stopped," and a mere 4.8 percent "registered a complaint with a superior."[7] Another survey by the Women's Career Foundation found that 43 percent of the women in management in the sample had experienced sexual harassment. The Labor Economics Bureau of the Tokyo metropolitan government published its first sexual harassment counseling statistics. Women's groups organized a Sexual Harassment Summit to celebrate the anniversary of the first sexual harassment trial in Fukuoka. Nikkeiren, the Federation of Business Employer Associations, published sexual harassment prevention guidelines. The pioneer Santama Group Concerned with Work and Sexual Discrimination initiated the "10,000 People Sexual Harassment Survey." Ninety percent of the respondents reported having experienced sexual harassment.

In 1991, the Second Tokyo Lawyers Association drafted a sexual harassment prevention bill. In 1992, the first sexual harassment case in Japan was won. The supervisor of a thirty-two-year-old woman working at a publishing company in Fukuoka was said to have made repetitive remarks about her sex life such as "She's a loose girl" in front of other colleagues and clients. The court ruled in favor of the plaintiff and awarded her $15,000. Although the award was modest, this became the landmark sexual harassment case in Japan. It was the first time the concept of a "favorable working environment" (*hataraki yasui kankyō*) was cited, despite the absence of a legal definition of sexual harassment at the time. It was also the first time that the court pinpointed the management's responsibility in failing to correct the situation. Above all, many women's groups were formed to support the case, groups that played an indispensable role in uncovering what was until then experienced and accepted by many women in Japan as an everyday part of working life.

In 1993, the Ministry of Labor first officially defined sexual harassment. In 1994, a noted professor at Kyoto University was charged with sexual harassment of a female student and an office staff member and resigned his post. In a

Kanazawa construction company case, the Japanese court used the term "sexual harassment" in the ruling for the first time. The Japanese Women's Studies Association organized the workshop Background on Campus Sexual Harassment in Japan. The Tokyo metropolitan government published the first public sexual harassment prevention manual. In 1996, a student from Thailand brought a complaint to the Chiba police about being sexually harassed by her Japanese professor. The Ministry of Labor set up a special study group to work on sexual harassment prevention guidelines. A pioneer group named No! Sexual Harassment set up the 24-hour Hot Line on Violence against Women. In 1997, the national Campus Sexual Harassment Network was formed. It successfully pressured the Ministry of Education to conduct a survey on campus sexual harassment. That same year, the Equal Employment Opportunities Law was revised. Article 21 stipulates that "Employers have the responsibility in their employment management to prevent sexual harassment at work,[8] which creates unfavorable working conditions or an unfavorable environment for women. Accordingly, the Ministry of Labor needs to set up guidelines concerning the employers' responsibility."

Since the law took effect in April 1999, there has been an explosion of sexual harassment prevention training activities and manuals. Initially a problem with no name, the issue of sexual harassment has been discovered, redefined, and institutionalized in Japan within the short span of a decade. Perhaps the resignation of the infamous mayor of Osaka, Yokoyama Knock, in 1999, is the best evidence that sexual harassment can no longer be considered "a mere detail" in Japan.

Military Sexual Slavery

Ha Sun Nyo was nineteeen years old when she was taken to an army base in Shanghai. She was assigned to a room in a dormitory where she was raped by soldiers all day every day. She was beaten constantly, once with a fifty-centimeter oak club on the head. After the war, she was abandoned at the station. When she eventually found her way back home, her father was dead and she told her mother that she had been working as a cook and a laundry woman.

Park Tu Ri thought she would be working at a factory in Japan but was taken to a rape center in Taiwan instead. She was forced to have sex with an average of ten men a day, with one day off per month. She was also beaten many times. She, too, hid her past from her family when she finally returned home after the war.

Lee Sun Dok was taken to a rape center in Shanghai by deception and force. She and fourteen to fifteen other girls were placed in small huts built around an army tent. She was raped by an officer shortly after arriving at the center. Afterwards, she was raped by eight or nine soldiers every weekday and seventeen or eighteen soldiers every Sunday for eight years. In one beating incident, a soldier kicked her in the stomach and slashed her back with his sword. She was abandoned after the war and returned home to find her parents had died. She, too, kept her past a secret.[9]

Between 1932 and 1945, an estimated 200,000 women were recruited and sent throughout the Asia-Pacific region where Japanese soldiers were present. Initially an isolated practice in Shanghai, the "comfort system," an institution believed to help reduce the spread of rape as well as sexual diseases, greatly expanded after the Nanjing Massacre in 1937. According to official sources at the Ministry of Foreign Affairs, by 1938 at least eighty-two "comfort stations" in nine Chinese cities could be identified.[10] By 1945, they numbered several hundred and existed practically everywhere Japanese troops were stationed. However, because most war documents were burned when Japan surrendered in 1945, no one knows the exact number and location of the comfort stations, the details of recruitment and operations, or what happened to the women who were drafted. There is evidence that Japanese, Korean, Taiwanese, Chinese, Filipino, Indonesian, Vietnamese, Burmese, Dutch, and Australian women were involved.[11] The percentage of each ethnic group varied from place to place, but Korean women are believed to have constituted the majority (80 percent) of this population. According to the testimonies of the women themselves, recruitment methods ranged from outright abduction by military personnel to deception by civilian recruiters. The comfort stations, too, ranged from exclusive ones open only to officials to more open military-run or civilian-managed houses for soldiers and civilian employees of the army. In general, the women were confined, made to serve between one to thirty men each day, and subject to the regular supervision of doctors.

Despite the fact that the U.S. military knew about the comfort women, the issue was not pursued at the Tokyo Tribunal, with the exception of cases concerning Dutch woman.[12] It was equally ignored in the bilateral treaties between the Japanese government and the Korean and Chinese governments. Grassroots organizing concerning Japanese war responsibility in Korea and China as well as in Japan throughout the postwar decades has also left out the issue. As Yoshimi argues, one cannot say that the Japanese were entirely unaware of the issue.[13] In 1947, the Korean comfort women were the central characters in a novel by Tamura Tajiro, and in 1973 Senda Kako wrote *Jugun Ianfu* (Military comfort women). But because the issue touches on four great taboos—war, colonialism, the emperor, and sexuality—most comfort women remained in complete silence until Korean women's groups supported their coming out in the early 1990s.[14] In fact, some Korean women's groups had already raised this issue in the 1970s, but it was not taken up by Japanese women's groups, which were busy fighting against sex tourism by Japanese men in Korea.[15] In 1988, at the conference Women and Tourism organized by Korea Church Women United in Seoul, representatives from the Japan Anti-Prostitution Association (JAPA) met Yun Chung-Ok, a Korean historian who was a pioneer in the research on comfort women. "Meeting with Professor Yun was our first encounter with the issue of military sexual slavery," remembers the executive director of JAPA.[16] Between 1988 and 1990, JAPA continued exchanging information with Professor Yun. In 1990, JAPA helped the Korean Council for the Women Drafted for Sexual Slavery by Japan (hereafter referred to as the Korean Council) to submit a letter to the Japanese government. In December, JAPA organized the first public meeting in Japan on the issue of comfort women, inviting Professor Yun as a guest speaker. The meeting, attended by about four hundred people, "was the turning point in Japanese society."[17] Forty-five years after the end of World War II, nongovernmental groups began to break their silence on the issue. Established Japanese women's groups, such as the fifty-two-member Liaison Group of International Women's Year, picked up the issue. New groups such as the Action Network for the Issue of Military Sexual Slavery Japan, a coalition of fifteen NGOs, were formed. They held rallies, sent petitions, met with government officials, and lobbied the Japanese Diet to recognize the issue and compensate the victims. The Japan Woman's Christian Temperance Union sent a letter to all 750 Diet members but received only three replies.[18]

In 1990, during the visit of the Korean president to Japan, the Korean Council submitted a declaration to the Japanese government requesting compensation for victims of the comfort system. The Japanese government responded in a Budget Committee meeting in the Lower House that the comfort system was run by civilians. In 1991, the coming out and visit of a Korean comfort woman, Kim Hak Shun, caused an uproar in Japan. In December that year, the first comfort women lawsuit was filed in Tokyo. But it was the publication of six pieces of evidence by a Japanese historian and professor, Yoshimi Yoshiaki, in *Asahi Shimbun* on January 11, 1992, that caused a dramatic turn. The next day, the cabinet secretary admitted the involvement of the Japanese army in setting up the comfort system. One week later, on January 17, Prime Minister Miyazawa Kiichi made a public apology at the Japan-Korea Summit. The Japanese government pledged to conduct research, collect testimonies, and disclose the results. In August 1992, in its first report, the Japanese government announced that it would do something in lieu of compensation.[19] One year later, in August 1993, the Japanese government admitted in another report that 1) the

Japanese army was directly or indirectly involved in the establishment, management, and moving of the comfort stations; 2) in many cases, the women were recruited by deception or force, and in some cases Japanese officials were involved; 3) woman at the comfort stations were subject to force and control; 4) in the case of Korean comfort women, most were recruited, moved, and managed against their will, by deception and force; 5) the military comfort system under the Japanese army deeply hurt the respect and dignity of these women; and 6) the Japanese government had apologized to these women.

The Japanese government, however, fell short of recognizing the issue as a crime that required more investigation, public education, and compensation for its victims.[20] In May 1994, the justice minister, Nagano Shigeto, had to resign as a result of his remarks that the Nanjing Massacre was an invention and that the comfort women were no more than licensed prostitutes. In August 1994, the prime minister announced that the comfort women would be given "support" and "atonement" money, historical research on this issue would be funded, and the Japanese people would be involved in these efforts.[21] In July 1995, the private Asian Women's Fund was established with donations from the public. Its principal activities consist of providing atonement funds to the victims, housing and medical assistance projects, research and publication of documents on comfort women, and education on contemporary women's human rights issues.

In 1996, the movement expanded to become a battle of discourse and memory.[22] Although backlash comments in the mainstream media had appeared since the early 1990s, it was not until 1996 that right-wing groups—a combination of academics, media and business groups, and politicians—became seriously organized and launched aggressive campaigns targeting the removal of texts on comfort women in textbooks. The Japanese Society for History Textbook Reform (Atarashii Rekishi Kyokasho wo Tsukuru Kai) and the Liberal Revisionist Research Institute (Jiyūshugishikan Kenkyūkai), headed by a professor of education at Tokyo University, Fujioka Hidenobu, were formed in 1996. The former has more than ten thousand dues-paying members. Its goals are to "portray Japan and the Japanese with dignity in reaction to what the society felt was an increasingly 'self-denigrating view' of Japan's national history."[23] The Bright Japan Diet Members Coalition (Akarui Nihon Kokkai Giin Renmei) within the Liberal Democratic Party and the New History Teaching Diet Members Coalition (Atarashii Rekishi wo Tsutaeru Kokkai Giin Renmei) within the New Japan Party (Shinshinto), as well as *Sankei Shimbun*, a business newspaper, have also been actively involved.[24] Their statements in Japanese newspapers and magazines can be summed up as follows: there is no proof of the existence or the coercive nature of the comfort system; the comfort women were voluntary prostitutes; rape is a natural part of war, and many other countries did the same thing; and the inclusion of Yoshimi Yoshiaki in textbooks is "dark, self-abusing, anti-Japanese, and apologizing."[25] According to these groups, the "brighter side" of history should be taught. The submission by Fujioka Hidenobu to *Sankei Shimbun* on September 27, 1996, typifies the position of the liberal revisionists. "All these sayings about the 'forced drafting' of the comfort women are awful. They mean that the Japanese state, through official order, recruited and moved Korean women like slaves, and that they were raped by the army. Was Japan such a grotesque country that committed these sexual crimes? Were Japanese such horny, dirty, and debased people?"[26]

In December 1996, the Okayama Prefectural Assembly adopted a petition submitted by the Committee of Education to delete the descriptions of comfort women in junior high school textbooks. The anti–comfort women campaign, which some activists called "secondary rape," spread to other local governments.[27] In April 2001, the Ministry of Education approved a new set of changes de-emphasizing Japan's wartime aggression, including the removal of references to comfort women in history textbooks,[28] which inspired a new diplomatic uproar with South Korea.[29]

Within the span of only a few years, an old wound had been reopened, reexamined, and temporarily healed. The Asian Women's Fund remains highly controversial. It splits academics as well as activists in Korea, Japan, and the Philippines. Although a few comfort women have accepted atonement money, many others, as well as their support groups, continue to press for a full apology, compensation, and prosecution of the Japanese government. Few would have predicted, however, that the Japanese government would publicly recognize the involvement of the Japanese army in setting up the comfort stations and admit that most of the women were forcibly recruited and lived in confinement. The comfort women movement not only ended the silence on the sexual abuse committed by the Japanese military, but it also opened up opportunities for research as well as lawsuits on a whole array of war responsibility issues, including forced labor[30] and the denial of pensions for Korean and Taiwanese soldiers.

Domestic Violence

Japanese literature on domestic violence first appeared in the 1980s, but the earliest works were either translations of foreign works or studies of violence of children within the family in Japan. In 1980, the Prime Minister's Office conducted a study on domestic violence, under the mandate of the Youth Policy Headquarters. At that time "domestic violence" had meant "family violence" (*kateinai bōryoku*), with its exclusive focus on the violence of children toward their parents, and especially their mothers. In the late 1980s, family violence was linked to an array of children's problems, including children dropping out of school (*tōkō kyohi*).

In the early 1990s, literature on "spousal violence" (*fufukan bōryoku*) emerged, but it was treated as a personal and family issue, dealt with primarily by anti-addiction groups. Domestic violence as a social structural issue was first raised by a nongovernmental group in 1992. This group—founded by eight feminists, including a member of the pioneer Network to Fight against Sexual Violence, a social worker who just completed her Ph.D. at UCLA, four women's studies scholars, a lawyer, and a woman counselor—introduced the concept of domestic violence by conducting the first survey on the subject in Japan, using "feminist action research" methods.[31] Critical of the traditional connotation of family violence (that is, violence of children against their mothers) in Japan, the group called themselves Otto (koibito) kara no Bōryoku (Violence from Husbands or Partners) Survey Research Group. They distributed 4,675 questionnaires and received 796 responses. Fifty-nine percent of the respondents had experienced some form of domestic violence. Among these women, 81.4 percent had suffered from forced sex. This pioneer survey broke the silence on domestic violence in Japan, which until then had been considered nonexistent. In fact, the concept of domestic violence was so foreign that a Japanese ambassador to the UN who had served on the Committee on the Elimination of Discrimination against Women in the early 1990s, when asked about the situation in Japan, answered simply that "I don't think we have this problem in our country."[32] "*Fufu genka*" (marital disputes) were considered by politicians and the public alike as a matter too personal and trivial for intervention.

Despite the new statistics, research, and advocacy, the issue of domestic violence remained largely marginalized even within the women's movement until 1994. That year, Nichibenren (the Japan Federation of Bar Associations) opened the first telephone hot line for battered women. The first scholarly work looking at sexual violence in Japan from a human rights point of view was also published in 1994.[33] In 1995, a local court in Nagoya recognized self-defense as a legitimate legal defense for victims of domestic violence who killed their husbands.[34] Large women's centers, including those in Yokohama and Kanagawa, started three-year projects on domestic violence, out of which came multiple surveys, cross-national comparisons, shelter studies, and networking workshops.[35] In 1996, the government incorporated "family violence" (*kateinai bōryoku*) in the Vision of Gender Equality.

But it was not until 1997 that things started to accelerate. The Tokyo metropolitan government conducted the first public survey on domestic violence in Japan. Two nongovernmental groups, the more established lawyer-dominated Japan Civil Liberties Union and the more recent advocacy group Beijing Japan Accountability Caucus (Beijing JAC), as well as some female members of the Social Democratic Party, each took on the task of drafting a domestic violence prevention bill. The Gender Equality Committee of the Kobe Lawyers Association published the first domestic violence consultation manual in Japan. Japan's Federation of Bar Associations held the first large-scale symposium on domestic violence in Japan in 1998, after creating a study group on the family and violence. Meanwhile, private feminist counseling centers spread throughout Japan, and the number of shelters created between 1993 and 1999 was double the combined total of those created up to 1992.[36] Further, eleven nongovernmental shelters formed a national network in 1997 and have been organizing an annual shelter symposium since 1998. In 1998, Japanese women outnumbered non-Japanese women for the first time in the oldest and largest nongovernmental shelter, HELP.[37]

By 1998 and 1999, domestic violence was taken on as an issue not only by women's groups, but also by men's groups and student groups. Established women's groups have added domestic violence to their traditional agenda focusing on peace, education, and democracy. The Women Democratic Congress, established in the postwar era, for example, created a subcommittee on violence against women in 1999 and organized a lecture on legal responses to domestic violence in other advanced countries. The National Women Counselors Network (comprised of public women's counselors), which has traditionally focused on problems related to prostitution, singled out domestic violence as a key concern. New advocacy, information, and self-help groups focusing uniquely on the problem of domestic violence, such as the Japan DV Prevention and Information Center, were formed. The first self-help group for batterers in Japan was also created in the autumn of 1998 after a workshop at the annual Men's Liberation Festival. The DV Prevention Project for Batterers organizes bi-monthly workshops for batterers and symposia for the public. Other men's groups such as Men's Lib Tokyo and Men's Lib Kanagawa have incorporated domestic violence as a theme for their consciousness-raising activities.[38] In 1999, the Women and Human Rights student group at Waseda University also organized a T-shirt campaign against domestic violence.

Between 1992 and 1997 not only was the term "*domesutikku baiorensu*," or "DV" for short, coined, but the issue became a legitimate topic in news[39] and television programs,[40] the subject of administrative and legal interventions, and the focus of research and publications.

Child Prostitution

Nongovernmental groups working on children's issues abound in Japan. According to Kodomo no Kenri Nettowākingu 97 (Children's Rights Network 97), there are more than 430 nongovernmental groups focusing on children's issues. About one third deal with educational issues, especially school refusal (*futoko*) and alternative schools ("free school"/"free space"). Another 12 percent deal with children with disabilities. Seven percent are the more recently established groups focused on the Convention of the Rights of the Child (CRC). Six percent focus on regional and international funding. Three percent of the groups link women's and children's issues, focusing on single mothers, working mothers, the revision of the Eugenics Protection Law in the mid-1980s, feminist counseling, and other subjects. Only ten groups (about 2 percent) focus on child sexual abuse and prostitution, for example, the CAP (Child Assault Prevention) networks. A similarly low percentage represents groups on minority children. The decade between 1986 and 1995 saw the most dramatic growth, witnessing a twofold increase in the number of children's groups that existed prior to 1985 (Fig 5.1).

The earliest nongovernmental organization on children's issues, the National Federation of UNESCO Association in Japan (1948), was founded immediately after the establishment of UNESCO. The pioneer Japanese NGO working on children's issues, the Japanese Society for the Protection of Children established in 1952, which remains influential today, typifies the approach of most other children's groups. It focuses on the protection of children and offers services on a wide range of issues such as education, day care, parenting advice, social gatherings, and information exchange. The 1970s saw an expansion of groups representing disabled children. The 1980s saw the emergence of diverse issues. The first group supporting refugee children was founded in 1980. The issues of minority as well as foreign children also started to be raised. Several regional and international children's friendship and funding groups were established. Linkages with women's groups started to be formed. In 1983, the first group focusing on single mothers and illegitimate children was formed in Osaka. The first organization looking at school refusal, the Medical Institute on School Refusal Culture, was already established in 1981. The decade between

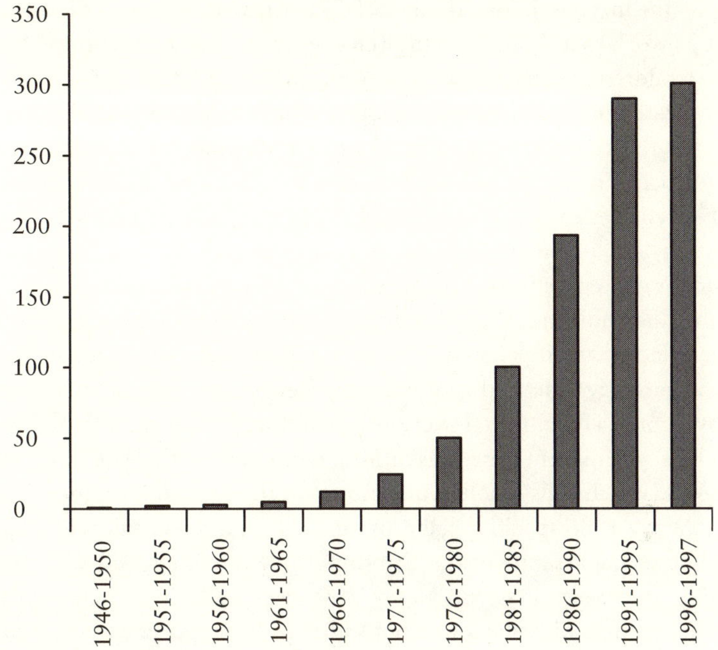

FIG. 5.1. Expansion of children's nongovernmental groups in Japan, 1946–97. Source: Kodomo no Kenri Nettowākingu (Children's Rights Network) 1997.

1986 and 1995 saw the dramatic expansion of two kinds of organizations: those concerned with alternative schools and those dealing with children's rights.

Although Japan has a Children's Constitution (Kodomo Kenshō), established in 1952, it was not until the late 1980s that groups adopted the point of view of children's rights. The first Japanese NGO using the Western term "children's ombudsperson," however, was established as early as 1981. In 1983, the Second Tokyo Bar Association set up the Commission on Children's Rights and was a pioneer in publicizing the issue of child abuse. But these two groups represented isolated efforts on children's rights until Kodomo no Jinken Ren (the Federation for the Protection of Children's Human Rights Japan) was formed in 1986. Largely an initiative of Nikkyōso (the Japanese Teachers' Union), this network today comprises more than sixty NGOs. The network represents a new type of internationally focused CRC advocacy and outreach children's rights group in Japan. It was instrumental in lobbying for the Japanese government's ratification of the convention in 1994 and remains the most important watchdog on the implementation of the CRC in Japan by conducting surveys, organizing symposia, and compiling alternative reports.

Despite the increase in the number of CRC-focused groups, however, few of the groups work specifically on children's sexuality and sexual abuse. In 1991, the Stop Children's Sexual Abuse group and the Child Abuse Prevention Center were created in Tokyo, but their work was mostly marginalized. It was not until 1992, after the founding meeting of ECPAT (End Child Prostitution in Asian Tourism) International in Thailand in 1990, that ECPAT Japan was formed; it remains to this date one of the very few groups that focus on child prostitution and pornography. "Assisted entertainment" (*enjo kōsai*), a euphemism for child prostitution, did get some media attention in the early 1990s, but neither the public nor the political parties thought anything should be done about it. In fact, many in Japan did not even consider *enjo kōsai* prostitution because it was mostly practiced voluntarily by teenage schoolgirls. Strictly speaking, prostitution with children over the age of thirteen was not illegal in Japan. Although prostitution in general is officially outlawed by the Anti-Prostitution Law of 1956 (which calls for the punishment of the prostitutes rather than the clients), there was no specific legal provision on child prostitution that fell under rape or sexual assaults in the Criminal Code and the Child Welfare Law. The same applied to child pornography, which was available in practically every convenience store, video shop, and bookstore in Japan. As late as 1996, 30 percent of the Japanese respondents to a survey conducted by the Japan Youth Research Institute to compare the values of high school students internationally thought that child prostitution and pornography were a matter of personal liberty.[41]

In 1993, when a Social Democratic Party member, Shimizu Sumiko, asked in a Diet session whether there were any plans to amend laws before ratifying CRC, the Japanese government's response was that "no amendment was necessary."[42] In 1993 and 1994, ECPAT Japan started to organize protests against child pornography in popular magazines, including *Shukan Gendai* and *Shukan Post*. In 1994, the first CAP group, modeled after CAP educational and outreach programs in the United States, was formed in Tokyo. Since then, it has spread nationwide. In August 1996, the issue of child prostitution and pornography took a dramatic turn in Japan. Japan had actually planned not to send any official delegation to the First World Congress against the Commercial Sexual Exploitation of Children. Only after lobbying by nongovernmental groups did it send a delegation, headed by a female politician from the Social Democratic Party, Shimizu Sumiko.[43] In January 1997, ECPAT Japan submitted a petition demanding legislation against child pornography and child sexual abuse that was presented through the support of female Diet members. In May, these female lawmakers set up a study group within the Diet on the issue. In the follow-up meeting of the Stockholm Congress in Tokyo that same month, a senior politician from the LDP, Tanigaki Shinichi, pledged publicly that the LDP "would enact necessary legal reforms" on the issue. Thus a coalition project team was formed in June 1997. Less than two years later, the law was unanimously passed in April 1999. In May 2000, the Child Abuse Prevention Law was also passed.

Global norms concerning women's and children's human rights have not only translated into changes on the legal and social movement fronts, but also in education. In the following chapter, I discuss how they have paradigmatically redefined women's and children's education in Japan.

CHAPTER SIX

Human Rights Education in Japan

> Human rights education has to move from the "universal" to the particular, from the abstract to the concrete, from the global to the local. Effective human rights education "shall be shaped in such a way to be relevant to the daily lives of the learners" and shall "seek to engage learners in a dialogue about the ways and means of transforming human rights from the expression of abstract norms to the reality of their social, economic, cultural and political conditions."
>
> Uprenda Baxi, "Human Rights Education: The Promise of the Third Millennium?"

In this chapter, I link the political developments I have discussed thus far to education in Japan. The impact of global human rights norms is not only restricted to the level of laws and policies but also extends to grassroots education. A major part of the work of domestic women's and children's human rights epistemic networks is the diffusion of global norms through education. For norms to be effective, knowledge about them needs to be produced and disseminated locally within Japan. Once global discourses are institutionalized in local knowledge, governmental actors, in turn, become educators of global human right norms. I begin by examining the redefinition of traditional Dowa (Buraku) education, women's studies, and children's education from the perspective of human rights education. I then briefly analyze a dozen examples of research, education, and training activities on reproductive rights, sexual harassment, domestic violence, comfort women, prostitution, and child sexual abuse by the domestic human rights epistemic network between 1995 and 2000. I further highlight five examples of outreach and training by the Prime Minister's Office, the Ministry of Foreign Affairs, the National Police Agency, a local government, and a private university. The new role of the Japanese state and other organizations as human rights educators could not be understood without considering the normative pressures generated by global human rights discourses. By the late 1990s, entire new fields of scientific inquiry had emerged in Japan. The number of legitimate educators had expanded, and the line between the educator and the learner had become blurred. New pedagogies and curricula in education have become available. In short, global norms have redefined what knowledge is in Japan.

Redefining Human Rights Education in Japan: First National Plan of Action for Human Rights Education

Education about and for human rights has been emphasized since the Universal Declaration of Human Rights in 1948, yet it received neither the resources nor mandate among international organizations. Successive world conferences on children, human rights, population and development, the environment, and women in the 1990s resuscitated the old belief that human rights can be achieved only through changing the minds of people. The 1993 Vienna Declaration and Platform for Action, the 1994 Cairo Declaration, the 1994 Declaration on the Elimination of Violence against Women, and the 1995 Beijing Platform for Action all emphasize the importance of incorporating world human rights standards in both formal and nonformal national educational efforts. The platform of the UN Decade for Human Rights Education (1995–2004) concretely calls for the creation of a national human rights education committee and a comprehensive plan of action. In particular, it stipulates that efforts should emphasize the grounding of global standards in local cultures and the collaboration of local nongovernmental organizations. To what extent have these global human rights norms been incorporated into national and local educational practices, especially in cultures that have traditionally been regarded as lacking a human rights tradition? In a country where group harmony sometimes takes priority over individual rights, how is the concept of human rights being taught?

The postwar Constitution represented a significant development in human rights in Japan, as human rights became one of the three guiding principles guaranteed in a national legal document (the other two were pacifism and the sovereignty of the people). In practice, however, the principle of human rights was often not translated into bureaucratic structures, legal norms, or judicial decisions. Until recently, the Civil Liberties Bureau within the Ministry of Justice and the private civil liberties commissioners, established in 1948, remained the only official bodies in human rights protection. Except for their posters created for the annual Human Rights Week in December, the bureau and the commissioners are little known either within or outside Japan. The Civil Liberties Bureau's marginal position within the Ministry of Justice and its limited budget and mandate (more public information than policy making)[1] make it largely a token human rights protection mechanism.[2] Human rights issues in Japan—the condition facing minorities, foreigners, the disabled, women, and AIDS patients, for example—are dealt with by different ministries largely in the absence of a human rights perspective.[3] Despite stipulations in the Constitution prohibiting discrimination based on race, creed, sex, social status, or family origin (Article 14), human rights violations have more often been handled by administrative guidance rather than legal procedures, that is, bureaucrats encourage companies and others through informal recommendations and advice to follow a desired policy rather than invoke formal legal mechanisms to compel such action.[4]

Despite the fact that human rights is one of the three guiding principles in the Japanese Constitution, Japan never had a human rights education policy until 1997. For decades, the term "human rights education" (*jinken kyoiku*) had uniquely meant Dowa education, that is, education for the integration of the Buraku, a caste minority from the Tokugawa era. Despite intermarriages with mainstream Japanese and social mobility, many Buraku could still be identified by their residence, place of birth, and (parental) occupations. Dowa education has been part and parcel of the Buraku liberation movement. Dowa education began in 1928, not long after the first nongovernmental Buraku group, Suihesha, was founded in 1922. It expanded in the postwar period with the establishment of the National Federation of Dowa Educators' Associations in 1953. Because of the high dropout rates and low attendance and performance of the Buraku, Dowa education had focused primarily on the education of and about the Buraku in their own communities. It became institutionalized in Buraku areas with government funding when the Japanese government passed three successive laws on specific government budgetary measures for Dowa area improvement in 1969, 1982, and 1987. Dowa education has also been called "liberation education" (*kaihō kyoiku*) since the 1960s and then "anti-discrimination education" (*han sabetsu kyoiku*) since the 1970s to include the struggles of other marginalized groups such as disabled people and Korean residents in Japan. The term "human rights education" actually emerged in the 1970s, when private companies and universities started to establish human rights departments and programs to handle Buraku discrimination issues after a series of high-profile discrimination scandals.

Prior to World War II, men and women followed separate educational tracks beyond elementary school, and women were denied access to universities. Since 1946, however, the Constitution has stipulated the equal right of all boys and girls to receive an education. In fact, since 1989 the percentage of women entering postsecondary institutions has exceeded that of men. However, women remain heavily concentrated in private two-year junior colleges that have little linkage to four-year universities.[5] Women's education is comprised not only of formal education in colleges and universities, but also of social education (*shakai kyoiku*) and lifelong education (*shōgai kyoiku*). First developed in the postwar period with the establishment of local civic centers and libraries throughout Japan, women's education became highly institutionalized under the influence of UNESCO recommendations on lifelong learning in the 1970s. In particular, women's studies (*joseigaku*) programs were set up in national and local women's education centers throughout Japan after the International Women's Year in 1975. In contrast to earlier "research on the woman question" (*fujin mondai kenkyū*) that focused on the differential educational and work needs of women, women's studies in the 1970s represented a new consciousness that challenged predominant gender norms. Since then, women's education developed into "gender research" (*jendā kenkyū*) in the early 1990s, "empowerment studies" (*empawāmento no tame no gakushū*), and "research on gender equality" (*danjo kyōdō sankaku kenkyū*) after 1995. "Women's human rights" also became part of "women 's studies" largely after the Beijing Conference in 1995.

Finally, children's rights education emerged in the late 1980s in Japan. In contrast to the other human rights education movements mentioned above, children's rights education in Japan is closely linked to the UN Convention on the Rights of the Child (CRC). Children's rights education in Japan has followed two main streams, one more focused on the CRC, and the other modeled after the Child Assault Prevention (CAP) programs in the United States, expanded in Japan after 1995. The two groups differ in focus as well as methodology. CRC groups emphasize the learning of the convention, while the CAP-influenced groups focus on the three core concepts of security, confidence, and freedom. CAP counselors believe that "human rights consciousness is not about knowledge. It is much simpler than that. It involves the heart."[6] In addition, the two groups are largely gender segregated, with a much higher proportion of men in the former[7] and women in the latter. Some CAP activists think that CRC groups have been mostly gender-blind and have largely ignored issues of children's sexuality that have differentially affected girls. CRC groups in the early 1990s did not take the issues of child sexual abuse, prostitution, and pornography seriously.

If CAP programs have enjoyed success in the classroom with funding from some local governments, the incorporation of CRC ideas into the formal curriculum has proven more difficult. Despite the Japanese government's ratification of the CRC in 1994, the Ministry of Education has done little more than produce a few new posters. The first poster, with the subtitle "For the Happiness of Children in the World," implies that the CRC is intended for developing countries rather than for Japan.[8] Some local education commissions have taken measures to promote the convention and children's participation through white papers, action programs, children's rights consciousness surveys, children's congresses, and children's human rights forums.[9] But many are still skeptical about the teaching of CRC ideas in schools. As a professor of education at Waseda University and a veteran CRC advocate voices his frustration,

> "*Kodomo no jinken*" (children's human rights) is still very much a taboo in Japan. We have encountered a lot of opposition in the process of drafting the first local CRC ordinance in Kawasaki city, which, if passed, will provide a legal mandate for an ombudsperson and a hot line. At least 70 to 80 percent of the teachers have heard of human rights in the Constitution, but few practice it. The common response I have heard is that "We need school rules to manage the kids." We have a tradition of "*kanri kyoiku*" (management education), by administrators, teachers, and parents. It is extremely difficult to connect children's human rights to the smallest things like hair and uniform. Teachers don't want to face these issues. It's easier to respond "It's a rule not to have dyed hair" than to explain why dyeing is bad. There is also pressure from the neighborhood on teachers to keep school rules. Yes, the concept of children's rights has become more known in the 1990s in Japan, but it has hardly penetrated into the school system. It remains mainly a grassroots movement.[10]

In 1995, the Japanese government established the Headquarters for the Promotion of Human Rights Education within the cabinet "under the influence of the UN Decade for Human Rights Education (1995–2004)."[11] The first Law for the Promotion of Human Rights Protection was passed in 1996. The first National Plan of Action for the UN Decade for Human Rights Education, emphasizing human rights education at four levels—formal education, lifelong education, corporate education, and specialized professions—was promulgated in 1997.[12] The National Plan of Action targets nine specific groups: women, children, the elderly, the disabled, Buraku, Ainu, foreigners, HIV patients, and former prisoners. Within less than a year, twenty-three prefectural and local governments had set up headquarters for human rights education, and seventeen had promulgated local plans of action for human rights education.[13] In 1998, the Tokyo metropolitan government funded the establishment of the Tokyo Human Rights Education Center. In November 2000, the Lower House passed the first Human Rights Education Law, mandating policy plans for human rights education at both national and local levels.

Since then, the different movements have to various extents embraced the new concept of "human rights education." Dowa educators, for example, have declared the end of Dowa education in favor of human rights education.[14] The

Category	Traditional approaches	New concept
1) Women	Women's studies	
2) Children	Protection	
3) The elderly	Welfare	
4) Disabled	Normalization	
5) Buraku	Liberation education	"Human rights
6) Ainu	Cultural promotion	education"
7) Foreigners	"Reasonable discrimination"	
8) AIDS patients	Welfare	
9) Released prisoners	Mainstreaming	

FIG. 6.1. Redefining Human Rights Education in Japan: Global Norms and Local Education

name of the long-standing *Liberation Education Review* has been changed to *Human Rights Education Review*, and, accordingly, the contents have been expanded to include other human rights issues.[15] The theme of the 1999 symposium of the Tokyo Buraku Liberation League was "Towards a Human Rights Policy for the Elimination of Buraku Discrimination." Many children's rights activists, too, have found the comprehensive concept of human rights education to help expand the scope of their work. Whereas "children's rights" had formerly been narrowly focused on school rules, corporal punishment, and bullying, "children's human rights" covers an expanded list of issues, including sexuality, children's participation, and the human rights of minority and foreigner children. In sum, despite disagreements about the interpretation of "human rights education" by the Japanese government and the lack of a common definition, the new discourse of human rights education has increased the legitimacy of the disparate education movements and opened up new ways to reconceptualize these movements. Above all, the comprehensive concept has forced each movement to be critical about its own exclusions and to connect to other movements. Feminists have started to link sexual violence to children's rights issues. Buraku organizations have begun to address the double discrimination faced by Buraku and other minority women.[16] Foreign workers' rights groups now look at issues of trafficking of women and children.[17] New networks have been formed. For example, Human Rights Forum 21, created in 1997, is a network of nine NGOs focusing on issues related to women, children, minorities, foreigners, the disabled, and the elderly. It remains to be seen how the new concept of "human rights education" will be used by the Japanese government in educational policy and applied by nongovernmental organizations in educational practice. Nonetheless, the new global discourse has created an unprecedented impetus for a more holistic conceptual approach to human rights education in Japan (Figure 6.1).

The "Discursive Revolution" by Domestic Human Rights Epistemic Networks

Women's movements worldwide have traditionally emphasized research, education, and the dissemination of information in achieving their goals. Instead of focusing only on formal political institutions and bureaucratization in the Michel-Weber tradition, these voluntary associations often extend their organizational repertoire through nonpolitical channels.[18] Pioneering Japanese feminists from very early on placed a great deal of importance on education.

> After the dissolution of the New Women Association in December 1922, Oku became frustrated with her political attempts to improve the position of Japanese women. . . . She felt that the real task was to educate Japanese women so they could understand and participate in politics in order to further their progress. Education was considered essential for socio-political enlightenment.[19]

In a country where the political representation of women remains low, the legal system is not always friendly to women, and feminism within academia is largely hidden, grassroots education becomes an important alternative form of politics. Most analyses of community education for women in Japan, however, have focused only on the role of public women's centers, that is, women's studies outside academe.[20] The role of nongovernmental organizations in promoting women's education remains relatively unknown.

Public information about women's human rights in Japan, in the form of research, publications, news, and government reports, is largely a phenomenon of the 1990s (Table 6.1). According to a National Women's Education Center database, there was scarcely a single book or journal article in Japanese on the topic of women's human rights prior to the 1990s, with the exception of publications on prostitution. Most of the titles prior to that period were either in English or were translations of foreign works. The most striking example of Japanese silence on the subject of women's human rights is the lack of a Japanese term meaning "reproductive health/rights." It entered the Japanese vocabulary only in 1993, right before the Cairo conference, and the number of books and journal articles on the subject, by both academics and nongovernmental organizations, quadrupled after the conference. The term "gender" also became part of the Japanese language largely in the 1990s, in contrast to "feminism," which was already common by the mid-1980s. Above all, "gender" mainstreaming occurred after the mid-1990s. The number of books on gender doubled, while the number of journal articles quadrupled. News articles on the subject increased almost a hundredfold, from 35 to 339 from the first half to the second half of the

TABLE 6.1

Explosion of Discourse on Women's Human Rights in Japan in the 1990s, by Issue

	1960–69	1970–79	1980–84	1985–89	1990–94	1995–99
I) Sexual violence (total)	0	1	6	10	235	702
Books	0	1	1	9	79	147
Journal articles	0	0	5	0	79	286
News articles	0	0	0	1	75	243
Government reports	0	0	0	0	2	26
II) Sexual harassment (total)	0	0	1	25	690	804
Books	0	0	1	7	68	133
Journal articles	0	0	0	17	123	168
News articles	0	0	0	1	470	441
Government reports	0	0	0	0	29	62
III) Comfort women (total)	0	0	1	1	345	140
Books	0	0	1	1	23	44
Journal articles	0	0	0	0	0	0
News articles	0	0	0	0	322	96
Government reports	0	0	0	0	0	0
IV) Domestic violence (total)	0	0	7	9	67	183
Books	0	0	2	9	18	67
Journal articles	0	0	5	0	15	48
News articles	0	0	0	0	33	46
Government reports	0	0	0	0	1	22
V) Shelter (total)	0	0	0	1	40	166
Books	0	0	0	1	4	27
Journal articles	0	0	0	0	6	47
News articles	0	0	0	1	29	81
Government reports	0	0	0	0	1	11
VI) Prostitution (total)	5	1	24	33	243	365
Books	0	0	1	12	92	125
Journal articles	0	0	23	16	114	195
News articles	0	0	0	5	32	42
Government reports	5	1	0	0	5	3
VII) Reproductive health/rights (total)	0	0	0	0	73	252
Books	0	0	0	0	22	68
Journal articles	0	0	0	0	38	172
News articles	0	0	0	0	11	9
Government reports	0	0	0	0	2	3
VIII) Feminism (total)	0	5	42	373	975	873
Books	0	3	18	268	415	371
Journal articles	0	1	16	81	390	308
News articles	0	1	8	21	166	190
Government reports	0	0	0	3	4	4
IX) Gender (total)	0	0	7	137	556	1775
Books	0	0	4	116	311	575
Journal articles	0	0	3	17	207	792
News articles	0	0	0	3	35	339
Government reports	0	0	0	1	3	69
X) NGO/NPO (total)	0	0	31	69	232	1151
Books	0	0	2	30	68	206
Journal articles	0	0	7	15	82	407
News articles	0	0	22	22	76	525
Government reports	0	0	0	2	6	13

Source: National Women's Education Center Database, November 1999.

1990s. Even government reports on gender increased twentyfold, from 3 to 69. Also worth noting is the dramatic increase of publications and news articles on nongovernmental or nonprofit organizations. Although terms for these organizations already existed in the 1980s, it was not until after 1995 that they became a common part of Japanese parlance. The Kobe earthquake in 1995 helped make the vibrant volunteer community more visible, and the nonprofit organization (NPO) law passed in 1998 also accounts for the expansion of publications concerning NPOs. The number of journal articles on NPOs quadrupled between 1994 and 1999. Above all, news coverage increased sevenfold, from 76 to 525 articles. The local epistemic women's and children's human rights network emerged in the mid- to late 1990s, when the environment for NGO work became slightly more favorable.

Media reporting of various women's human rights issues is highly selective. Sexual harassment, for example, captured far more attention (470 news articles between 1990 and 1994 and 441 between 1995 and 1999) than any other issue. The coming out of comfort women in the early 1990s also attracted considerable media attention, though interest in the subject quickly subsided after the government created the Asian Women's Fund in 1995 (96 news articles appeared between 1995 and 1999, compared to 332 between 1990 and 1994). Meanwhile, the Japanese government has all along been a laggard in researching and publishing about women's human rights. Between 1990 and 1994, it published only one report on domestic violence, another one on shelter, and two on reproductive health/rights. In the latter half of the 1990s, despite an explosion of news articles and publications concerning women's human rights, the government remained largely passive, publishing only three reports on reproductive health/rights, eleven on shelter, and twenty-two on domestic violence.

A new pattern of education that is qualitatively different from traditional education for women and children has emerged in Japan in the 1990s. Since the early 1990s, nongovernmental women's groups, women's studies scholars, female politicians, women's center staff members, lawyers, counselors, doctors, and men's liberation groups have formed a knowledge-based community. They share a common framing of human rights issues, control and disseminate information and knowledge of global human rights standards in Japan, and are often involved in policy formation. When the need arises, network members call upon foreign experts for help. Their educational activities have drastically redefined the purpose, subject, categories of trainers and learners, pedagogy, curriculum, and space of education in Japan. Below I discuss a dozen examples of this new kind of research, education, and training (Examples 1–12).

What is new in these examples of educational activities, a fraction of hundreds that were organized throughout Japan in the 1990s? Without exaggeration, one can say that each of the twelve activities would have been inconceivable a mere decade ago. Education has expanded to include topics that were taboo as late as the 1980s: child sexual abuse, domestic violence, sexual harassment, gender equality, male consciousness of prostitution, the pill, and the emperor system and women's human rights. New subjects have not only emerged as legitimate, but they have also been defined according to global standards. As the first two examples, the symposium on sexual violence against children from the point of view of the Convention on the Rights of the Child and the translation of "UN Rapporteur on Violence against Women: Special Report on Domestic Violence" show, child sexual abuse and domestic violence are no longer considered local issues but rather global problems defined and regulated by UN conventions and recommendations.

One of the most drastic changes concerns educating the Japanese about children's sexuality. As one lawyer who has worked on the issue of child abuse since the early 1990s said, "even though we did deal with children's rights before 1994 when the Japanese government signed the Convention on the Rights of the Child (CRC), back then there was no standard to refer to, especially for action. Now, it has become much easier to act according to international standards."[21] Although some nongovernmental groups had long pushed for a more holistic approach to sex education that reached beyond the narrow focus on menstruation and the reproductive system, it was not until 1997, with the National Plan of Action for Human Rights Education, that it became legitimate to talk about children's sexuality in Japanese schools. Since sex education is now part of human rights education, its boundary has been stretched to include issues of gender, transgender, drug use, AIDS, domestic violence, sexual harassment, and comfort women.[22] As recently as 1995, it was unthinkable to introduce child sexual abuse education in schools in Japan. Child Assault Program (CAP) groups were virtually unknown. By around 2000, CAP programs had become increasingly institutionalized in schools and communities. A national network of CAP counselors and organizations, many legally registered as NPOs, has trained 3,000 Japanese to become CAP counselors, who in turn have trained 160,000 children in schools and 200,000 adults.[23] Some more progressive city and prefectural governments, especially in the Osaka region, have started to fund CAP groups. As a CAP pioneer recounts,

> When I started introducing CAP to Japan in the early 1990s, people were not interested, even people in the field of welfare and education. Public schools were very closed, and

EXAMPLE 1

Theme	*Sexual Violence against Children from the Point of View of the Convention on the Rights of the Child*
Organization	Forum on Sex Issues (1965)
Date	July 22, 1995
Format	Symposium, group discussions
Target	General public (80)
Trainers	CAP (Child Assault Prevention) counselors
Program	I) "You Are Not Bad: Child Discrimination and Sexual Abuse"; II) "Recovering the Inner Child"
Remark	Right to self-expression; teaching children to say no

EXAMPLE 2

Theme	*UN Rapporteur on Violence against Women: Special Report on Domestic Violence*
Organization	Beijing Japan Accountability Caucus (JAC) (1995)
Date	July 22, 1995
Format	Translation
Target	NGOs and the general public

EXAMPLE 3

Theme	*Male Consciousness of Prostitution*
Organization	Association on Men and Prostitution (1996)
Date	August 1 to October 31, 1997
Format	Survey
Sample	Men (2,502)
Remark	"Prostitution is violence against women."

EXAMPLE 4

Theme	*Sexual Harassment Prevention: Training of Trainers*
Organization	Japan Civil Liberties Union (1947)
Date	February 3, 9, and 10, 1998
Format	Lecture and practicum
Target	Companies, judges, educators, labor unions, local governments, NGOs, and individuals (19 women and 12 men)
Trainers	Human rights educator (former affirmative action chief analyst at the University of California)
Content	Lecture: I) Ice-breaker, II) Empowerment and human rights, III) Diversity training, IV) Trainer skills, V) Sexual harassment prevention measures Practicum: I) Consciousness quiz, II) Video, III) Role play

EXAMPLE 5

Theme	*Domestic Violence Legal Manual*
Organization	Japan Domestic Violence Prevention and Information Center (1998)
Date	October 1998
Format	Manual
Target	NGOs, victims, and general public
Writers	Lawyer and feminist counselor
Content	Legal procedures, insurance, mental care, criminal case procedure, civil case procedure, model letter to the police, supplementary information

EXAMPLE 6

Theme	*Basic Training Course on the Basic Law on Gender Equality*
Organization	Tokyo Women Foundation
Date	November 8, 1999
Format	Seminar and practicum
Target	Women's centers staff members (50 women and men)
Content	I) Gender mainstreaming in Japanese social policies, II) The UN and women's policy in Japan, III) Local ordinance on gender equality by the Tokyo metropolitan government

EXAMPLE 7

Theme	*Let's Talk about Sexuality: Assertiveness Training*
Organization	Feminist Therapy Research Association
Date	November 13, 1999
Format	Consciousness raising and assertive training
Target	Women (25)
Trainer	Feminist counselor

EXAMPLE 8

Theme	*Empowerment Is the Password to the Twenty-first Century: Towards a New Relationship of Sharing the Joy of Living*
Organization	National Women's Education Center
Date	November 1, 1999
Format	Keynote address, symposium, and workshops
Target	Women (250)
Trainer	Swedish minister of industry, employment, and communications, Canadian adult education expert, U.S. director of Asian Development Bank, legal experts, women's studies scholars, lifelong education experts, etc.
Content	I) Keynote address "Women and Human Rights," II) Symposium called "Women and Human Rights in Politics, Employment, and Education," III) Workshops
Remark	To "examine the issues important to the creation of a gender-equal society from an international perspective and create national and international networks that contribute to the promotion of women's empowerment" in order to prepare for the UN conference Women 2000: Gender Equality, Development, and Peace in the 21st Century, in June 2000.

EXAMPLE 9

Theme	*The Pill and Reproductive Health/Rights*
Organization	Women's Online Media
Date	November 5, 1999, to March 10, 2000
Format	Online lecture series
Target	General public
Trainers	Sociologist (Ph.D., Princeton University), gynecologist, and NGO representative
Content	I) The sociology of reproductive health/rights and the pill, II) What do and don't we know about the pill, III) Exchange of opinion between the "cautious" and the "tolerant"
Remark	"Although the pill is finally legalized, there is a lot of misinformation. We have gathered a lot of information on reproductive health/rights, and we want to organize a study meeting through the Internet."

EXAMPLE 10

Theme	*The Emperor System and Women's Human Rights*
Organization	Association for Research on the Impact of War and Military Bases on Women's Human Rights (1998)
Date	April 29, 2000
Format	Study meeting
Target	General public
Discussant	Feminist historian

EXAMPLE 11

Theme	*This Life Is Mine: Eradication of Violence against Women and Children*
Organization	National Women's Shelters Network (1996)
Date	June 24–25, 2000
Format	Symposium, sessions, workshops, and videos
Target	General public
Trainers	Lawyer, psychiatrist, poet, and U.S. shelter representative
Program	I) Keynote speech: "Learning from 25 Years of Experience of the U.S. Shelter Movement," II) "This Life Is Mine: For Women's Safety and Freedom Now," III) Sessions on: 1) Domestic violence prevention law survey results, 2) Networking, 3) Postshelter life, 4) Support training for shelter management, 5) Self-help groups, 6) Mental care of women and children
Remark	"Let's expand the shelter movement"; eradication of violence against women and children

EXAMPLE 12

Theme	*Women's International War Crimes Tribunal on Japan's Military Sexual Slavery and Public Hearing on Current War Crimes against Women*
Organization	Violence against Women-Net Japan, Korean Council for the Military Sexual Slavery by Japan, Asian Center for Women's Human Rights, Women's Caucus for Gender Justice (U.S.)
Date	December 8–12, 2000
Format	Symposium, tribunal, public hearing, video, and panels
Target	General public, international, regional, and national (800)
Trainers	UN special rapporteur on violence against women, former president of the Yugoslavia War Crimes Tribunal, legal advisor for gender-related crimes in the Office of the Prosecutor for the International Criminal Tribunal for the Former Yugoslavia, professors of law and history, eight country prosecution teams (North Korea, South Korea, China, Taiwan, the Philippines, Indonesia, Japan, and the Netherlands), etc.
Content	I) Tribunal: country prosecution team presentations, testimony of expert witness, comfort women, and soldiers, judgment, II) Public hearing, III) Panel discussion on the impact of the International Criminal Court on women in Asia
Remark	"No other movement has decided to look at the war crimes and crimes against humanity under international law on the issue of sexual slavery and sexual violence such as that of the comfort women."

they would not allow external people to go into the schools, especially if you asked to have curriculum time. Most schools simply would not let us in. They asked for credentials and all that. CAP counselors had to work hard to gain their credibility. Our programs were also extremely precarious, as constant funding was rare. In Japan, the tendency to rely on government is strong; "state issues" are not handled by people. But CAP has now built a good reputation. I think CAP represents a victory for NPOs in Japan. Schools have to learn from NPOs! The role of NPOs in human rights education has been progressing gradually. It urges people to think about the role of civil society and about school–NPO partnerships.[24]

As reflected in a recent survey by the Health, Labor, and Welfare Ministry in August 2001, however, the problems of child sex education in Japan have barely begun to be addressed. Nearly 90 percent of young couples surveyed in Tokyo say that they are dissatisfied with the sex education they receive at school and elsewhere, and they feel adults should not hesitate to teach them how to avoid contracting sexually transmitted diseases. The survey also showed that 77.1 percent of female respondents, all in their teens, have had sex, and 62.6 percent said that they think it is ridiculous that adults believe junior high and high school students do not have sex.[25] It remains to be seen how CRC and CAP initiatives are integrated into the mainstream sex education curricula.

What is also drastically new is the purpose of education: it is now considered less about the "banking" of knowledge and more about the transforming and empowering nature of knowledge.[26] In the words of bell hooks, "Urging all of us to open our minds and hearts so that we can know beyond the boundaries of what is acceptable, so that we can think and rethink, so that we can create new visions, I celebrate teaching that enables transgressions—a movement against and beyond boundaries. It is that movement which makes education the practice of freedom."[27] One of the traditional key characteristics of adult education is its transforming rather than forming nature. As the feminist scholar Sattler explains,

The kind of education I care about is the kind that changes lives. In the dreadful balance that maintains the lives of battered women, education can make all the difference in saving emotional and spiritual—and all too often physical—lives. This book is about that kind of education, which is profoundly feminist, profoundly engaged with women's lives, and virtually unnoticed by all but the immediate circle of those whose lives have been saved or changed. No school boards fight over this curriculum, and no protesters wave signs or chant rosaries in opposition. There is no training in domestic violence to be a "teacher"; instead shelter workers and volunteers from all walks of life teach without teaching, without textbook or classroom. Their "lectures" are punctuated by hotline calls and children's cries, by laughter and tears. The theme, however, remains the same: how to save the lives in the balance. . . . The application of this book is not only to expand the concept of feminist spaces and feminist pedagogy but to expand our understanding of the connections between education and politics (particularly the political economy of social knowledge) and non-school-based educational space.[28]

Example eleven shows that the goal of the diverse activities of an emergent shelter network in Japan—from domestic violence prevention training and research to networking—is to work for "women's safety and freedom now." The first example, concerning child sexual abuse, also shows that transforming learning activities with children have emerged in Japan. The CAP group has introduced in Japan child assertiveness training modeled after a popular program in the United States started at the Ohio State Rape Crisis Center in 1978, with the objective of teaching children to say no. In fact, since 1995, action-oriented "empowerment education" has spread throughout Japan.[29] There is, however, little consensus on what the term really means, as its Japanese translation, "*chikara wo tsukeru*," is as vague as its English original. According to the National Women's Education Center, NWEC, which has organized hundreds of grassroots women's studies programs, empowerment education consists of five components and steps: the learners' experience, learning, communication and participation, action, and evaluation.[30] However, as the NWEC director admits, evaluation of "empowerment education" is not an easy task. "When we use foreign concepts such as women's rights or empowerment, many women might understand the words but not the meaning. Our objective is vague. We don't know at what level we should evaluate."[31]

Not only are the subjects, definitions, and objectives of learning now different, but the categories of trainers and learners have also expanded. Whereas women's studies specialists, invited by women's centers, have traditionally been the trainers, a wide range of actors—nongovernmental groups, lawyers, counselors, doctors, nurses, and politicians—are now seen as legitimate educators. These new educational activities now target not only women, but also children, civil servants, victims, and the general public. As the twelve examples illustrate, the new trainers include research associations such as the Association for Research on the Impact of War and Military Bases on Women's Human Rights, politician-led NGOs such as the Japan DV Prevention and Information Center, shelter networks, feminist therapy centers, cyber groups, and men's groups such as the Association on Men and Prostitution. The last category is particularly interesting. Since the establishment of women's centers in Japan, "women's studies" had been conceived as a subject concerning women, for women, by women. It was not until the early 1990s that a men's movement emerged in Japan. In 1989, the Japan Women's Studies Association held a forum entitled "Can Men Be Feminists?" In 1991, the first "men's lib" group was formed in Osaka. That same year, "men's studies" was first offered at Kyoto University. In 1996, the first annual men's festival was organized. Since then, classes, workshops, and symposia targeting men have expanded throughout Japan.[32] For example, the themes covered by the Men's Liberation Research Association from 1991 to 1996 included violence, prostitution, sexuality, contraception, men's studies in Korea, and sex education. In the absence of government-funded men's centers in Japan, men's group activities most often take place in women's centers and hence are often linked to women's issues. Some male women's studies scholars have actually criticized the exclusion of men from feminism. Since the goal of feminism is gender justice, "women's studies cannot be of women, by women, and for women."[33] Since the concept of "gender equality" emerged in Japan in the 1990s, there has been more emphasis on the "men side" of the problem. Self-help groups for batterers, for example, were first organized in Japan in 1998. However, one should not exaggerate the size and impact of this budding movement. As one men's lib activist told me, the obstacles are myriad. "It is difficult for men to talk about themselves. To begin with, the trouble is how to get them to come. There is still a strong prejudice against the men's liberation movement in Japan. The men involved are seen as losers."[34]

Finally, the pedagogy, the curriculum, and the "classroom" also differ in the new kinds of education. Until the early 1990s, lectures were the predominant form of educational activity in women's education in Japan. In recent years, feminists and human rights scholars alike have called for a more "participatory type" (*sankagata*) of education.[35] Lectures have been criticized as too didactic, reinforcing the hierarchy that separates the teacher and the student. Instead, participatory workshops, role play, and group discussions are encouraged. In particular, group consciousness raising and assertiveness training have spread throughout Japan, among women's and men's groups as well as children's rights groups. Unlike in the United States where consciousness raising (CR) and assertive training (AT) were products of the women's liberation movement, in Japan they were introduced by Japanese who studied in the United States in the early 1990s. Despite the expansion of CR and AT groups and programs, participatory education faces formidable challenges in Japan. As several of my interviewees admitted, "Japanese don't respect their own emotions,"[36] and "Japanese are not at ease expressing themselves."[37] A child rights advocate also reckons that one of the most important yet most difficult areas for the advancement of children's rights in Japan is the promotion of children's voice and participation.[38]

Not only have nongovernmental groups introduced new pedagogy, but they have also generated a new body of curriculum materials. They range from direct translation of UN materials, "alternative reports," domestically compiled or written manuals or guidelines, videos, and "mini communications"—group newsletters—of all shapes and sizes. In fact, NGOs have played a pioneering role in providing resource materials concerning women's human rights in Japan. One should not underestimate the obstacles posed by the language barrier in making UN and foreign materials accessible to the Japanese public. As a board member of the Japanese Association of International Women's Rights (JAIWR, 1988)—modeled after the International Women's Rights Action Watch (IWRAW), a network of international NGOs monitoring the implementation of the Convention on the Elimination of All Forms of Discrimination against Women (CEDAW)—told me, "although the Japanese people contribute to the UN through their taxes, few have direct access to UN information. Japanese is not one of the six official languages in the UN, and UN information has been until recently monopolized by the Ministry of Foreign Affairs."[39]

The act of translation is a highly political one. The government and the nongovernmental community even disagree on how terms such as "children," "reproductive health/rights," and "gender equality" should be translated. Since the Japanese government has been highly sensitive in avoiding Anglo-Saxon terms in its official policy papers and laws, translation has become a highly disputed exercise. In non-English-speaking countries such as Japan, the language barrier poses a real challenge to norm diffusion. Terms such as "violence against women," "gender-based violence," "sexual harassment," "domestic violence," "shelter," "sexual slavery," and "women's human rights" existed in Japanese about a decade ago. "Violence against women," for example, has been translated in many ways, including "*josei e no bōryoku*" (violence against women), "*josei ni tai suru bōryoku*" (violence targeting women), and "*sei bōryoku*" (sexual violence). The meaning of "violence against women," then, depends on which translation is used. Sometimes "violence against women" has been, perhaps politically, equated with or reduced to domestic violence, with its nearly exclusive focus on Japanese families, thus marginalizing other issues such as trafficking and prostitution.

The Japanese government does not always provide timely access to translated UN documents; NGOs instead often translate the documents, making them accessible to the Japanese public. The Japanese government even credits, in its Beijing-Plus-Five report, JAIWR with promoting awareness of CEDAW in Japan. The members of JAIWR have gone around the country to teach schoolchildren about CEDAW in different ways, including by using *manzai* (comedy). Similarly, the Domestic Violence Legal Manual by the Japan DV Prevention and

Information Center in 1998 was the first comprehensive legal manual on domestic violence in Japan before the Anti–Domestic Violence Law was passed in 2001.

However, alternative curricula rarely go unchallenged. When the director of the Forum on Sex Issues was featured on a popular NHK morning program using an actual condom in a segment on sex education, "groups of housewives came to her office and banged her windows and doors."[40] In the case of the comfort women, the curriculum has become a battlefield of political representation. In Japan, all formal curriculum materials are produced by private groups that present their textbooks to the Ministry of Education for examination and approval. Since 1996, the right-wing, conservative Atarashii Rekishi Kyokasho wo Tsukuru Kai (Japanese Society for History Textbook Reform) has been campaigning for the elimination of war references in history textbooks. Their efforts culminated in the latest approval by the Ministry of Education of fewer references to war in textbooks starting in 2002. Another nongovernmental network, Kodomo to Kyokasho Net 21 (Children and Textbooks Japan Net 21), a network formed in 1998 of 110 groups that previously supported the famous textbook trials of Professor Saburo Ienaga from 1965 to 1997, has been trying to reverse this movement.[41]

Finally, new spaces for training and learning have also emerged. Although most of the new kinds of educational activities still take place in women's centers, they are no longer the only legitimate space for learning. Three new spaces are particularly worth noting. First, despite their limited physical, economic, and personnel resources, Japanese nongovernmental organizations have become important sites of feminist research and human rights training. Because of institutional and disciplinary obstacles, women's studies scholars in Japan often do a substantial amount of their research and training work outside the academic setting. As a feminist legal scholar told me, "I include as many materials on sexual violence as I can in my classes. But within the legal discipline in Japan, it has been considered as non-academic, and is hence illegitimate."[42] Little systematic information, let alone evaluation, of the work by these NGOs is available. Second, training activities are no longer confined within Japan. UN conferences, their parallel NGO forums, and workshops outside conference venues have become popular sites of education. Since the Beijing Conference, Japanese women have learned not only to attend world conferences, but to organize workshops at conference sites as well. During the Beijing-Plus-Five Conference in June 2000, for example, more than three hundred Japanese women organized and participated in more than twenty panels and workshops on diverse themes—from sexual discrimination at the workplace to the political par-

TABLE 6.2
Embedded Knowledge: Global Human Rights Norms Redefining Local Education in Japan

	Pre-1990s	1990s
Name and approach	Women's education	Human rights education
Subject and definition	Local	"Glocal"
Objective	Forming	Transformative
Educators	Women's studies scholars	Epistemic network members
Learners	Women	Women, men, children, parents, teachers, civil servants, etc.
Pedagogy	Lectures	Participatory workshops, role play, group training
Curriculum	Local	Global and local, "alternative"
Location	Women's centers	UN, international, regional, national, and local spaces, and cyberspace

ticipation of women and violence against women—in the parallel Beijing-Plus-Five Feminist Symposia at the City University of New York. Third, women's and men's groups alike are increasingly organizing online classes and web-based group consciousness training. As example nine, "The Pill and Reproductive Health/Rights" by Women's Online Media shows, one can download information, follow lectures, and engage in group discussions about sexuality, the pill, and reproductive rights on the web. By bringing their educational activities to UN sites and cyberspace, Japanese NGOs have stretched the traditional boundaries of educational institutions within Japan and connected themselves to a larger global human rights education community. Table 6.2 summarizes the characteristics of new human rights education in Japan in the 1990s.

Japanese State Actors as Educators of Global Human Rights Norms

The number of foreign terms concerning women and gender that has entered mainstream Japanese media and politics in the past decade is astounding: *reipu, seku hara, domesutikku baiorensu, sherutā, repurodakutibu raitsu, enpawāmento, josei no jinken, josei e no bōryoku, jendā, and torafikkingu.*[43] Yet the majority of Japanese probably still do not fully understand these terms. If nongovernmental educational efforts began in the early 1990s, the Japanese government took up its new role as an educator of women's human rights only in the late 1990s. The need to educate the public as well as train civil servants on (women's) human rights is clearly stipulated in four major policy document—the Vision of a Gender Equality (1996), the National Plan of Action for the Pro-

TABLE 6.3

Policy and Legal Stipulations on Human Rights Education in Japan

I) 1996 Vision of Gender Equality

It is necessary to improve the training of such people as police officers, the staff of prosecutor's offices, correctional officers, immigration control officers, and medical/welfare staff who are directly concerned with the investigation, prosecution, court procedure, consultation, and relief from the viewpoint of protecting women's rights.

Enlighten the people on the importance of the elimination of violence against women so that it may infiltrate the minds of each member of society.

The Declaration on the Elimination of Violence against Women, which expresses the determination of the international community to abolish violence against women, should be made widely known by the use of phrases that can be easily understood by everyone.

II) 1996 National Plan of Action for the Promotion of a Gender-Equal Society

Conduct informative and educational campaigns through initiatives related to the "United Nations Decade for Human Rights Education," Human Rights Week, etc., while making reference to international trends related to the problem to promote understanding of the human rights of women among the general public and to prevent violence against women.

III) 1997 National Plan of Action for Human Rights Education

"Human rights education" is defined in the Plan of Action for the UN Decade for Human Rights Education as "training, dissemination, and information efforts aimed at the building of a universal culture of human rights through the imparting of knowledge and skills and the molding of attitudes."

IV) 1999 Report on Violence against Women

For the prevention of violence against women, it is important that everyone in society understands that violence against women is a violation of human rights. For that purpose, the government needs to promote outreach activities through the media. The government also needs to make sure that information on counseling is available to victims; and, in the case of foreign women, that information is available in foreign languages. In addition, sex education from childhood on, education for gender equality, and the education of teachers and parents are needed in order to promote respect for women's human rights and to promote understanding of sexuality.

V) 1999 Basic Law for a Gender-Equal Society

Article 18: The state shall make efforts to promote necessary study and research for the formulation of policies related to the promotion of the formation of a gender-equal society, including study and research on the effect of social systems and practices on the formation of a gender-equal society.

VI) 2000 Law to Promote Human Rights Education

Article 8: The national government shall present its report to the Diet every year on measures that it has implemented to promote human rights education and the increase of human rights awareness.

Article 9: The national government can provide financial assistance to local governments that implement measures on human rights education and the raising of human rights awareness, by entrusting related projects and other means.

motion of Gender-Equal Society (1996), the National Plan of Action for Human Rights Education (1997), and "Towards a Society with Zero Violence against Women," a report to the prime minister by the Council for Gender Equality (1999)—and legally mandated in the Basic Law for a Gender-Equal Society (1999) as well as the Law to Promote Human Rights Education (2000) (Table 6.3).

TABLE 6.4

Japanese State Actors as Educators of Global Human Rights Norms: Some Examples

Institution	Theme	Date	Target	Format	Participants
Prime Minister's Office	Violence against women	Oct. 1999	General public	Symposium	600
Ministry of Foreign Affairs	Human rights education Trafficking	Jan. 2000	Asia-Pacific governments General public	Workshop Symposium	50 200
Police Policy Research Center	Domestic violence Child abuse	Apr. 2000	General public	Symposium	300
Local government	Sexual harassment	Oct. 1999	Staff training	Lecture	60
Waseda University	Sexual harassment	Apr. 1999	University community	Pamphlet	40,000

There has been a small explosion of conferences, lectures, and training workshops organized by various branches of the Japanese government, particularly after 1999, with the revision of the Equal Employment Opportunity Law and the passage of the Basic Law for a Gender-Equal Society and the Child Prostitution and Pornography Prohibition Law. In the last section of this chapter, I discuss five such examples of outreach and training that I attended during my fieldwork between September 1999 and May 2000. They include activities organized by the Prime Minister's Office, the Ministry of Foreign Affairs, the National Police Agency, a local government, and, finally, a private university (Table 6.4).

Examples of Outreach and Training

The impact of global norms is hardly uniform across different ministries, agencies, and local governments. Although UN relations have traditionally been the domains of the Ministry of Foreign Affairs, the Office for Gender Equality within the Prime Minister's Office, a weak liaison body, has transformed itself into the main carrier of women's human rights norms within the government after the Beijing Conference. In 1999, the Office for Gender Equality organized a contest for translating CEDAW.

> Japan signed in June 1985 the Convention on the Elimination of All Forms of Discrimination against Women, which is often referred to as the World Constitution for Women. Although fourteen years have passed, it still cannot be said that this treaty is sufficiently well known within Japan. In 1999, in commemoration of the twentieth anniversary of the adoption of this convention by the United Nations, a contest for translating the complicated phrases used in the treaty into clear and comprehensible Japanese was held with

the aim of making this treaty more widely known. This translation contest was proposed by a citizens' group from Kitakyushu City that was studying the treaty at the time. Ten translations were selected from a rich variety of unique entries that included illustrated translations in everyday language, Marchen-style stories, and male-female dialogues incorporating social conditions. It is hoped that the collection of winning entries in Japanese can be used to promote understanding of the spirit of the treaty by citizens in all walks of life and the use of this treaty in their daily lives.[44]

Since 1998, the office has also organized the annual Symposium on Violence against Women. On October 12, 1999, I attended one such half-day symposium. More than six hundred people, including government officials, the media, nongovernmental groups, and the general public, attended the event. After an opening speech by the deputy director of the Prime Minister's Office, a women's studies professor delivered the keynote address, "The Status of Violence against Women and Measures," in which she chronicled the influence of the Vienna Conference in 1993 and the Beijing Conference in 1995. She further noted the dearth of information and statistics in Japan. Two panel discussions followed: "Support for Sex Crimes Victims" and "Support for Victims of Domestic Violence." Panelists included a local police chief under the National Police Agency, directors of a private women's clinic, a nongovernmental legal network, counseling center, and shelter, and finally a local government representative from Sapporo City. The Nogata Police Station in the Tokyo metropolitan area has become an exemplar of police initiatives on violence against women. The police chief showed the new designated space for sex crime victims and introduced a new team of female police officers. The director of the Kansai Counseling Center, who had studied in California, mentioned the increasing demand for sex crime victim counseling, which has just begun in Japan. The director of the Matsushima women's clinic, a founder of the first nongovernmental group linking sexual violence and the medical institutions, noted the low consciousness among doctors, nurses, and counselors about sexual violence and urged for more training of medical personnel. The executive director of a nongovernmental shelter in Kanagawa Prefecture noted the difficult working conditions of a private shelter and the insufficiency of policies addressing immigrant women victims of domestic violence. A feminist lawyer and founder of the influential nongovernmental Lawyers' Network against Violence against Women discussed the urgency of passing a domestic violence prevention law in Japan. Finally, the director of the Women's Planning Section of the Sapporo city government presented a progressive network model, "Council of Related Institutions on Violence against Women / Domestic Violence," adopted in 1997. Although the impact of such an annual event is hard to evaluate, the symposium carries a high symbolic significance: it is no longer taboo to talk about sex and violence. In addition, considering the traditional opposition between the administration and civil society in Japan, the invitation of several nongovernmental groups to participate as panelists in this important public symposium perhaps signals a new era of increased cooperation between the government and NGOs, the exact terms of which remain to be negotiated.

MINISTRY OF FOREIGN AFFAIRS

The Ministry of Foreign Affairs has traditionally been the primary agency handling Japan's relationship with the UN. In particular, the Human Rights and Refugee Section oversees the participation of the Japanese government in UN human rights commissions and conferences. As the CEDAW chief within the Human Rights and Refugee Section explains, "the Ministry of Foreign Affairs is outward-looking, that is, it introduces the UN to Japan and is responsible for the Japanese government's policy to the UN, whereas the Office of Gender Equality within the Prime Minister's Office only coordinates."[45] Until very recently, the Ministry of Foreign Affairs had such a monopoly on information and power that, as one human rights scholar remarked, "in Japan, human rights issues [were] treated as diplomatic issues."[46]

In January 2000, I attended two events organized by the Ministry of Foreign Affairs. The first one, the Workshop on National Plans of Action for Human Rights Education in the Asia-Pacific Region, was a closed intergovernmental regional workshop organized by the Office of the High Commissioner for Human Rights and hosted by the Ministry of Foreign Affairs of Japan. Representatives from twenty-seven Asia-Pacific countries, as well as some NGO representatives,[47] attended the three-day workshop. As the director-general of the Multilateral Cooperation Department of the Ministry of Foreign Affairs said in his opening remarks,

> Putting matters in the historical perspective, the year 1998 was the fiftieth anniversary of the Universal Declaration of Human Rights, in which many commemorative events, including those of the United Nations, took place. In that year, the Ministry of Foreign Affairs of Japan organized the Symposium on Human Rights in the Asia-Pacific Region in Tokyo with the presence of the High Commissioner for Human Rights, Mrs. Mary Robinson. The symposium reaffirmed the contemporary significance of the Universal Declaration of Human Rights in today's world. . . . [T]he objective of this workshop is to provide a forum in which states in the Asia-Pacific region can explore and discuss the strategies and components for the development of a national plan of action for human rights education, to identify the purposes of the plan of action at the national and regional level, and to encourage states to develop and implement the plan of action. It is my sincere hope that the experience of Japan, and the way in which it has developed a national plan of action, will also contribute in the discussions.

At the time of the workshop in January 2000, Japan was one of two countries in the Asia-Pacific region that had a national plan of action for human rights education. Some other countries, such as Australia, have a national plan of action for human rights that includes provisions on human rights education. Japan's Asian neighbors were pleasantly surprised that Japan had become, at least in form, a leading human rights educator.

> Japan, as a member of the international community, has joined a number of international human rights instruments, such as the International Covenant on Civil and Political Rights and the International Covenant on Economic, Social, and Cultural Rights. In addition, Japan has recently ratified the International Convention on the Elimination of All Forms of Racial Discrimination, which has long been an issue of concern for Japan. As we approach the Century of Human Rights, it is vital for Japan, as a peace-loving state, to play an active role in the internationally concerted efforts to accord full respect for the human rights of every individual and to eliminate discrimination of any kind.[48]

The three-day workshop concluded with a four-page statement urging states to integrate human rights education into all levels of formal education, to train professionals, to conduct public awareness campaigns, to produce and revise materials, and to carry out research, policy, and legislative reforms.

Immediately following this intergovernmental workshop, the Ministry of Foreign Affairs organized its first public Asia-Pacific Symposium on Trafficking in Persons. It was a high-powered event, with the executive director of UNICEF, the UN special rapporteur on the sale of children, the president of the International Criminal Police Organization and director of the International Criminal Affairs Division of the National Police Agency, the director-general of the Immigration Bureau of the Ministry of Justice, and the former chief cabinet secretary and legislator of the recent Child Prostitution and Pornography Prohibition Law in attendance. As the senior state secretary for foreign affairs remarked in his keynote address,

> The word "trafficking" is still very much unknown in Japan. Despite the fact that there is no accepted definition at the international level, trafficking generally refers to the smuggling of people across borders for the purpose of sexual exploitation and forced labor. . . . Although the Convention on the Elimination of Discrimination against Women and the Convention on the Rights of the Child have provisions on trafficking, they have not been widely understood, and the problem has only been dealt with partially.

The director of the International Criminal Affairs Division of the National Police Agency affirmed that "trafficking in persons is a violation of human rights as well as a violation of domestic law" and that only international efforts will be able to cope with the problem. The director-general of the Immigration Bureau also noted the importance of the decriminalization of the trafficked, contrary to prevailing practices of the Ministry of Justice. Almost all speakers emphasized the importance of cooperation between the government and NGOs, even though some of the participating NGOs complained that few NGOs were present because the event was poorly publicized.

POLICE POLICY RESEARCH CENTER

Since violence against women became an issue in Japan in the 1990s, the Police Policy Research Center and the research arm of the National Police Agency have carried out different research, training, and outreach activities. On April 11, 2000, I attended a public symposium organized by the Police Policy Research Center entitled "Criminal Law Responses to Domestic Violence and Child Abuse: Measures in the US." More than three hundred people, including government officials, NGO representatives, the general public, and the media, attended the event. It was the first public outreach event on the issues of both domestic violence and child abuse organized by the police. The half-day symposium included speeches by three overseas speakers, two district attorneys and a Domestic Violence Task Force Commissioner from Massachusetts, and comments by two Japanese criminal law scholars. In addition to the overview of the legal provisions on domestic violence and child abuse in the state of Massachusetts, the focus was on prevention through education and outreach, including classroom visits and the training of prosecutors, police, and nongovernmental groups. Perhaps the calling upon of foreign experts, especially from the United States, could be interpreted as a reminder of the dearth of information on the subject in Japan, as well as Japan's reliance on external legitimacy.

LOCAL GOVERNMENT

In addition to central ministries and agencies, local governments have become important carriers of new legal norms, especially in terms of the training of local civil servants. Since April 1999, sexual harassment prevention training has been mandated for all civil servants in Japan. On October 29, 1999, I attended one such training seminar organized by the Women's Planning Section of the Chuo-Ku ward government within Tokyo. The two-hour seminar, "Stop the Sexual Harassment," targeting local government staff and held inside the government building, was the third in a series of sexual harassment prevention training seminars. The first two, specifically targeting the management and attended by one hundred participants each, were held the month before, in the format of lectures by a lawyer. The first one introduced the legal framework under the revised Equal Employment Opportunity Law, and the second one focused on prevention, counseling, and education about sexual harassment. The third one was a more general treatment of the problem of sexual harassment in Japan, focusing in particular on the recent emergence of sexual harassment in academia. The format was a ninety-minute lecture by a well-known feminist scholar, Ueno Chizuko, of Tokyo University, who wrote *Stop the Academic Harassment*. The room was filled with about sixty participants, mostly local government staff; more than 80 percent of the participants were men. Ueno distributed a five-page handout, two typed pages of her exposé and three pages containing a university sexual harassment prevention guideline checklist, an evaluation of existing guidelines, and results of a survey by nongovernmental organizations. The complete silence after the lecture was a vivid reminder that this kind of training is still novel in Japan.

WASEDA UNIVERSITY

The final example of outreach activity is in the form of guidelines distributed to faculty, staff, and students at Waseda University, a leading university in Tokyo that has more than forty thousand faculty and students. Although it is private, it is nonetheless under the mandate of the Rule 10–10 of the Personnel Authority on sexual harassment prevention. Since April 1999, Waseda has created three independent committees on sexual harassment prevention, information, and investigation. The committees have published a pamphlet in Japanese and a more detailed guideline available in four languages (Japanese, English, Chinese, and Korean) for the entire university body. Its introduction reads:

> Waseda University is committed to the creation of a comfortable educational and working environment based on its founding principles of respect for the individual rights of faculty, staff, and students. As part of this commitment, the university strives to prevent sexual harassment as both a grave violation of human rights and a form of sexual discrimination. Waseda University also strives to take prompt, effective, and appropriate action in response to incidents of sexual harassment. . . . A clear statement of sexual harassment policy shall be published and disseminated through university newspapers, booklets, and posters. Sections on sexual harassment shall be included in the student guidebooks, faculty manuals, and employment regulations distributed to students, faculty, and staff. Seminars and lectures shall be held to raise awareness of sexual harassment and thus contribute to its prevention and eradication. Furthermore, the Sexual Harassment Information Committee shall publish and distribute an annual report describing its activities, listing the results of its surveys and giving examples of case histories. (Waseda University Guidelines on Sexual Harassment)

In their first year, between April 1999 and April 2000, the committees have heard a total of forty cases, although no penalties have been applied. As the president of the Sexual Harassment Guideline Working Group, a professor of education, admits,

I have been at Waseda for forty years; I must say that this is quite a change. In November 1999, when we drafted the first sexual harassment prevention guideline and sent it out to the entire university community for feedback, I was worried that there would be little response. Some six hundred letters came from professors, staff, and students. I was very surprised. . . . We now conduct surveys every year and include sexual harassment prevention in our orientation activities. But I must admit that sexual harassment is only the tip of an iceberg. We need more holistic education on sexuality and sex discrimination in order to solve problem of "*sekuhara*," but the Ministry of Education does not seem to want to recognize the problem.[49]

Successive world conferences and their resultant platforms for action in the 1990s have emphasized the importance of human rights education in ensuring that those norms are not mere proclamations but are translated into local realities. In particular, the 1993 Vienna Declaration and Platform for Action on Human Rights, the 1994 Cairo Declaration on Population and Development, the 1994 Declaration on the Elimination of Violence against Women, and the 1995 Beijing Platform for Action all emphasize the importance of incorporating world human rights standards in national educational efforts. The UN Decade for Human Rights Education (1995–2004) further calls for the creation of a national human rights education committee and plan of action.

What one observes is not just an incorporation of global human rights norms in policy papers and laws, but training and outreach activities by diverse state and substate actors throughout Japan. One cannot comprehend these changes without understanding the emergence of norms concerning women's and children's human rights at the global level. By the late 1990s, not only was it legitimate to talk about issues such as sexual harassment, domestic violence, child sexual abuse, and trafficking, but the Japanese state was also expected to actively conduct research, disseminate information, and educate about them. Although it seemed inconceivable not long ago, the Japanese state has turned itself into an ardent educator of global women's and children's human rights standards.

Global human rights norms do not impact Japan uniformly. To understand better the changes concerning women's and children's rights discussed thus far, I will now turn to the contrasting case of the development of minority rights in Japan.

CHAPTER SEVEN

Japanese Nongovernmental Mobilization at the World Conference against Racism

Perhaps the litmus test for the impact of global norms on Japan is the recognition of minority rights in Japan. There is a long tradition of politically motivated and accepted *nihonjinron* (ideology of the Japanese as a homogenous race). For the purpose of providing a case that is contrary to the central thesis of this book—that global human rights norms have exerted a considerable impact on women's and children's rights—this chapter traces the development of minority rights in Japan. First, I look at the construction of Japanese racial identity in modern Japan. Second, I discuss three changes in Japan since the early 1990s that have brought the issue of racism to the forefront, namely the "foreign labor problem," a resurgence of right-wing nationalism, and the visibility and internationalization of Japanese nongovernmental organizations (NGOs). Finally, I discuss at length the latest development in Japanese NGO mobilization at the 2001 UN World Conference against Racism, Racial Discrimination, Xenophobia, and Related Intolerance.

Between August 23 and September 9, 2001, around 15,000 government delegates and 8,000 NGO representatives attended WCAR in Durban, South Africa. Although the conference was not much reported by Japanese media, more than a hundred people from Japan went as part of the first pan-racial nongovernmental coalition, Durban 2001 Japan, itself representing more than twelve NGO networks of Burakumin, Ainu, Okinawans, Koreans, migrant workers, and Japanese returnees from China. Although it is too early to suggest that WCAR resulted in paradigmatic legal changes concerning racial relations in Japan like the Beijing conference did for women's rights, I aim to show how five formerly distinct movements—concerning Burakumin, Ainu, Okinawans, Koreans, and migrant workers—became part of transnational advocacy networks on caste, indigenous peoples' rights, colonization, and migrants' rights and redefined racism as an issue in Japan at WCAR. I further analyze how women within these minority communities mobilize around the concept of "multiple discrimination," which challenges the race-neutral assumptions of the mainstream Japanese women's movement as well as the gender-neutral assumptions of minority movements in Japan.

Constructing Japanese Racial Identity

To argue for a multiracial Japan is to assume that minorities exist within Japan. Estimating the size of the minority population in Japan, however, largely remains guesswork, as the Japanese government "does not conduct population surveys from an ethnic viewpoint."[1] There are approximately 3 million Burakumin, 50,000 Ainu, 1.2 million Okinawans, 950,000 Koreans, and 750,000 other registered foreigners in Japan, in addition to several hundreds of thousands of illegal overstayers.[2] These estimates would put the minority population somewhere around 5 percent of the total population of 126 million as of 1997. The problem lies not only in the lack of statistics, but also in the representation of the minority population in Japan. On the one hand, various minority groups are underrepresented in mainstream establishments such as the education and political systems. On the other hand, they are often overrepresented in the media, where they are often linked with criminality.[3]

It is important to underline the contemporary nature of the creation of racial minorities in Japan. As Neary notes, "discrimination [against the Burakumin] was part of the institutional structure of Tokugawa Japan. There were rules regulating the dress and behavior of the four main classes—samurai, peasant, artisan, and merchant. Intermarriage was prohibited."[4] Though the 1871 Emancipation Edict abolished the caste system, prejudice against the former outcastes remained. Many scholars have argued that the official discourse of Japanese ethnic homogeneity is itself a sociopolitical construction of modern Japan. Weiner deconstructs the "invention" of the Japanese *minzoku* (people) by the Meiji state, under which "race" and "nation" became naturalized and merged under the ideology of *kazoku kokka* (family state) under the emperor.[5] Since to be modern and civilized is to be Japanese, the colonial subjects of Hokkaido, Okinawa, Taiwan, Korea, and China were considered inferior Others, to be brought under Japan's civilizing influence. As Weiner puts it,

> It was within the context of the political, economic, and social processes which developed under colonial rule in Hokkaido, Korea, and Taiwan that the new Japanese identity was most fully expressed. If a strong collectivistic nationalism allowed the Japanese to partake of a modern and progressive identity, the existence of empire confirmed their own manifest superiority vis-à-vis the peoples of Asia.[6]

Lie also details the contemporary construction of the "class, cultural, and ethnic others" as a result of Japan's territorial expansion since the late nineteenth century.[7] The Ainu people were forcibly assimilated after Hokkaido became part of Japan in 1869 with the establishment of the Hokkaido Development Agency. Traditional Ainu cultural practices such as ear piercing and tattooing were banned in 1871. The fishing right of the Ainu was banned in all rivers in the 1880s, and their hunting right was completely prohibited in 1889. The Hokkaido Former Aborigines Protection Act, passed in 1899, completed the assimilation policy. The Ainu were consequently forced to be peasants in the Japanese agricultural system, and the Ainu children were forced to attend the Aborigines Elementary School, where use of the Ainu language was completely prohibited. Okinawa, an independent kingdom with its own culture and language, was annexed by the Meiji state in 1879. As the historian George Kerr notes, "the educational system took the lead in the 'Japanization' program. Virtually every home in the island could be reached through the children at school. . . . By the end of World War I, the major obstacles of assimilation had been overcome."[8] Taiwan became a Japanese colony after the Sino-Japanese War in 1895. As for the Ainu, Japanese seized land and forced aborigines in Taiwan to become rice cultivators. Korea was colonized in 1910, and Manchuria became a Japanese puppet state in 1931. Although the Japanese government promoted Japanese emigration to these colonies, population flows in the reverse direction were far more significant.[9] As Lie argues, the "proximate origin of the Korean minority in postwar Japanese society is therefore due to the labor demands of prewar Japan."[10] After the mid-1930s, Japan initiated a policy of complete Japanization. In 1938, the Korean school curriculum became the same as the Japanese curriculum.[11] By 1944, the Korean population in Japan had reached 2.4 million, more than half of whom were forcibly located because of the war effort. Although Koreans were considered nationals under colonial rule, they were stripped of their citizenship after the war. By the conclusion of the 1965 peace treaty, South Korean citizenship was imposed on most ethnic Koreans in Japan.[12]

Most studies of Japanese minorities involve in-depth analysis of individual minority groups, including the Burakumin, Ainu, Okinawans, Koreans, and foreign workers.[13] Often, domestic explanations focusing on the Japanese bureaucracy, interest groups, and party politics are invoked to explain change.[14] Little research has looked at the connections between these movements and their international dimensions under the umbrella discourse of human rights. From 1983 on, the Buraku Liberation League began to attend meetings of the UN Commission on Human Rights and formed close relationships with international NGOs such as the Minority Rights Group.[15] It led a campaign for Japan's ratification of the International Convention on the Elimination of All Forms of Racial Discrimination, which was finally successful in 1995. As for the Ainu, Narita Tokuhei became the first Ainu to attend the NGO-led World Conference of Indigenous People in 1981, an event that would prove to be consequential in making the Ainu people visible at the international level and within Japan.[16] In 1984, Narita Tokuhei also started forging alliances with other domestic groups, using the language of universal human rights.[17]

Korean residents in Japan who had been denied access to welfare and pensions because of their foreigner status also took advantage of international human rights law. In 1982, they became entitled to pension plans as a result of Japan's ratification of the Refugee Convention, whereby discrimination based upon nationality was prohibited.[18] Migrant workers' organizations continue to mobilize around the 1990 Convention on the Rights of Migrants, despite the fact that the Japanese government has not ratified it. In contrast to the Burakumin, Ainu, and Koreans, Okinawans began to use international human rights mechanisms only in the 1990s. Until 1972, "'reversion' to Japan, rather than independence, [was] the rallying cry of Okinawan activists," since Okinawa came under U.S. rule after Japan's defeat.[19] According to one young activist, "it has not been easy to find a common human rights frame. Most Okinawans do not perceive themselves as a 'minority,' for example, as they are the majority within Okinawa. Few people, including activists, understand the concept of 'indigenous peoples' rights.' There is a tremendous amount of education to be done."[20]

Meanwhile, women within these minority groups in Japan, "the minorities within minorities," have been silenced both within the mainstream Japanese women's movement and the minority movements. Despite criticisms from Japanese feminists, scholars and activists alike, the mainstream Japanese women's movement has mostly ignored the issue of race. Fujime, a feminist historian, criticizes the lack of a more holistic approach integrating class, race, and gender in Japan's second-wave feminism of the 1980s.[21] Ogoshi describes the "discrimination within Japanese feminism" and warns against a feminism that "espouses Japanism."[22] Suzuki calls the comfort women movement representative of a paradigm shift in Japanese feminism, from its habitual focus on women as victims (Japanese women being discriminated against within Japan) to a focus on women as aggressors or victimizers (Japanese women being complicit in Japan's war efforts in Asia).[23] Matsui argues for the responsibility of the Japanese women's movement in addressing the plight of Asian women in Japan. She writes:

> It is crucial for feminism to recognize and trace the complexity of the multiple contexts that generate gender politics. It is true that Japanese women are oppressed within their

own society; it is also true that some Japanese women occupy positions of relative power, from which they oppress, or are implicated in the oppression of, other Japanese women. But it is not enough. We need to go one step further and look at the relationship of Japanese women to the women of countries that are economically dominated by Japan. What price do other Asian women pay for the prosperity and daily comfort of so many Japanese women? How do we as Japanese women stand in relation to the thousands of Filipino hostesses working in Japanese bars? Then there is the whole question of the Filipino, Korean, and Sri Lankan brides who are imported to Japan to overcome the shortage of women.[24]

Whose Japan? Changes in the Racial Scene since the 1990s

Since the early 1990s, the juxtaposition of three developments—the "foreign labor problem," a resurgence of right-wing nationalism, and the visibility and internationalization of Japanese NGOs—has put the issue of racism at the forefront. The first change concerns demographics, or at least the political implications of an unintended demographic shift. Though Japan continues to have the lowest percentage of immigrants and expatriate workers of any advanced industrialized nation—about 1 percent of the population—since the early 1990s the country has seen the creation of permanent migrant communities, a phenomenon that was much feared by the Japanese. Sellek describes three stages of foreign worker migration into Japan.[25] The first phase, from the late 1970s to around 1986, was dominated by illegal female migrant workers from South East and East Asia. However, since most of these women work in the sex industry, an industry regulated by law and supported by corporations, their presence was never regarded as a problem. The second wave, from the mid-1980s to 1990, was marked by an influx of illegal male migrant workers from Iran, Pakistan, Bangladesh, the Philippines, China, Malaysia, Thailand, and South Korea who took low-skilled jobs. The third stage, a response to the problem of illegal migration, was marked by the revision of the Immigration Control Act in 1990. Although it imposed severe penalties on employers who used illegal migrants, it also made it legal for South Americans of Japanese descent and their spouses (Nikkeijin) to reside and work in Japan, a so-called "side door" provision that would ease Japan's demand for unskilled labor without disturbing the ethnic homogeneity of Japanese society.[26] The number of Nikkeijin jumped from 14,528 in 1989 (1.5 percent of total registered aliens) to 201,795 in 1996 (14.3 percent of total registered aliens).[27]

Meanwhile, the number of illegal migrant workers/"overstayers" continues to increase. Although the number of illegal workers in Japan peaked in 1993, their average length of stay continued to increase. At the end of 1999, the Ministry of Justice estimated that there were 270,000 illegal residents in Japan, many of whom are married and have children.[28] The presence of a large migrant population, legal and illegal, during times of recession has generated polarized debates about their rights and role in Japan. Herbert summarizes the various positions in favor of the admission of foreign labor in terms of sectoral labor shortage, internationalization, multiculturalism, and human rights.[29] On the other side, objections to foreign labor are related to issues of labor market competition and unemployment, crime and insecurity, social costs, and cultural conservation, as well as the precedent set by Western European nations, where the admission of foreign laborers has been seen as a failure.

Since the mid-1990s, several foreign residents have taken their cases to the Japanese courts. In November 1999, a Brazilian won a case against a jewelry store that refused her entry because she was a foreigner and was awarded 4.7 million yen in damages. In the absence of Japanese laws covering the treatment of foreigners, the judge in this case ruled, "the country must abide by its international treaties. In 1996, 31 years after the Convention on the Elimination of All Forms of Racial Discrimination was adopted by the United Nations, Japan finally signed it, becoming the 148th country to do so. . . . Since the judgment was based on international law, it cannot be appealed under Japanese law." In November 2002, the Sapporo District Court ordered a bathhouse in Otaru, Hokkaido, to pay 3 million yen in damages to two foreign residents and one naturalized Japanese citizen for refusing them entry because they are not Japanese. In December 2000, the bathhouse had a posted sign in English reading "Japanese Only," citing as a reason the recent trouble with drunken Russian sailors turning Japanese customers away. In the ruling, presiding judge Sakai Mitsuru claimed that "the action of barring foreigners from the defendant's company is a form of racial discrimination, and refusing to allow people to bathe is beyond the limit of permissible conduct in society." The court, however, rejected the damages claim against the Otaru government, which the plaintiffs argued had a duty to meet the requirements of the International Convention on the Elimination of All Forms of Racial Discrimination, which Japan signed in 1995. The judge said the convention did not require local governments to institute an ordinance to stamp out discrimination, and there had been no omission on the part of the city.[30]

A second related development in the 1990s was the resurgence of right-wing nationalism. No one really knows how large the extreme right is in Japan. It is made up of political elites, intellectuals, private corporations, the media, and the *yakuza*. Szymkowiak and Steinhoff trace the origins of the Japanese radical right to the state ideology of the emperor being at the pinnacle of an all-encompassing family united by blood.[31] Though the emperor system was officially dismantled after the war, the retention of the emperor as a figurehead, a largely intact prewar bureaucratic structure, and one-party rule by the conservative Liberal Democratic Party (LDP) from 1950 until 1993 mean that a nationalist legacy never quite faded in postwar Japan. According to Szymkowiak and Steinhoff, right-wing groups in Japan are organized around a few issues—restoration of the emperor to his pre-1945 status; the Yasukuni Shrine, where Japan's 2.5 million war dead are worshiped; denial of war responsibility; and territorial claims (the Kurile island chains occupied by Russia)—and a core ideology of racial purity. Because radical right ideas are, with a few exceptions, legitimate in LDP circles, their public utterance has rarely been considered a political liability. There is a long tradition of explicit nationalist exclamations by top Japanese politicians. In 1986, Prime Minister Nakasone Yasuhiro said publicly that Japan was a homogeneous country. In May 1994, Justice Minister Nagano Shigeto, in the coalition government of Hata Tsutomu, said, at the price of his dismissal, that the Nanjing Massacre never occurred and that Japan had no war responsibility toward its Asian neighbors. In 1999, despite tremendous opposition from local school boards and teachers, the Hinomaru was formally adopted by the Diet as Japan's national flag and "Kimigayo" as the national anthem, imposing a legal duty on all schools to use both.[32]

In April 2000, the Tokyo governor, Ishihara Shintaro, in addressing the Self-Defense Forces, used a derogatory term from colonial Japan in referring to Koreans, Taiwanese, and Chinese:

> In Tokyo today, many of the Sangokujins and foreigners who have illegally entered this country commit atrocious crimes. The nature of crimes in Tokyo differs from that in the past. Considering these situations, it is possible that a big riot may occur during a big natural disaster. In order to deal with such riots, the capability of the police force is limited. I hope you will not only fight against disasters but also maintain public security on such occasions.[33]

The following month, Prime Minister Mori Yoshiro stunned the country with his utterance that Japan was a divine country with the emperor at the center. In August 2001 and April 2002, Prime Minister Koizumi Shinichiro paid a "private" visit to the Yasukuni Shrine, which angered both China and Korea. As China's Foreign Ministry reproached, "China resolutely opposes visits by Japanese leaders, in whatever form and at whatever time, to the Yasukuni Shrine, which honors Class A war criminals."[34] Accompanying these incidents was an intellectual undercurrent of historical revisionism to portray a bright Japanese national history. As already discussed in chapter 5, in 2002, right-wing groups led by the Japanese Society for History Textbook Reform (Atarashii Rekishi Kyokasho wo Tsukuru Kai) successfully campaigned for the elimination of war clauses in history textbooks, which was finally approved by the Ministry of Education. Even more worrisome was a special measures law that was passed in a record six months in the name of anti-terrorism after the September 11th attacks in the United States. The law renewed the questioning of Article 9 of the Constitution banning Japan's right to use force.

A third crucial development in the 1990s was the increasing visibility and internationalization of Japanese NGOs. Though many attribute the expansion of NGOs in Japan to the Kobe earthquake in 1995 and the subsequent passage of the NPO law in 1997,[35] Japanese NGO mobilization within the UN actually began in the late 1980s. Several scholars have argued that Japan is known as a silent observer or reluctant participant in the human rights activities of the UN.[36] Japan has, often with delays, ratified most UN conventions,[37] even though that itself tells us little about the translation of those standards in Japan.[38] The Japanese government consistently argues that the Constitution guarantees fundamental human rights to all and hence passed a minimum of laws after ratifying international human rights conventions. In turn, Japanese courts, characterized by legal conservatism, often invoke Article 30 of the Civil Code, which invalidates any judicial act that is "contrary to public order or good morals."[39]

In response to Japan's sluggishness in conforming international human rights norms, Japanese NGOs formed several networks in the 1990s to lobby for Japan's ratification of UN conventions and monitor its compliance to the conventions and declarations that it has signed. For example, an initiative of Nikkyōsō (the Japanese Teachers' Union), Kodomo no Jinken Ren (the Federation for the Protection of Children's Human Rights, Japan), comprised of sixty NGOs, was formed in 1986 to lobby for Japan's ratification of the UN Convention of the Rights of the Child (CRC), which it did in 1994. It remains the most important watchdog for the implementation of the CRC in Japan, conducting surveys, organizing symposia, and compiling alternative reports. The mega–world conferences of the 1990s also became galvanizing opportunities for Japan's embryonic NGO networks. In 1990, the International Human Rights NGO Network was formed to coordinate Japanese NGO activities in relation to the UN human rights mechanisms, as well as to liaise with the Japanese government. In 1992, in preparation for the Vienna conference, the network became the NGO Liaison Group for the World Conference on Human Rights. By June 1993, sixteen human rights groups, including Korean, Buraku, women's, and AIDS groups, had joined and participated in Vienna.[40] The liaison group has since then actively lobbied for Japan's ratification of CERD in 1995 and CAT in 1996. It continues to provide shadow reports to the CCPR

(Covenant on Civil and Political Rights) and CESCR (Covenant on Economic, Social, and Cultural Rights), as well as the CERD (Convention on the Elimination of All Forms of Racial Discrimination) committees each time the Japanese government files its own reports. Perhaps the Fourth World Conference on Women in Beijing exerted the most dramatic influence on Japan. Rallying around the discourses of women's human rights, the women's movement in Japan was able to press for a series of unprecedented legal changes, including the revision of the Equal Employment Opportunity Law (1997), legalization of the pill (1999), and the passage of the first Basic Law on Gender Equality (1999), the Anti-Stalking Law (2000), and the Domestic Violence Prevention Law (2001). The children's rights movement also capitalized on the violence against women campaign and pushed for the passage of the Child Prostitution and Pornography Prohibition Law (1999), as well as the Child Abuse Prevention Law (2000), neither of which the Japanese government had intended to pass after its ratification of the CRC.

Japanese NGO Mobilization in WCAR

The five official themes of WCAR focus on the causes of racism, victims, measures of prevention, remedies, and strategies. In the context of a growing migrant population in Japan, resurgence of the right, and emerging NGO advocacy, the World Conference against Racism provided a timely opportunity for a wide spectrum of Japanese NGOs to coalesce into a larger anti-racism network. The NGO coalition Durban 2001 Japan, comprised of Buraku, Korean, Ainu, Okinawan, migrant, and women's groups, was formed in October 2000. Despite divergent interests, the coalition agreed on three common goals for mobilization: the enactment of an anti-discrimination law in Japan, the creation of an independent national human rights protection machinery, and the development of an individual complaint procedure for ICERD.[41] Prior to departure for Durban, the coalition held five press conferences in Japan and organized three public lecture series: Gender and Racism, Anti-Discrimination Law, and Establishment of a National Human Rights Protection Machinery.[42]

In Durban, Japanese NGO mobilization took the form of educational workshops and lobbying. At the NGO forum the group Durban 2001 Japan organized its own booth, disseminating information on racial discrimination in Japan. The coalition also organized a press conference and several workshops, Work and Descent-Based Discrimination, Multiple Discrimination against Minority Women in Japan, Promoting Human Security: Trafficking in Women and Children, and Colonialism, Nationalism, and Racism in Japan. A young

Ainu woman from the coalition also spoke on a panel called Voices of Indigenous Women, organized by a network of indigenous women groups and attended by the high commissioner, Mary Robinson. In addition, Buraku groups organized a demonstration to protest the exclusion of caste in the official outcome documents. More importantly, members of the coalition lobbied with the Dalits, Indigenous Peoples, Reparation and Slavery, Migration and Refugees, Trafficking, and Asians and Asian Descendants caucuses. Below I examine the process of lobbying and its impact on the outcome documents concerning each of the five groups.

BURAKUMIN

Despite its long history of mobilization in Japan, the Buraku movement continues to face three obstacles. First, the traditional approach of the movement focused on denunciation of specific incidents. Most Japanese have little consciousness of Buraku discrimination. As Lie argues, "for many people, Burakumin status is a historical relic that holds no contemporary relevance. Even when differences were acknowledged, ethnic status was denied because ethnicity is racialized in Japan."[43] Until the new discourse of caste discrimination at WCAR, the Buraku liberation movement lacked a global human rights frame.[44] Second, the movement itself has been plagued by political divisions along party lines, which further the indifference of the majority of the Japanese. Finally, the Japanese government has also consistently denied that they constitute a "minority" within Japan. In its first report to the Human Rights Committee (HRC) in 1980 (under the requirement of ICCPR, ratified by Japan in 1979), the Japanese government maintained that there were no minorities on its soil. The Buraku issue continued to be omitted from the government's subsequent reports to the HRC in 1987, 1991, and 1997, as well as from its first and second reports to the CERD Committee in 1999.[45] The attitude of the Japanese government to this date remains that the Buraku issue represents discrimination from within a homogeneous population and that "special measures" had been put in place to improve the situation.[46]

In March 1999, Human Rights Watch published its first survey report on violence against the "untouchables" in India, breaking the silence on the issue in the Western world. The following year the Indian NGO National Dalit Human Rights Campaign connected with Human Rights Watch, Amnesty International, and the Migrant Rights Group to form the International Dalit Solidarity Network.[47] The Tokyo-based International Movement against All Forms of Discrimination and Racism (IMADR) and its members from the Buraku Liberation League soon joined this global network. A global anti–caste discrimination campaign ensued, including eighteen months of intensive lobbying at both the international and national levels, until the Durban conference. In August 2000, the global advocacy network on caste successfully lobbied for the adoption of the first UN resolution on work- and descent-based discrimination by the Subcommission on the Promotion and Protection of Human Rights. It specifically stated that Buraku discrimination in Japan, together with discrimination based on the caste system in South Asia and Africa, is prohibited by international human rights law. In its final observations on the first and second reports by the Japanese government in March 2001, the CERD Committee reiterated that the Buraku people fall under the definition of "descent" within Article 1 of the Convention, that is, they are discriminated against on the basis of their descent.[48]

The International Dalit Solidarity Network then further engaged in "information politics," mobilizing global public support through publication of facts. Human Rights Watch issued a major report entitled "Caste Discrimination: A Global Concern," as well as press releases. It maintained a special focus page on ending caste discrimination on its web site.[49] The issue of caste figured prominently in the WCAR Asia-Pacific NGO Declaration in Tehran/Kathmandu in February and April 2001.[50] At the second world preparatory committee (prepcom) in Geneva in May and June 2001, the International Dalit Solidarity Network managed to get the Swiss government to sponsor a text that urges states to "ensure that all necessary constitutional, legislative, and administrative measures, including appropriate forms of affirmative action, are in place to prohibit and redress discrimination on the basis of work and descent, and that such measures are respected and implemented by all state authorities at all levels."[51] At the third world prepcom in Geneva in August, however, the Indian and U.S. governments pressured Switzerland to withdraw the proposed text, while Guatemala, together with ten other countries, voiced the strong opinion that only the paragraph on work and descent-based discrimination be kept.[52] As India refused to settle the issue by the predominant consensus method, paragraph 73, as it became known in the final draft Programme of Action, was bracketed. Intense lobbying ensued in Durban. During the intergovernmental conference, the caste question was relegated to a special working group, headed by India, instead of the plenary drafting committee. India received support from a number of Asian countries and the United States in exchange for its support for Israel.[53] Despite the visibility of some five hundred Dalits and Buraku at the conference and the backing of the European Union, paragraph 73 was deleted from the final outcome Programme of Action. In the words of Kinhide Mushakoji, the director general of IMADR who served as an NGO representative in the Japanese governmental delegation, "the issue of descent became sacrificed in WCAR because of the Middle East question."[54]

Throughout the negotiations in Durban, the Japanese government adopted a neutral position. It neither actively supported the retention of paragraph 73 nor objected to the inclusion of the term "work and descent-based discrimination" in the final outcome document, as long as the Buraku issue was not included under "descent."[55] Though caste discrimination is excluded in the intergovernmental outcome document, WCAR nonetheless became the first occasion on which the issue of caste was substantively raised in international law. In addition to a large body of information generated by the global campaign, eighteen paragraphs (including two specifically on the Buraku) in the final NGO Declaration and Programme of Action concern caste discrimination, an issue that was little known even within the global NGO community until Durban.

AINU

The issue for the Ainu people is not so much the absence of a global human rights frame, as it is for the Buraku. Since the 1993 International Year of the World's Indigenous Peoples, the Ainu people have more or less successfully built solidarity with other indigenous peoples of the world. The problems they face are the consistent denial by the Japanese government of their status as indigenous people of Japan, on the one hand, and the slow progress toward the recognition of indigenous peoples' rights at the international level, on the other. The traditional approach of the Japanese government toward the Ainu people was one of, in Siddle's words, "welfare colonialism."[56] Ironically, the Meiji government did consider the Ainu aboriginals, albeit "former aboriginals," as reflected in the Hokkaido Former Natives Protection Act of 1899. The act mandated a policy of colonization, forced relocation, and assimilation, with the single objective that the Ainu would become a dying race. In 1974, the Japanese government established the Hokkaido Utari Welfare Policy, which aimed at improving the livelihood of poor people in Hokkaido without recognizing the ethnic minority status of the Ainu. In 1981, in response to the final observations by the Human Rights Committee based on its First Periodic Report, the Japanese government stated, "the establishment of a rapid communication system had made the difference in their way of life indiscernible. The Utari were Japanese nationals and treated equally with other Japanese."[57] In 1988, in response to the observations by the Human Rights Committee concerning its second report, the government conceded that the Ainu people should be able to preserve their culture as as any other Japanese could.[58] By 1992, when Japan filed its third report, as a result of Ainu mobilization at the UN, the Japanese government finally recognized the Ainu as an ethnic minority and suddenly shifted its "area policy" to "ethnic policy."[59] The report stated, "as for the question of the people of Ainu raised in relation to Article 27, they may be called the minorities of that Article, because it is recognized that these people preserve their own religion and language and maintain their own culture." The question of whether the Ainu constitute an ethnic minority was not raised again in Japan's Fourth Periodic Report under the ICCPR in 1997. That same year, the first Law for the Promotion of Ainu Culture was passed. However, to this date, the Japanese government continues to deny the Ainu people their status as indigenous people of Japan. As the Federation of Bar Associations in Japan states in its alternative report in 1997, the Ainu culture promotion law falls short in recognizing the rights of the Ainu people as described in Article 27 of the ICCPR, including compensation for past violations of economic rights and the right to traditional use of land and resources as part of their right to enjoy their indigenous culture. In 1997, the Sapporo District Court made a landmark judgment on the Nibutani Dam case in which the Ainu were clearly defined as indigenous people.[60]

Despite this historic ruling, the Japanese government continued in its first and second reports to the CERD Committee in 1999 its position that the Ainu were a completely assimilated race, stating that "at present, the Ainu people lead lives that differ little from those of any other constituents of the society, linguistically as well as culturally; moreover, that there is an extremely limited number of people who can speak the Ainu language." In July 2001, shortly before the Durban conference, the former deputy chief cabinet secretary from Hokkaido, Suzuki Muneo, referred to the Ainu as a "completely assimilated people," while the trade minister, Hiranuma Takeo, remarked in Hokkaido that homogeneity accounted for the excellence in Japanese society.[61]

The problem of the advancement of the Ainu's rights is not only a domestic one. There has yet to be a fight for the rights of indigenous peoples within the framework of a UN convention, in contrast to the rights of women and children or racial discrimination in general. Despite tremendous local and international mobilization since the early 1980s, states could not agree on a declaration, much less a convention, on indigenous peoples' rights. In 1982, the UN Working Group on Indigenous Populations was set up under the Subcommission on the Prevention of Discrimination and Protection of Minorities within the Commission on Human Rights. In 1985, a UN Voluntary Fund for Indigenous Populations was established to assist indigenous peoples in participating in the working group meetings. The year 1993 was designated the International Year of the World's Indigenous Peoples, followed by a UN Decade between 1995 and 2004. In 1995, the working group submitted a draft Declaration on the Rights of Indigenous Peoples, and an open-ended intersession working group was set up to review the text. Unfortunately, negotiations have been stalled due to a lack of resources as well as opposition from states.[62] Between 1995 and 2001, the working group met only annually but was able to adopt two articles in the first three years and eleven more in the subsequent three years. In 2001 a special rapporteur on the rights of indigenous peoples was appointed, and in 2002 the Permanent Forum on Indigenous Issues was established by the Economic and Social Council, which allows, for the first time, indigenous representatives to address the UN officially.

Short of having a UN convention, the International Labor Organization (ILO) Convention 169 on the conditions of life and work of indigenous and tribal peoples becomes the only international instrument to which indigenous peoples have access. Few states, however, have ratified the convention, leaving important gaps in the protection of indigenous peoples' rights at the international level. In Durban, the fierce "battle of the 's,'" that is, over the inclusion of the term "indigenous peoples" in its plurality with implied rights under customary international law, unfolded around paragraph 27 in the final draft declaration (paragraph 24 in the final declaration). It states:

> The use of the term "indigenous peoples" in the declaration and Programme of Action cannot be construed as having any implications as to rights under international law. Any reference to rights associated with the term "indigenous peoples" is in the context of ongoing multilateral negotiations on texts that specifically deal with such rights and is without prejudice to the outcome of those negotiations.

The text originally appeared as a footnote in the second world prepcom in May 2001. By the third world prepcom, however, it appeared as a full-blown paragraph in the declaration and was adopted (and therefore theoretically not to be reopened for further negotiations). In Durban, the Indigenous Peoples' Caucus lobbied for the deletion of the text. The GRULAC group (Latin American and Caribbean countries) and Canada supported amending it. The EU (and France in particular) proposed that the term "person belonging to an indigenous population" be used in the rest of the outcome document as a condition for its support for the deletion of paragraph 27.[63] Though the paragraph was finally retained in the outcome declaration, for many young Ainu activists, WCAR represented an important opportunity to network with other indigenous groups around the world.

OKINAWANS

If the Buraku movement suffered from the lack of a global human rights frame, and the Ainu movement suffered from both the Japanese government's denial that they constituted an indigenous people and the absence of a UN convention, then the Okinawan movement seems to have been afflicted by all three of the issues. Activism in and on Okinawa has for decades largely been associated with the anti-militarism movement and inseparable from issues of the U.S.–Japan security alliance. On the tenth anniversary of the reversion, Okinawans and their Japanese supporters drafted a constitution for an independent Republic of the Ryūkyūs, even though self-determination has never been a controlling principle in solving Okinawa's international political status.[64] In the early 1990s, some younger Okinawan activists began to reconsider their movement from an ethnic minority perspective.[65] Reframing the Okinawan movement from an ethnic, and especially an indigenous peoples', perspective, is not devoid of problems, however. As Kikuzato notes, although the Okinawan movement shares some similarities with the Ainu movement—both were subjected to a policy of colonization and assimilation, for example—there are significant differences between the two. Unlike the Ainu in northern Japan, few within Okinawa consider themselves a minority. How to pursue the right to self-determination without inflaming Okinawan nationalism and ethnocentrism is another major issue.[66]

The continual denial of their culture and language by the Japanese government no doubt contributed to many Okinawans' sense of a troubled national identity.[67] Compared to the movement for the rights of the Ainu, who, though not recognized as indigenous people, were nonetheless officially accepted as an ethnic minority within Japan, the movement for Okinawans' rights as an indigenous minority has barely begun. There is a great deal of debate, including from within the movement itself, about the national and ethnic origins of the Okinawans.[68] The Japanese government has consistently denied that the Okinawans constitute a minority within Japan. Similar to its policy toward the Buraku and Ainu, the Japanese government's approach to Okinawa is to provide economic aid, through the Okinawa Development Agency set up in 1972. In all of the periodic reports by the Japanese government to the Human Rights Committee and the CERD Committee, the Okinawan issue was categorically omitted.

Compounding the problem of a human rights frame that Okinawan activists hesitate to use as a frame for their movement, and of the Japanese government's denial of minority status, is the lack of institutionalization and legitimation of the rights of indigenous peoples at the international level. A significant difference here between the Ainu and the Okinawan movements concerns the disproportionate use of the Ryūkyū Islands for military purposes. As many have observed, about 75 percent of all American troops in Japan are stationed in Okinawa, even though it constitutes less than 1 percent of Japan's total territory. Under the Land Appropriations Law, due process requires that records of land and property to be taken for public use be signed by the owners.[69] In the mid-1990s, several owners refused to yield their land, and mayors who were supposed to step in refused to fulfill their duties. The prefectural governor also refused to intervene, resulting in legal action by the prime minister against the governor.[70] The governor, Ota Masahide, lost his case in the Supreme Court in 1996. The following year, the Special Measures Regarding the U.S. Military Use and Expropriation of Land were revised to allow for unconditional governmental expropriation of land in Okinawa. In Durban, members of the Okinawa Citizens Center rallied, without success, against paragraphs 23 and 43 in the final declaration, which state respectively:

> We fully recognize the rights of indigenous peoples *consistent with the principles of sovereignty and territorial integrity of States*, and therefore stress the need to adopt the appropriate constitutional, administrative, legislative and judicial measures, including those derived from applicable international instruments (emphasis mine).
>
> We also recognize the special relationship that indigenous peoples have with the land as the basis for their spiritual, physical and cultural existence and encourage States, wherever possible, to ensure that indigenous peoples are able to retain ownership of their lands and of those natural resources *to which they are entitled under domestic law* (emphasis mine).

Land seizure was not the only issue. Okinawan activists in WCAR also lobbied around the Environmental Racism and Women Caucuses. Though the retention of paragraphs 23, 24, and 43 concerning the definition of indigenous people and their land usage represented a setback for the Indigenous Caucus, the Durban conference provided an opportunity for young Okinawan activists to reconceptualize their movement from an indigenous peoples' perspective.

KOREANS

If the Japanese government policy toward the Burakumin, Ainu, and Okinawans is typified by "welfare colonialism," the approach toward Korean residents in Japan is one of colonialism *tout court.* Since Koreans in Japan were stripped of their Japanese nationality at the conclusion of the San Francisco Peace Treaty in 1952, many Koreans remain as "aliens" and hence are not entitled to welfare protection. Those who have obtained Japanese nationality have access to welfare but are nonetheless denied their minority status in Japan. In 2001, there were an estimated 951,000 Koreans living in Japan. More than 90 percent were second-, third-, fourth-, and fifth-generation Koreans and Korean-Japanese who were born and raised in Japan. More than 61 percent, however, did not possess Japanese nationality. In 1991, the Japanese government passed the Special Law on the Immigration Control of Those Who Have Lost Japanese Nationality and Others on the Basis of the Treaty of Peace with Japan. Korean "aliens" in Japan have since then become "special permanent residents" who require re-entry permits and are subject to deportation under certain conditions. Despite the abolition of a formal policy forcing Koreans to adopt Japanese names in 1983, Koreans who wish to become naturalized Japanese citizens continue to face pressure to change their names, as demonstrated in the entry samples in the "Application Guide for Naturalization."[71]

Since the Constitution of Japan "guarantees fundamental human rights to foreign residents in Japan except the rights that, owing to their nature, are interpreted to be applicable only to Japanese nationals,"[72] these Korean residents continue to face discrimination in all areas of daily life, including pensions, social security, and education, as well as local voting rights. When Japan ratified the UN Convention Relating to the Status of Refugees in 1982, the nationality clause in the National Pension Act and other social security systems (which excluded all foreign residents, including Koreans, from accessing national pension and welfare) was finally scrapped. However, elderly Koreans who do not meet the contribution requirements (because of the nationality clause) continue to be denied a pension. The issue of education for Korean children also causes concern. Korean schools were once banned by the state. To this date, the Ministry of Education still favors assimilation. About 10 percent of Korean resident children attend North or South Korean schools that are approved by prefectural governors as "miscellaneous schools." In its First and Second Periodic Reports to the CERD Committee, the government maintains that "because no specific legal provisions have been stipulated on the educational content of these schools, and because it is difficult to confirm that the graduates of these schools have an academic ability equal to or higher than the graduates of regular high schools, these graduates are not considered to meet college entry requirements." Further, most Koreans, except for those in a few cities, remain banned from the ballot.

The Japanese government has consistently denied that Koreans constitute a racial minority in Japan. The earlier justification, reflected in the government's response to the HRC comments on its First Periodic Report in 1981, was that Koreans were foreigners who did not have Japanese nationality and hence did not qualify as a minority under Article 27 of the ICCPR.[73] As the Japanese government insisted on omitting Koreans in their subsequent periodic reports while the HRC continued to mention Koreans in their comments, the section chief of the Human Rights and Refugees Bureau in the Ministry of Foreign Affairs responded in 1998 that since many had been assimilated in Japan, they were in effect no longer Koreans.[74]

If the domestic battles have been focused mostly on issues of nationality, welfare, and education, the World Conference against Racism in Durban opened up a new channel for Koreans in Japan to make their claims. Until then, it was almost impossible for Korean residents to address the issue of colonization and war compensation. In Durban, Korean groups from Japan, including the Research Action Institute for the Koreans in Japan (RAIK), worked closely with the Reparation and Slavery, African and African Descendents, and Asia and Asian Descendents caucuses to press for an apology and reparations from former colonial powers. Issues of "the past," of colonization and slavery, had remained bracketed until Durban. Since the third world prepcom, JUSCANZ countries (Japan, the United States, Canada, Australia, New Zealand, Norway, and Switzerland) have maintained that they would not recognize slavery as a crime against humanity, apologize, or award reparations.[75] At WCAR, negotiations on the "past" issue were relegated to a special working group. Many African and Asian governments backed the Slavery and Reparation Caucus, while the European Union threatened the host country, South Africa, that if African countries insisted on the colonization and slavery issue, the United States and Europe would not agree on anything.[76] In the final outcome Declaration and Programme of Action, paragraphs 14 and 99 recognized, respectively:

> Slavery and the slave trade are a crime against humanity and should always have been so, especially the transatlantic slave trade and are among the major sources and manifestations of racism, racial discrimination, xenophobia and related intolerance, and that Africans and people of African descent, Asians and people of Asian descent and indigenous peoples were victims of these acts and continue to be victims of their consequences;

> We acknowledge and profoundly regret the massive human suffering and the tragic plight of millions of men, women and children caused by slavery, the slave trade, the transatlantic slave trade, apartheid, colonialism and genocide, and call upon States concerned to honor the memory of the victims of past tragedies and affirm that, wherever and whenever these occurred, they must be condemned and their recurrence prevented. We regret that these practices and structures, political, socio-economic and cultural, have led to racism, racial discrimination, xenophobia and related intolerance.

Though reparations were excluded, the recognition of slavery as a crime against humanity was considered by the global coalition a major step forward.

On this and other issues, however, the Japanese government was mysteriously silent. Despite the fact that the Durban conference was heavily focused on the transatlantic and Indian slave trade, Korean and Japanese NGOs were able to use the "reparations for the past" frame to challenge the Japanese government on a whole range of issues, including forced labor, pensions for war veterans, wartime sexual slavery, and history textbooks. In its statement to the plenary session on September 2, 2001, the head of the Japanese governmental delegation recognized:

> Building from our deep remorse over our past colonial rule and aggression, Japan is determined to eliminate self-righteous nationalism, promote international cooperation, and thereby advance the principles of peace and democracy throughout the world. Regarding the concerns expressed by some neighboring countries, I would like to reiterate here that the government of Japan firmly maintains the above-mentioned acknowledgment of history. Based on this recognition, the government requires that schoolchildren understand through history education that World War II caused disaster to all humankind.

MIGRANT WORKERS

As of 1999, an estimated 1.2 million migrant workers lived in Japan. About 20 percent of those were overstayers. Since the revision of the immigration law in 1990, Japan technically no longer imports unskilled labor, except for Nikkeijin. The composition of migrant workers has changed dramatically since then. Brazilians of Japanese descent constituted only 1.5 percent of all registered aliens in Japan in 1989, but accounted for 14.3 percent in 1996.[77] Japanese nongovernmental groups have charged that the current immigration policy based on bloodline violates Article 2 of ICERD in making explicit "distinction, exclusion, restriction, or preference based on descent." Meanwhile, illegal migrant workers in Japan are not eligible for national insurance or public assistance. The traditional approach of the Japanese government toward migrant workers and their families in Japan is one of "reasonable discrimination."[78] In 1991, the government started reporting on the status of migrant workers in Japan in its periodic reports to the HRC. When challenged about the denial of basic social services to overstayers, a Ministry of Health and Welfare official responded that giving medical insurance and public assistance to illegal foreign workers would promote the overstaying of foreign workers.[79]

In Durban, the National Network in Solidarity with Migrant Workers, formed in 1997 with more than eighty-nine Japanese and international NGOs, became part of the Migration and Refugees NGO Caucus. Negotiations on the issue of migrant workers centered on the recognition of the 1990 Convention on the Protection of the Rights of All Migrant Workers and Members of Their

Families, which had been adopted but was not yet in force; the distinction between documented and undocumented workers; the inclusion of migrant workers in the list of victims of racism; and, lastly, the treatment of families of migrant workers.[80] A main battle for the Migration and Refugees NGO Caucus was to lobby for the inclusion of the 1990 Convention in the outcome document, thereby pushing states to recognize the convention as part of international human rights norms. The caucus did succeed in putting the convention in paragraph 78, which "urges those states that have not yet done so to consider signing and ratifying all the major international human rights conventions." In the rest of the texts, however, the European Union and the United States were unwilling to expand the list of instruments beyond ICERD.

The Migration and Refugees NGO Caucus also lobbied, albeit unsuccessfully, for the inclusion of both documented and undocumented migrant workers.[81] Recipient states, however, refused to recognize undocumented migrants in the texts.[82] Except for a preamble paragraph, which reminds states of the vulnerability of migrants, especially undocumented ones, all other provisions apply only to legal migrant workers. Another major issue was the inclusion of migrants as victims of racism. However, as most states prefer not to strengthen the capacity of CERD, no other categories, with the exception of women, trafficked persons, and Romas/Gypsies/Sintis/Travellers, were included as victims or other victims of racism.

There were also heated debates concerning the status and treatment of the families of migrant workers. Singapore, for example, vocally opposed extending any measures in the outcome Programme of Action to family members of migrant workers. Any mention of families was subsequently dropped from the texts.[83] Not all was lost, though. Paragraph 12 explicitly recognizes the relationship between globalization and migration ("interregional and intraregional migration has increased as a result of globalization, in particular from the south to the north, and . . . policies toward migration should not be based on racism, racial discrimination, xenophobia, and related intolerance"). Paragraph 47 affirms that immigration policies "should be consistent with applicable human rights instruments." Further, despite objections from the EU, paragraph 16 recognizes, for the first time in international law, xenophobia against non-nationals as a source of racism ("xenophobia against non-nationals, particularly migrants, refugees, and asylum-seekers, constitutes one of the main sources of contemporary racism and that human rights violations against members of such groups occur widely in the context of discriminatory, xenophobic, and racist practices").[84] In the context of the jewelry shop and public bathtub lawsuits as well as xenophobic remarks by the Tokyo governor, this paragraph was a particularly significant victory for Japanese migrant worker NGOs.

MINORITY WOMEN

If minority groups discussed thus far have been made invisible in Japan, women within these communities suffer from double silence. As a minority, they are invisible within larger Japan; as women, they are further silenced within their own communities. Although the Fujin Suiheisha, or the Women Section of the Buraku liberation group, was established in as early as 1926, "it was to support the men who were involved in the movement."[85] Similarly, although Ainu women suffer equally from the colonization and assimilation policies of Japan proper, they also endure sexism within their own culture.[86] In Okinawa, the issue of violence against minority women came to the fore because of the 1995 rape incident in Okinawa. At the time when several thousand women from Japan were attending the Fourth World Conference on Women in Beijing, a twelve-year-old Okinawan girl was raped by three U.S. Marines. Women from Okinawa and beyond rallied around the central theme of violence against women at the Beijing conference to denounce the structural sexual violence in U.S. military bases.[87] Okinawan women suffer not only from racism within larger Japan, but also from racialized sexism in Okinawa. In this regard, Korean as well as migrant women living in Japan also encounter multiple discrimination. While the larger Korean struggle traditionally focuses on issues of homeland reunification, immigration, and education, violence against Korean women and girls receives little attention. The comfort women issue is a prime example of this compound discrimination. Despite the scale of the operation (extending throughout Asia wherever Japanese troops were present during the Second World War) and the enormous harm done (an estimated 200,000 women, more than 80 percent of them Korean, were drafted as sexual slaves), nothing was done to bring justice to these women until the 1990s. The Tokyo Tribunal did not mention the issue. The Japanese and Korean governments omitted it in their postwar bilateral treaty. The postwar Korean movement in Japan focused on reunification, and the mainstream Japanese women's movement ignored the issue until the Korean women's movement brought it up in the late 1980s. Violence against migrant women in Japan equally had only begun to attract attention in Japan. Although many non-Japanese women suffer domestic violence at the hands of their Japanese husband or partners, they often hesitate to report the violence to the police because of their status as undocumented residents or workers.[88] A commonality in the situations of Buraku, Ainu, Okinawan, Korean, and migrant women is the absence of data.[89] They are mentioned in none of the reports filed by the Japanese government with the HRC or CERD. They were also omitted from both the minority movements and the mainstream Japanese feminist movement until the Fourth World Conference on Women in Beijing in 1995. The marginalization of minority and indigenous women at the conference precipitated the establishment of the Research Group on Multiple Discrimination against Minority Women within IMADR in 1999, which represented the first cross-NGO effort to address the issue of multiple discrimination (*fukugo sabetsu*) in Japan.[90]

At WCAR, Buraku, Ainu, Okinawan, Korean, and migrant women from Japan spoke out on the theme of multiple discrimination. Together with Dalit women from India and Nepal, Buraku women talked about their experiences of intersectional discrimination at the Work and Descent-Based Discrimination and Multiple Discrimination against Minority Women in Japan workshops, while an Ainu woman spoke on the Voices of Indigenous Women panel. A Korean woman from Japan also gave her testimony in the World Court of Women against Racism, organized by the India-based Asian Women's Human Rights Council and the Tunisia-based El Taller International with the support of 120 other human rights and women's groups. Despite significant resistance from several states,[91] feminist groups managed to insert the concept of intersectional and multiple discrimination into the final outcome document, which became the first UN instrument to recognize the intersectionality of gender, race, and other variables.[92] The preamble urges states to "apply a gender perspective, recognizing the multiple forms of discrimination which women can face." Paragraph 2 affirms that "victims can suffer multiple or aggravated forms of discrimination based on other related grounds such as sex, language, religion, political or other opinion, social origin, property, birth or other status." Although gender is not listed as a ground for racism, states recognize that racism and racial discrimination "reveal themselves in a differentiated manner for women and girls" (paragraph 69). In particular, in the final Programme of Action, paragraph 31 addresses the intersectional discrimination faced by migrant women; paragraph 50 recognizes indigenous, migrant, and other women as "other victims" of racism; and paragraph 54 explicitly links gender-based violence to racism:

> 31. Urges States, in the light of the increased proportion of women migrants, to place special focus on gender issues, including gender discrimination, particularly when the multiple barriers faced by migrant women intersect; detailed research should be undertaken not only in respect of human rights violations perpetrated against women migrants, but also on the contribution they make to the economies of their countries of origin and their host countries, and the findings should be included in reports to treaty bodies.

> 50. Urges States to incorporate a gender perspective in all programmes of action against racism, racial discrimination, xenophobia and related intolerance and to consider the burden of such discrimination which falls particularly on indigenous women, African

women, Asian women, women of African descent, women of Asian descent, women migrants and women from other disadvantaged groups, ensuring their access to the resources of production on an equal footing with men, as a means of promoting their participation in the economic and productive development of their communities.

54. Urges States:

To recognize that sexual violence which has been systematically used as a weapon of war, sometimes with the acquiescence or at the instigation of the State, is a serious violation of international humanitarian law that, in defined circumstances, constitutes a crime against humanity and/or a war crime, and that the intersection of discrimination on grounds of race and gender makes women and girls particularly vulnerable to this type of violence, which is often related to racism, racial discrimination, xenophobia and related intolerance.

Although it remains difficult to gauge the impact of the discourse of multiple discrimination on the Japanese state, Japanese NGOs are already incorporating an intersectional framework in their follow-up lobbying efforts. In December 2002, IMADR focused its entire shadow report to the Fourth and Fifth

TABLE 7.1

Mentioning of Racial Minorities in International Human Rights Instruments and Conferences by the Japanese Government, 1980–2001

Minority groups	ICCPR 1980 (Report 1)	ICCPR 1987 (Report 2)	ICCPR 1991 (Report 3)	ICCPR 1997 (Report 4)	ICERD 1999 (Reports 1 and 2)	WCAR 2001 (Government Statement)[a]
Buraku				X[c]		X
Ainu		X[b]	X	X	X	X
Okinawans						
Koreans					X[d]	X
Migrant workers			X	X	X[e]	X
Minority women						[f]

Source: International Human Rights NGO Network 1999 and the First and Second Report by the Japanese Government on the International Convention on the Elimination of All Forms of Racial Discrimination (June 1999).

[a]It states, "Based on the above principles [embodied in the Constitution of Japan], we have been fighting against various forms of discrimination based on race and other reasons in Japan, which include: the people of Dowa regions, who have been historically discriminated; the Ainu people, who have maintained their ethnic identity; Korean residents, the majority of whom came to reside in Japan during 36 years of Japan's rule. . . . A gender-equal society is another goal to be achieved. In addition, there are reported incidents of human rights violations against foreigners among individuals including discriminatory treatment, often due to the difference in language and culture and lack of mutual understanding." Japanese government address to WCAR plenary, September 2, 2001 (http://www.mofa.go.jp/index.html).

[b]Ainu as an ethnic, rather than indigenous, minority.

[c]Emphasized that the Special Measures Laws were sufficient in dealing with Buraku discrimination.

[d]Emphasized that the situation of Koreans in Japan has been regularized by their "special permanent resident" status.

[e]Maintained that certain rights are applicable only to Japanese nationals.

[f]The statement did not specifically address minority women, although it mentioned that "a gender-equal society is another goal to be achieved."

TABLE 7.2

Redefining Racism in Japan: Domestic Mobilization of Global Frames

Minority groups	Year (issue origin)	Population	Japanese govt. approach	Global frames	Domestic networks
Buraku	1603	3,000,000	"Special measures"	Caste	Buraku Liberation League; IMADR
Ainu	1872	30,000	"Cultural promotion"	Indigenous peoples' rights	Ainu Association of Hokkaido; Shimin Gaiko Centre
Okinawans	1879	1,000,000	U.S.–Japan Security Alliance and Economic Development	Indigenous peoples' rights	Okinawan Citizen Info Center
Koreans	1905	950,000	"Special permanent residents"	Reparation for colonization and slavery	Research Action Institute for the Koreans in Japan
Migrant workers	1970s	1,000,000	Ilegal overstayers	1990 Convention on Migrant Workers and Families	National Network in Solidarity with Migrant Workers (89 NGOs)
Minority women	—	~3,000,000	Nonexistent	Multiple discrimination	IMADR–Research Group on Multiple Discrimination against Minority Women

Periodic Reports by Japan on the situation of minority women in Japan.[93] To sum up, Table 7.1 summarizes the mentioning of racial minorities by the Japanese government as reflected in its periodic reports to the HRC and CERD, as well as in its statement to the WCAR plenary in Durban. Table 7.2 shows the redefinition of racial discrimination in Japan through NGO mobilization of global human rights frames.

How do we explain the extensive changes concerning women's and children's human rights at both the state and grassroots levels on the one hand, and the limited development in minority rights in Japan on the other? In the following chapter, I provide an explanatory framework, focusing on Japanese NGO mobilization of global human rights frames at world conferences, local education, and Japanese NGO alliance with key politicians.

CHAPTER EIGHT

Domestic Mobilization of Global Human Rights Norms

Issue Reframing, Advocacy Education, and Leverage Politics

What do the developments in five seemingly distinct movements—concerning the pill, sexual harassment, military sexual slavery, domestic violence, and child prostitution—have in common? In this chapter, I first briefly discuss how predominant domestic political and social movement approaches are insufficient to explain the changes concerning women's and children's human rights since the mid-1990s. I then provide a constructivist explanatory framework focusing on three mechanisms of norm diffusion, namely issue reframing at world conferences, local advocacy education, and leverage politics through alliances with key domestic politicians. The lack of institutionalized global human rights frames before the Durban conference and, in turn, the failure to garner key political support by Japanese nongovernmental networks accounts for the limited development of minority rights in Japan.

Domestic Political Approaches

BUREAUCRATIC DOMINANCE

The bulk of theoretical work that has examined the power of the Japanese bureaucracy has focused on two ministries, the Ministry of International Trade and Industry and the Ministry of Finance. However, there is little evidence that changes concerning women's and children's human rights in the 1990s were the result of bureaucratic dominance or battles, unlike changes in trade and the budget. No single central ministry or agency has overseen a coherent policy on women's human rights in Japan. The Council for Gender Equality within the Prime Minister's Office, which has been responsible for drafting the Vision and Plan for a Gender-Equal Society, is primarily an advisory and liaison body with no administrative power. The Ministry of Labor has responsibility for sexual harassment prevention. The Ministry of Education promotes gender-equal education. The National Police Agency drafts new measures for victims of sex crimes. Local governments create their own structures to handle domestic violence. It is thus hard to argue that a single dominant bureaucratic structure or bureaucratic struggle explains the varied changes across many other ministries, agencies, and local governments concerning women's human rights. Even though the Council for Gender Equality has taken up the role of coordinating various ministries and agencies, the bureaucratic dominance model cannot explain why the council itself has suddenly become an ardent advocate for women's human rights in the first place. In the case of children's human rights, until the Child Prostitution and Pornography Prohibition Law and the Child Abuse Prevention Law were passed in 1999 and 2000, respectively, there simply was no administrative section within the Children and Family Bureau in the Ministry of Health, Labor, and Welfare that took care of children's sexuality issues. Further, the bureaucratic informalism model described by Upham can hardly account for the recent extensive use of the court in the case of sexual harassment, comfort women, and, more lately, child prostitution,[1] and the sweeping legal changes concerning women's human rights in the late 1990s.

PARTY POLITICS

Some might point to the collapse of the "1955 setup" (the dominance of the Liberal Democratic Party, or LDP) in 1993 as a major reason for political change. In 1993, after bitter factional struggles over who would succeed Kanemaru, who stepped down as the vice president of the LDP because of a corruption scandal, a new group called Reform Forum 21, headed by Ozawa and Hata, successfully brought a resolution of nonconfidence in the cabinet. Just before the general election, the group left the LDP to form the Japan Renewal Party. Another ten members of the Lower House had also left to form another new party, Sakigake (Harbinger). A third new party, the Japan New Party, was established by the former governor of Kumamoto Prefecture, Hosokawa Morihiro, in 1992. When the LDP failed to come up with concrete proposals for political reform, the Japan New Party and Sakigake pushed ahead to establish a non-LDP coalition government with seven parties and one parliamentary group, putting the LDP bitterly into the opposition.[2] As a political scientist notes,

> The LDP's loss of control of the government to a seven-party coalition in the summer of 1993 was indeed the end of an era. The dynamics and the logic of the political system would be different in the future from what they were during the period of the so-called '55 system, the long era of LDP dominance that began in 1955 when the conservative parties came together to form the LDP and the right and left wings of the Socialist Party reunited.[3]

A year later the LDP managed to regain power, but only in coalition with its long-time opponent, the Social Democratic Party of Japan (the SDPJ, which was headed by an outspoken and well-known woman, Doi Takako), and the new party Sakigake (led by another female politician, Domoto Akiko). The demise of the LDP and the rise of multiparty politics certainly opened up new opportunities for political change. As Osawa, a feminist scholar and member of the drafting committee of the Basic Law for a Gender-Equal Society, argues, coalition politics rather than a sudden metamorphosis of the LDP was the cause of the improved political environment for gender equality since 1993:

> The Liberal Democratic Party has not generally been known as a champion of gender equality, yet here was the party leader and prime minister of Japan, describing gender equality as "one of the pillars of 'reform and creation' in every field of society", in a formal speech, made in an official capacity and with the media in attendance. Is the feminist LDP a reality, or just a chimera? . . . The three-party accord under which the SDPJ and Sakigake pledged extra-cabinet support for the LDP included, among other items, augmentation of gender-equality–promoting national machinery and the establishment of a basic law on gender equality (Josei Seisaku Joho Nettowāku 1996). That law was finally passed in June 1999, as the Basic Law for a Gender-Equal Society (Danjo Kyōdō Sankaku Shakai Kihon-ho). . . . [I]t is probably safe to say that legislation on gender equality would never have come this far without the influence of the SDPJ and Sakigake during the brief period of the relatively left-leaning coalition.[4]

Similarly, the private Asian Women's Fund was created when Murayama Tomiichi of the SDPJ was prime minister between 1994 and 1996. Coalition politics, however, cannot successfully explain the continuation of legal changes on gender equality and children's rights after the end of the LDP–SDPJ–Sakigake coalition in 1996–98.[5] After 1998, the influence of the SDPJ and of Sakigake had entirely vanished. The ruling coalition after 1999 (comprised of the LDP, Komeito, and the Liberal Party) was much more conservative. The legalization of the pill in 1999, for example, was the result of lobbying by multipartisan female politicians. By the time the Child Prostitution and Pornography Prohibition Law was passed in 1999, the larger normative environment had changed so much that the points of contention between the different parties were related to scope and definition rather than the nature of child prostitution and pornography as a violation of children's human rights.

INTEREST GROUP POLITICS

Did interest groups, then, play a role in pushing for the extensive policy, institutional, and legal changes concerning women's human rights in Japan? Most of the interest-group-dominance theorists have focused on the power of business groups. Women's groups in Japan have rarely been conceived as powerful interest groups successfully pushing for political changes. In fact, in each case—the legalization of the pill, sexual harassment prevention, redress for "comfort women," the prevention of child prostitution, and the prevention of domestic violence—the law was passed or the measure was taken in spite of significant interest group opposition.

Until the legalization of the pill in 1999, it was often argued that interest group politics accounted for Japan's conservative contraceptive policy.[6] For more than three decades, powerful interest groups had continuously blocked the low-dose contraceptive pill for diverse reasons, arguing it endangered women's health, would lead to sexual immorality, would increase the incidence of AIDS, and could even cause the destruction of the environment (citing estrogen's role as an endocrine disrupter). These interest groups included the Japan Association for Maternal Welfare (Nihon Bosei Hōgō I Kyōkai, commonly known as Nichibo, a professional organization that included almost all practicing obstetricians and gynecologists and that had a monopoly on the lucrative Japanese abortion market), the Japan Midwives Association, and pro-life groups such as the Association for the Day for Respect for Life (Seimei Sonchō no Hi Jikko Jinkai). In 1985, Nichibo, which had long opposed the pill, and other medical groups reversed their position and submitted requests to the Ministry of Health and Welfare for clinical testing on the pill. In 1992, when clinical trials finally supported the legalization of the pill, however, deliberations within the Central Pharmaceutical Advisory Council at the Ministry of Health and Welfare were, once again, suddenly stopped for fear of the spread of AIDS. The fact is that, despite the elimination of significant opposition by medical groups, the pill never won the support of the majority of Japanese bureaucrats, politicians, and feminists.[7] Although the elimination of interest group opposition represented a significant breakthrough and no doubt facilitated the eventual legalization of the pill, it alone could not explain the reframing of the pill as a reproductive rights issue or the timing of the pill's legalization in 1999.

In the case of sexual harassment, both the Keidanren (Federation of Economic Organizations) and Nikkeiren (Japan's Federation of Employers Associations) were opposed to the revision of the Equal Employment Opportunity Law, which mandated sexual harassment prevention in the workplace. Once the law took effect in 1999, however, both employers associations have responded to the issue.[8] In the case of comfort women, after almost fifty years of silence, the government in 1992 admitted its involvement and set up a private fund to help compensate the victims, despite strong ties between the LDP and nationalist right-wing groups, including the million-strong Japan Association of the Bereaved Families of the War Dead.[9] Similarly, the Child Prostitution and Pornography Prohibition Law was passed in 1999 in spite of significant opposition from the powerful entertainment and media businesses that control the multibillion-yen child prostitution and pornography market. Hence, although interest group politics might explain the limits of change, as is particularly evident in the case of comfort women, it cannot satisfactorily address the emerging larger consensus around issues of women's and children's human rights and the subsequent legal changes in the late 1990s.

A Domestic Social Movement Approach

Domestic social movements in the United States, Korea, and Japan played a crucial role in the emergence of the pill, sexual harassment, military sexual slavery, domestic violence, and child prostitution as issues in Japan, but their influence was most acute in the initial phases of the movements. The women's movement in the United States, in particular, had a significant impact on the development of sexual violence issues in Japan. As one veteran feminist activist puts it plainly, "we have always had a special relationship with the United States," suggesting the influence that the United States has exerted on Japan since the days of the Allied occupation. The increased attention given to rape, sexual harassment, domestic violence, and child prostitution in Japan in the 1990s was related to the development of rape crisis centers, the battered women's movement, efforts to prevent child sexual assault, and sexual harassment trials in the United States. In 1987, two Japanese women returned from California and founded the first rape crisis center in Japan. The word for "rape" in Japanese, "*gōkan*," had been legally prohibited from use in the media until very recently. Even today the media prefers the vague word "*bōkō*," which suggests violence but not rape. Intending to demystify the word "*gōkan*," the two founders of the group called their organization Gōkan Shien Center (Rape Crisis Center). As one veteran lawyer told me, "in those days, my clients would describe their experiences to me without using the word '*gōkan*,' and they were hesitant to use the hot lines because they were not sure that they had really been raped." Similarly, the Child Assault Prevention (CAP) programs in Japan were started by veteran feminists who were involved in the CAP movement in the United States.[10] In the case of the pioneering domestic violence survey in 1992, the feminist action research method brought back by a Japanese feminist scholar who studied in the United States proved essential to its launching.[11]

Japanese who have been influenced by movements in the United States are not limited to those who have lived or worked there. Many Japanese, activists and academics alike, participate in overseas study tours and conferences. Japanese activists might travel to shelters in the United States, for example, then appropriate the word and adapt the know-how for use in Japan.[12] Those who cannot travel can access print materials from the United States. The translation of books, handbooks, manuals, pamphlets, and government reports is an important part of the work of Japanese nongovernmental organizations because of the dearth of materials on human rights issues in Japan. The translation of the American handbook "Stopping Sexual Harassment" in 1989 by the Santama Area Group Concerned with Work and Sexual Discrimination, for example, helped stir the debate. However, movements on rape, domestic violence, child sexual assault, and sexual harassment in the United States in the 1970s and 1980s cannot explain the timing of events in Japan. Why did domestic violence emerge as an issue in Japan almost two decades later, in the mid-1990s? Similarly, the child assault prevention movement in the United States had very little impact on Japan until after 1995.

The Japanese and Korean women's movements also played a significant role in bringing forth various issues. Sexual harassment captured the attention of the Japanese media in the late 1980s, largely as a result of Japanese nongovernmental women's groups support of court cases. The first survey on domestic violence in Japan was also conducted by a Japanese nongovernmental group, the DV Survey Research Group, and the shelter movement was likewise an NGO-led effort. Similarly, the issues of child prostitution and child sexual abuse were first raised by nongovernmental groups such as the Stop Children Sexual Abuse group and End Child Prostitution in Asian Tourism (ECPAT) Japan in the early 1990s. The women's movement in Korea was central in breaking the silence on comfort women that had lasted for forty-five years. The Korean Council for the Women Drafted for Sexual Slavery by Japan, created in 1990, pioneered research and publications on Korean comfort women and supported their court cases, leading to a movement that has since spread to other Asian countries.[13] Women from Taiwan, China, the Philippines, Malaysia, Indonesia, East Timor, and the Netherlands have come forward to give their testimony, and domestic groups and networks addressing the issue of comfort women have been formed in each of these countries.

Several scholars, however, have noted that the perception that the abuse suffered by the comfort women is a "national shame" has perpetuated their silence.[14] In fact, for fifty years social movements in Japan have failed to consider the comfort women as a human rights issue, from either a racial or a sexual point of view. The movements instigated by Korean residents in Japan have largely focused on unification and democratization; they did not focus on the issue of comfort women until it was pursued by women's groups in Korea and

Japan in the early 1990s. As the former president of the Korean Democratic Women's Club told me,

> The Korean resident movement in Japan has traditionally been split along the North–South divide. Since 1972, with the North–South Agreement, we have worked together for unification. The national struggle has always been intertwined with the women's struggle, but men were at the top and women prepared meals. *Minshuka suru no ni, naze josei wo minshuka shinainoka?* [If we work on democratization, why are the relationships between men and women not democratized?] When we started supporting the comfort women, there was no response from male Korean residents, who thought that they had nothing to do with these comfort women. Only when it became a political issue did they link it to their larger war compensation agenda.[15]

Women's movements in Japan had equally ignored the issue until Korean women's groups spearheaded the efforts in the early 1990s. Although domestic social movements in the United States, Korea, and Japan, then, might explain the "discovery" of violence against women in Japan, they cannot explain the acceleration of change in the latter half of the 1990s. In particular, a domestic social movement approach cannot address why formerly disconnected movements concerning the pill, sexual harassment, military sexual slavery, domestic violence, and child prostitution were suddenly unified under the new definition of women's and children's human rights after 1995. Before the Vienna and Beijing conferences, sexual harassment was defined in terms of sexual discrimination in the workplace. Only after the conferences, when sexual harassment was redefined as an issue of violence against women and a violation of women's human rights, did sexual harassment become a subject of legal revision and an extensive body of administrative guidance by the Ministry of Labor, the Ministry of Education, the National Police Agency, and the Personnel Authority. Similarly, the Japanese government started to commission surveys on domestic violence and revise old policies to accommodate the "new" problem only after the Beijing Conference in 1995. As a veteran feminist activist of one of the biggest women's groups in Japan simply says, "some of us had already thought of legal changes on violence against women in Japan as early as 1993. But the timing was not right. There was too little consciousness about violence against women issues in Japan until the Beijing Conference."[16]

Issue Reframing, Advocacy Education, and Leverage Politics

A constructivist interpretation of the Japanese state, instead of relying on domestic political and social movement approaches, allows us to understand how domestic NGO mobilization of global norms on women's and children's human rights provided the redefinitions for the five issues addressed in this volume. The reconsideration of domestic issues through a global human rights frame alone is insufficient, however; the case of limited change concerning the issue of comfort women shows how vital NGO alliance with key politicians is. The glacial pace at which minority rights in Japan progresses stands in further contrast because of the absence of a global human rights frame and the inability of NGOs to garner political support despite emerging advocacy education on racial discrimination.

Four successive world conferences in the 1990s—the 1993 World Conference on Human Rights in Vienna, the 1994 International Conference on Population and Development in Cairo, the 1995 Fourth World Conference on Women in Beijing, and the 1996 First World Congress against Commercial Sexual Exploitation of Children in Stockholm—stood in sharp contrast with earlier UN conferences on human rights, women, and children, which were sporadic and disconnected. The Beijing Conference, in particular, has exerted a huge influence on many Japanese.[17] "Many women returned from Beijing and started all kinds of projects—surveys, shelter, outreach, and advocacy—in their own region."[18] "Beijing was a very important experience to me as an activist. We organized workshops, carried out signature campaigns, and lobbied against the Japanese government. Above all, I felt solidarity across national boundaries that I never felt in Japan. In Japan I was a minority. At the Beijing Conference, I was the majority."[19]

One of the most dramatic illustrations of how a world conference exerted an influence on the Japanese government relates to the pill. For more than three decades after the Japanese government first looked into the issue in 1961, numerous reasons were put forward to block the legalization of the low-dose contraceptive pill, including concerns about its negative impact on sexual morality, health, the population crisis, AIDS, and even environmental destruction.[20] It was the International Conference on Population and Development (ICPD) in 1994 and its follow-up meeting (ICPD+5) in 1999 that proved decisive. In preparation for the conference, a nongovernmental advocacy network, Japan's Network for Women and Health, Cairo 94, was founded in 1994 by eleven feminists, including veteran activists, scholars, and politicians.[21] As the network's purpose is explained in its report,

> The UN has urged that each country's respective NGOs be involved in deciding the agenda for the ICPD [International Conference on Population and Development], and further that the national report submitted by the various governments at the conference incorporate and reflect accurately the opinions and views of the NGOs. . . . To our regret, women and citizens of Japan have had little or no access to information pertaining to the preparatory process leading up to ICPD. . . . To address these serious omissions in Japan, we have established Japan's Network for Women and Health, Cairo 94 with the

purpose of sending Japanese women's voices on to Cairo. We feel strongly that the "population problem" should not be discussed in terms of numbers or statistics. Instead, we feel that the "population problem" should be redefined from the perspective of reproductive health, placing an emphasis on a women's self-determination of her own fertility, as well as a woman's physical, social, and mental well-being throughout her life cycle. . . . Speaking in more concrete terms, we plan to conduct the following activities as part of the preparatory process for Cairo: 1) to spread and publicize the concept of reproductive health within Japan; 2) to ensure that the Japanese government's national report reflects accurately the opinions of Japanese women; 3) to participate in the NGO forum in Cairo; 4) to ensure that women NGO members are included in the government delegation to ICPD; and 5) to establish domestic and international solidarity with concerned women's NGOs both within Japan and overseas.[22]

At the conference Japan was seriously ridiculed, as it was the only industrialized country where women did not have access to the low-dose pill.[23] As Ashino Yuriko, the deputy executive director of the Family Planning Federation of Japan, explains,

The 1994 International Conference on Population and Development (ICPD), held in Cairo and championing reproductive rights and reproductive health as keys to sound development, put pressure on the Japanese government to speed up its sluggish approval process, in large measure by encouraging Japanese women to be more outspoken in support for the cause. Official foot dragging began to look almost ludicrous when, in January 1999, the anti-impotence pill Viagra was approved for prescriptive use after a mere six months of deliberation. "Unbelievable!" exclaimed foreign critics at the international conference held at The Hague earlier this year to review progress in the five years since the Cairo meeting. Official Japan stood before an international forum, accused of sexual discrimination.[24]

But shaming tactics at the ICPD and the reframing of access to the pill as a women's human rights issue were not sufficient. Few Japanese—bureaucrats, politicians, and the public alike—had ever heard of the term "reproductive health/rights." Upon their return to Japan, members of Japan's Network for Women and Health, including several female politicians such as Owaki Masako, Shimizu Sumiko, and Domoto Akiko, became active carriers of this revolutionary concept that linked, for the first time in Japan, sexuality, self-determination, women's health, violence against women, women's human rights, population, and development. The concept of reproductive health/rights was so foreign that the Japanese government did not know how to translate it and had to use the literal translation "*repurodakutibu herusu/raitsu*" in all its policy papers after its heavily criticized attempt to use the much narrower "maternity health." Hence, an immediate follow-up activity for the network after the ICPD was to conduct local research and disseminate information about reproductive health/rights.

It was doubtful, however, that the ridicule that the Japanese government experienced at the Cairo conference and grassroots education about reproductive health as a women's human rights issue alone would have led to legalization. What proved critical was leverage applied by Japan's Network for Women and Health. The network maintained strong linkages with target politicians from its inception. Domoto Akiko, for example, the party leader of Sakigake in the ruling coalition at the time, was a founding member of the network. The network also included thirty-seven Diet members, in addition to several well-known academics, including Hara Hiroko, also a founding member. In 1998, thirty-eight nonpartisan female politicians signed a petition submitted to the Ministry of Health and Welfare demanding their "reproductive rights" through the legalization of the pill. In early 1999, when the Ministry of Health and Welfare approved Viagra within less than six months, many female politicians together with members of Japan's Network for Women and Health organized a highly effective protest. A few months later, the low-dose pill was finally legalized in Japan.

The impact of the reframing of issues at world conferences on the case of child prostitution in Japan is equally astounding. One might perhaps expect the Japanese government to attend UN conferences and comply with UN standards. But why should the Japanese government care about the largely NGO-led World Congress on the Commercial Sexual Exploitation of Children in 1996? If UN institutions such as the Commission on Human Rights and the special rapporteur on violence against women proved crucial in the case of comfort women, global norms exerted their impact on the issue of child prostitution largely through nongovernmental organizations. Unlike the Vienna and Beijing conferences, the First World Congress against Commercial Sexual Exploitation of Children in 1996 was largely an NGO initiative. Although UNICEF (United Nations Children's Fund), ESCAP (the Economic and Social Council for the Asia-Pacific Region), and the Swedish government were involved, the First World Congress was by and large the result of six years of lobbying by a nongovernmental network, ECPAT, formed after a founding meeting of Asian and international NGOs in Thailand in 1990. In fact, the Japanese government had no intention of sending a delegation to the congress, deeming the issue of child prostitution not important enough. Japanese policies concerning children emphasized protection. Although the Japanese government finally signed the Convention on the Rights of the Child in 1994 (and Article 34 deals specifically with the sexual exploitation of children), the concept of "children's human rights" (*kodomo no jinken*) has yet to take root in Japan. Since child pornography was outlawed in most North American and European countries in the 1980s, Japan has become a leading trafficking country, especially within Asia, as well as one of the world's leading producers of child pornography.[25]

At the First World Congress against Commercial Sexual Exploitation of Children in Stockholm, the Japanese government was heavily criticized for its lack of consciousness and its insufficient response to child prostitution and pornography in Japan and elsewhere in Asia. The fact was that at that time few in Japan considered child prostitution and pornography a problem. In addition, few among the Japanese children's nongovernmental groups focused on these issues. ECPAT Japan was formed in 1992 as part of a global network to engage in advocacy education against child prostitution and pornography. According to its mission statement,

> ECPAT is a global network of organizations and individuals working together for the elimination of child prostitution, child pornography and the trafficking of children for sexual purposes. It seeks to encourage the world community to ensure that children everywhere enjoy their fundamental rights free and secure from all forms of commercial sexual exploitation. The ECPAT network consists of groups of organizations and individuals from over 35 countries around the world working together to end commercial sexual exploitation of children. Its activities include: monitoring the implementation of the Agenda for Action adopted at the World Congress Against Commercial Sexual Exploitation of Children in Stockholm in 1996; working closely with non-governmental organizations, intergovernmental organizations and other individuals and groups; providing expert consultancy to governments on legal changes needed to protect children; working closely with Interpol and local law enforcers to ensure laws are implemented; providing training for personnel working to rehabilitate child victims of sex abusers; involving young people in seeking solutions to commercial sexual exploitation of children; motivating local communities to find strategies which will protect children; seeking ways to control the flow of child pornography in shops and on the Internet; and assisting the tourism industry in its campaign to end sex tourism.[26]

Since 1994, CAP groups, which were modeled after CAP educational and outreach programs in the United States, also spread nationwide. After the Stockholm Congress, the outreach activities of ECPAT Japan intensified. In April 1997, it organized the seminar Stop Child Prostitution and Child Pornography, inviting three female Diet members, Noda Seiko of the LDP and Shimizu Sumiko and Owaki Masako of the Social Democratic Party. The following month, these lawmakers set up a study group on the issue within the Diet. In a follow-up meeting of the Stockholm Congress in Japan that same month, a senior politician from the LDP pledged publicly that the LDP "would make necessary legal reforms" on the issue. A coalition project team was thus formed in June 1997. Despite initial disagreements on several issues, including the age, rationale, and the legality of mere possession of pornographic materials for personal consumption,[27] a draft was submitted to the Upper House in March 1998. However, the Lower House election in July 1998 and the passing of urgent financial reform measures prevented the draft from being debated in the Diet. In December 1998, the coalition project team decided to invite opposition parties to join their efforts. Despite major disagreement between the coalition and the opposition on the definition of prostitution and pornography, the penalty, and the provision on personal possession of pornographic materials,[28] the law was unanimously passed in April 1999. As Domoto Akiko, a project team member, exclaims, "in Japan all laws relating to children's rights treat children as subjects to be protected. This is the first time that the focus is not on the protection element, but on the prosecution of those who violate the rights of children."[29] Party politics might explain the detailed content of the law, but not the larger normative environment. By 1999, it was widely recognized that no politician could possibly say no to the defense of children's human rights. In a press conference, the project team leader, Moriyama Mayumi, was asked if there had been resistance from male parliamentarians, and she simply answered, "the reality was that they were very cooperative and all went smoothly."[30] The most significant opposition actually came from the media, as they argued for freedom of expression, but they were told that "to protect children's human rights had become part of international understanding, [and] there was no objection possible."[31] Similar to the case of the legalization of the pill, it is unclear whether Japan's attendance at the First World Congress against CSEC and the educational outreach by ECPAT Japan and CAP groups alone would have led to the subsequent passage of the Child Prostitution and Pornography Prohibition Law. As Shimizu Sumiko, a key politician behind the law, reflects, "I have attended lots of international conferences and usually there is little follow-up. But this one has been different. In the first follow-up meeting in Tokyo, we managed to get a high-level LDP politician to commit to do something."[32] As an ECPAT Japan activist told me, "it was doubtful how far NGO efforts alone would have gone. The support of the female Diet members was key to our success."[33]

Although the 1989 Convention on the Rights of the Child, which the Japanese government ratified in 1994, provided a favorable background for the issue to emerge, the Japanese government repeatedly declared that it had no intention of amending any domestic laws. However, as soon as child prostitution, pornography, and trafficking were redefined as commercial sexual exploitation at the World Congress, the Japanese government was put on the defensive overnight. Less than three years later, the normative environment had shifted so dramatically that debates on the bill centered on details such as age and penalty rather than the underlying principle of protecting children's human rights. By 2000, the issue was finally officially adopted by the UN through the Optional Protocol on Sexual Exploitation of Children to the Convention on the Rights of the Child. One would expect the Japanese government to sign and ratify the protocol with minimum delay. In December 2001, the Japanese government further showed its commitment by hosting the follow-up Second World Congress against Commercial Sexual Exploitation of Children.

The dramatic effect of leverage politics can best be demonstrated by contrasting the extent of change in issues of child prostitution, domestic violence, and comfort women. Three years elapsed between the definition of child prostitution and pornography as a violation of children's human rights at the First World Congress and its legal prohibition in Japan in 1999. Similarly, in the case of domestic violence, NGO-supported nonpartisan female politicians, despite great skepticism,[34] drafted the anti–domestic violence law, which was passed by the Lower House in March 2001. The Japanese position on the issue of comfort women, in contrast, has hardly evolved since the government established the private fund in 1995, despite mounting international pressures and domestic mobilization; the bitterly divided movement has failed to garner the united support of female politicians.[35]

Although the public testimonies of the comfort women aroused a great deal of public attention in Japan in the early 1990s, neither the government, the Diet, nor the courts recognized the existence of the problem.[36] The rapid change of the government's position—from outright denial in 1990 to partial recognition in 1992 and to massive intervention (however inadequate) in 1995—cannot be understood without considering the dramatic shifts at the international level.[37] Before 1992, few within the UN even knew about the existence of the comfort women. In February 1992, the Korean Council submitted a letter to Secretary-General Boutros-Ghali requesting investigation, research, and compensation by the Japanese government, and full investigation by the UN. In March, the Japanese government responded to the Commission on Human Rights that its prime minister had already made an apology and that trials were going on in Japan, but that it had no intention of compensating the victims. In May, the Working Group on Contemporary Forms of Slavery within the Human Rights Subcommission on the Prevention of Discrimination and the Protection of Minorities adopted a resolution urging the secretary-general to appoint a special rapporteur to look into the matter of comfort women. In February 1993, the Japanese government responded that all compensation matters were solved by bilateral treaties and challenged the jurisdiction of the UN on issues that predated its founding. In June 1993, the World Conference on Human Rights adopted the Vienna Declaration and Platform for Action, which states that "violations of the human rights of women in situations of armed conflict are violations of the fundamental principles of international human rights and humanitarian law. All violations of this kind, including in particular murder, systematic rape, sexual slavery, and forced pregnancy, require a particularly effective response."

One year later, in June 1994, the Working Group on Contemporary Forms of Slavery recommended the Japanese government solve the issue through the UN Permanent Court of Arbitration in The Hague. In July, eleven comfort women and their supporting organizations followed the suggestion and filed a case with the Permanent Court of Arbitration. In November 1994, the nongovernmental International Commission of Jurists published the 208-page Report on Comfort Women, with twenty-one conclusions and seven recommendations, among which were:

Conclusions:

1) The Japanese government has responsibility for the sexual abuses suffered by the women under the Japanese army and government of the time.

2) The Japanese government has not conducted sufficient investigation, and has the tendency to keep quiet rather than to solve the issue.

3) Neither the Korean nor the Philippine bilateral agreements with the Japanese government could prevent the comfort women from seeking personal compensation.

Recommendations:

1) The Japanese government should conduct victim hearings within six months, set up an institution, as well as draft legislation to solve the matter.

2) If the Japanese government fails to do the above, it should take all measures to help these women to recover including providing medical and housing assistance.

3) If the Japanese government fails to take these measures, it should set up a tribunal made up of international legal experts or a court of arbitration.

4) If the Japanese government refuses to act, the supporting nongovernmental organizations representing these women should seek recommendations from international judiciary institutions.

5) Concerning the interpretation of bilateral treaties, the Korean and Philippine governments should bring their case directly to international judiciary institutions.

6) All relevant member states of the UN should disclose information in their country on this subject.

The report was seen by the Japanese media as "a reflection of world opinion."[38] In March 1995, the Commission on Human Rights adopted the preparatory report on Violence against Women by the UN special rapporteur on violence against women, Radhika Coomaraswamy, in which the comfort women issue is linked to current forms of military sexual slavery and is described as a violation of international humanitarian law for which the Japanese government has both legal and moral responsibility. That same year, the Japanese government created the private Asian Women's Fund to provide atonement money and assistance to victims. Though the issue of comfort women was dramatically redefined, from an issue of bilateral foreign policy to one of international human rights,[39] the Japanese government continued to deny legal responsibility.

In February 1996, in accordance with the Commission on Human Rights resolution in 1994, the special rapporteur on violence against women issued the Report on the Mission to the Democratic People's Republic of Korea, the Republic of Korea, and Japan on the Issue of Military Sexual Slavery in Wartime, in which she clarified at the beginning that she considers the case of women forced to render sexual services in wartime by or for the use of armed forces a practice of military sexual slavery. The report concludes with the following recommendations:

A. At the national level

137. The Government of Japan should:

(a) Acknowledge that the system of comfort stations set up by the Japanese Imperial Army during the Second World War was a violation of its obligations under international law and accept legal responsibility for that violation;

(b) Pay compensation to individual victims of Japanese military sexual slavery according to principles outlined by the Special Rapporteur of the Sub-Commission on Prevention of Discrimination and Protection of Minorities on the right to restitution, compensation and rehabilitation for victims of grave violations of human rights and fundamental freedoms. A special administrative tribunal for this purpose should be set up with a limited timeframe since many of the victims are of a very advanced age;

(c) Make a full disclosure of documents and materials in its possession with regard to comfort stations and other related activities of the Japanese Imperial Army during the Second World War;

(d) Make a public apology in writing to individual women who have come forward and can be substantiated as women victims of Japanese military sexual slavery;

(e) Raise awareness of these issues by amending educational curricula to reflect historical realities;

(f) Identify and punish, as far as possible, perpetrators involved in the recruitment and institutionalization of comfort stations during the Second World War.

B. At the international level

138. Non-governmental organizations working at the international level should continue to raise these issues within the United Nations system. There should also be an attempt to seek an advisory opinion of the International Court of Justice or the Permanent Court of Arbitration.

139. The Governments of the Democratic People's Republic of Korea and the Republic of Korea may consider requesting the International Court of Justice to help resolve the legal issues concerning Japanese responsibility and payment of compensation for the "comfort women."

140. The Special Rapporteur urges the Government of Japan in particular to take into account and act upon the above recommendations at the soonest possible time, bearing

in mind the advanced age of the surviving women, as well as the fact that 1995 is the fiftieth anniversary of the ending of the Second World War. The Special Rapporteur feels that not only have fifty years passed since the end of the war but that it is time to restore the dignity of those women who have suffered so much.

Further, in March 1997, the International Labor Organization Committee of Experts released a report that claimed that the Japanese system of military sexual slavery violated the 1930 Convention No. 29 on Forced Labor that the Japanese government had ratified in 1932. In 1998, the UN special rapporteur on systematic rape, sexual slavery, and slavery-like practices during armed conflicts, Gay McDougall, also issued a report on wartime slavery, using Japanese military sexual slavery during World War II as a case study. "In fact, the issue of the former 'comfort women' was a major impetus for the United Nations deciding to commission the study on systematic rape, sexual slavery and slavery-like practices in armed conflict."[40]

For the purpose of terminology, the Special Rapporteur concurs entirely with the view held by members of the Working Group on Contemporary Forms of Slavery, as well as by representatives of nongovernmental organizations and some academics, that the phrase "comfort women" does not in the least reflect the suffering, such as multiple rapes on an everyday basis and severe physical abuse, that women victims had to endure during their forced prostitution and sexual subjugation and abuse in wartime. The Special Rapporteur, therefore, considers with conviction that the phrase "military sexual slaves" represents a much more accurate and appropriate terminology.[41]

In December 2000, three Asian NGOs, the Violence against Women in War Network-Japan, the Korean Council for the Women Drafted for Military Sexual Slavery by Japan, and the Philippine-based Asian Center for Women's Human Rights, co-organized the Women's International War Crimes Tribunal on Japan's Military Sexual Slavery, which attracted more than a thousand international participants. The four judges at the tribunal found that "rape and sexual slavery, when committed on a widespread, systematic or large-scale basis, constitute crimes against humanity . . . [b]ased on our consideration of the evidence submitted to this Tribunal." The judges also found Emperor Hirohito criminally responsible for crimes against humanity, and that the state of Japan had acted in violation of both its treaty obligations and its obligations under customary international law. The final judgment released in The Hague in December 2001 further emphasized the racial aspects of gender discrimination endured by the comfort women.

The evidence demonstrates multiple violations of both the requirements for the protection of women as well as the prohibitions on race and sex discrimination. Most fundamentally the evidence shows that women were targeted for the provision of forced sexual services because they were women, thus denying them gender equality as well as their rights to respect for their physical, mental and sexual integrity and human dignity. The creation of the "comfort women" system, reflects the intersection of extreme discrimination based on both gender and race/ethnicity. The ethnocentrism and racism of the Japanese military and government resulted in the prevailing philosophy that it was more acceptable to make colonized and conquered women into "comfort women" than Japanese women.

The redefinition of the Japanese comfort system as sexual slavery by the UN links the old, forgotten issue to present-day military sexual slavery in various parts of the world. For many years, "as a survival strategy of the women's movement in the national struggle," Korean activists cast the comfort women issue as an ethnic, rather than gender, struggle.[42] They have insisted on a distinction be-

TABLE 8.1

Domestic Mobilization of Global Norms Redefining Women's and Children's Human Rights in Japan

Local definition (1970s–1990s)	Global redefinition (1990s)	Interest group opposition	Local NGO epistemic networks	Institutional/ legal changes
		THE PILL		
Health, population, AIDS, environment	Reproductive health/rights	Pro-life groups such as Association for the Day for Respect for Life	Japan's Network for Women and Health	Legalization (1999)
		SEXUAL HARASSMENT		
Unpleasant sexual experiences	Violence against women	Federation of Economic Organizations and Japan's Federation of Employers Associations	Lawyers' Network against Violence against Women; Campus Sexual Harassment Network	Revised Equal Employment Opportunity Law (1999)
		MILITARY SEXUAL SLAVERY		
Licensed "comfort stations"/ prostitution	Sexual slavery	Association of the Bereaved Families of the War Dead and other extreme right groups	Violence against Women in WarNet-Japan; Action Network for the Issue of Military Sexual Slavery Japan	Asian Women's Fund (1995)
		DOMESTIC VIOLENCE		
Marital dispute	Violence against women	Right-wing conservative groups	DV Survey Research Group; National Shelter Network	Domestic Violence Prevention Law (2001)
		CHILD PROSTITUTION		
Assisted entertainment	Commercial sexual exploitation	Federation of entertainment and media businesses	ECPAT Japan; Child Assault Prevention networks; Federation for the Protection of Children's Human Rights	Child Prostitution and Pornography Prohibition Law (1999)

tween the Korean comfort women who were drafted and Japanese comfort women who were prostitutes under the state-licensed system, a distinction that many Japanese feminist scholars find problematic.[43] By redefining "comfort women" as sex slaves, as victims of a violation of their right to their sexuality, it breaks down the artificial divide between the Japanese and non-Japanese. Although the 2000 NGO-led tribunal attracted considerable international and Japanese media attention, its impact on the Japanese state seems limited. Despite its reframing of the comfort system as military sexual slavery and its sustained outreach activities in the 1990s, the inability of the national, regional, and international movement on the comfort women issue to garner domestic political support within Japan accounts for the stalled progress. To this date, the Japanese women's movement remains bitterly divided over an issue that involved few Japanese women and that happened in wartime more than fifty years ago. Table 8.1 summarizes my explanatory framework.

Similar to the case of comfort women, in which international pressure led to the establishment of a private fund without a full-fledged apology and compensation, Japanese NGO mobilization on minority issues at the UN led to some minimal legal changes without corresponding recognition by the Japanese government. The case of the Ainu is an excellent example. As discussed in chapter 7, Ainu mobilization within the UN in the early 1990s led to the significant change from area to ethnic policy, and from economic aid to cultural promotion. Although the 1997 Ainu Culture Promotion Act is a milestone in itself, it does not provide for the recognition of the Ainu people as indigenous people with territorial rights. Similarly, in the case of advancement of Koreans' rights in Japan, though the ratification of the Refugee Convention in 1982 led to pension reforms, many Koreans remain aliens in Japan. As for the Okinawans, migrant workers, and minority women, the inaccessibility of global human rights frames until the World Conference against Racism and, in turn, the inability of Japanese NGOs to obtain political support account for the continuous policy of denial and invisibility implemented by the Japanese government.

CHAPTER NINE

Conclusions

Reconstructing Japanese Political Culture in the Age of Globalization

The 1990s were an exceptional decade for the advancement of human rights and feminist politics at the global level. In a series of successive world conferences on children, the environment, human rights, population, social development, and women, the global women's movement produced a body of discourses that paradigmatically redefined women's human rights. The global campaign against violence against women also generated spillover effects on the children's human rights movement. This book has examined how these discourses arise as norms and how they are reproduced locally by epistemic networks, that is, how education has effected political change in Japan. In this concluding chapter, I briefly summarize my argument and discuss the implications of this study on the engendering of global governance, the connections between transnational social movements and grassroots education, and the reconstruction of Japanese political culture from a globalization perspective.

Globalization of Human Rights Norms and Domestic Political Change: The Case of Japan

Between 1997 and 2001, eight laws concerning women's and children's human rights were enacted in Japan: the revised Equal Employment Opportunity Law, prohibiting sexual harassment at the workplace (1997); the legalization of the pill (1999); the Basic Law for a Gender-Equal Society (1999); the Child Prostitution and Pornography Law (1999); the Child Abuse Prevention Law (2000); the Anti-Stalking Law (2000); the Law to Promote Human Rights Education (2000); and the Anti–Domestic Violence Law (2001). These changes concerning gender and human rights politics present a challenge to the major paradigms that focus on the bureaucracy, political parties, and interest groups in order to understand political change in Japan. The 1990s did witness a major reconfiguration of the predominant triumvirate in Japan: the LDP, the bureaucracy, and interest groups. The demise of the LDP and the rise of multiparty politics opened up new political opportunities for domestic advocacy networks. To a certain extent, coalition politics since 1994 had been an important factor behind the changes concerning women's and children's human rights. For example, the private Asian Women's Fund for former comfort women was created when Murayama Tomiichi of the Social Democratic Party of Japan (SDPJ) was prime minister between 1994 and 1996. However, coalition politics alone can not explain the continuation of changes concerning women's and children's rights after the end of the LDP–SDPJ–Sakigake coalition in 1996–98. Traditional party politics cannot explain why female politicians across party lines (including Domoto Akiko of Sakigake, Moriyama Mayumi of the LDP, Shimizu Sumiko, Owaki Masako, Tsujimoto Kiyomi, and Fukushima Mizuho of the Social Democratic Party, and Kawahashi Yukiko and Komiyama Yoko of the Democratic Party, to name just a few) have become crucial agents of change by introducing global norms on women's and children's human rights to Japan, on the one hand,[1] and allying with nongovernmental groups within Japan, on the other.[2] Despite the fact that, by 1999, the ruling coalition of the LDP, Komeito, and the Liberal Party was much more conservative than the non-LDP coalition in 1993, major legal changes concerning child prostitution, stalking, and domestic violence continued.

Nor can a domestic social movement approach satisfactorily address the sudden changes concerning women's and children's human rights in Japan in the 1990s. Grassroots mobilization for the pill, for example, started in the early 1970s, but it virtually disappeared until the early 1990s. Mobilization against both sexual harassment and domestic violence began in the late 1980s and early 1990s but attracted little political attention until after the 1995 Beijing Conference.[3] The demands made by the Korean and Japanese women's movements on the issue of comfort women at the beginning of the 1990s also fell on deaf ears until the UN intervened and issued a report on wartime Japanese sexual slavery in 1994, which led to the establishment by the Japanese government of the private Asian Women's Fund.

In contrast to these predominant domestic explanations, this study uses a constructivist perspective and situates Japan within global human rights standards. I show how Japan has become an embedded network state, that is, embedded in global human rights norms that are mobilized by domestic epistemic nongovernmental networks. Few would have predicted the significant discursive impact of four world conferences between 1993 and 1996 on Japanese society. Indeed, the Japanese government sent low-level delegations to the 1993 World Human Rights Conference in Vienna, the 1994 International Conference on Population and Development in Cairo, and the 1995 Fourth World Conference on Women in Beijing, and planned not to attend the 1996 First World Congress against Commercial Sexual Exploitation of Children in Stockholm altogether. With the exception of the Beijing Conference, relatively few Japanese NGOs participated in these conferences, yet, the global discourses of women's and children's human rights were powerful enough to provide new frames for members of domestic Japanese human rights networks.

The historic acclamation by feminist activists at the 1993 World Human Rights Conference in Vienna that "women's rights are human rights" helped redefine sexual harassment and domestic violence in Japan as human rights issues. The global redefinition of access to the pill as a "reproductive right" at the 1994 Cairo Conference on Population and Development paved the way for the end of the three-decade ban on the pill in Japan in 1999. The redefinition of the "comfort system" as "military sexual slavery" by the UN special rapporteur on violence against women in 1994 was sufficient to put both legal and moral responsibility for the system squarely on the Japanese government. Almost six thousand Japanese women attended the 1995 World Conference on Women in Beijing, then returned to Japan demanding their human rights. Last but not least, the redefinition of child prostitution as "commercial sexual exploitation" at the 1996 First World Congress against Commercial Sexual Exploitation of Children in Stockholm resulted in the swift passage of the Child Prostitution and Pornography Prohibition Law in 1999. Five separate and marginalized movements were suddenly unified under the category of human rights.

Signatures by Japanese officials on conference outcome documents are little more than promises until they are followed up domestically. Members of the women's human rights epistemic networks hold the Japanese government accountable for what it utters or signs in front of the world. As one bureaucrat told me, "Japan cares where it stands internationally."[4] Although there are few female activists who have become politicians in Japan, increasing numbers of female politicians have either founded their own nongovernmental groups, become board members of NGOs, or developed close working relationships with NGOs through expert hearings and study meetings. Similarly, an increasing number of feminist scholars have not only been invited to lead seminars and workshops for NGOs, but have themselves either founded NGOs or become board members or donors of NGOs. By the mid-1990s, the domestic epistemic networks learned the art of accountability politics, not only by participating in world conferences, but also by compiling alternative reports to the UN, attending annual meetings, and strategically using various UN institutional mechanisms, including the special rapporteur system. The 1990s saw an explosion of NGO-led advocacy education, research, information dissemination, and training on human rights in Japan. I have highlighted and discussed some examples on a range of issues, including child sexual abuse, domestic violence, sexual harassment, prostitution, comfort women, reproductive rights, and assertiveness training. These outreach activities represent a paradigm shift in the traditionally narrowly conceived areas of women's and children's education. The purpose and subjects of study, definition of issues, categories of trainers and learners, pedagogy, and curricula have all expanded to include men and women, children and adults, civil servants and the general public, and victims and victimizers alike. Once global human rights norms were institutionalized locally through domestic laws and policies, the Japanese government in turn changed itself into an educator of global human rights. Below I address the implications of this research.

Engendering Global Governance

Although the study of nongovernmental organizations was once marginalized within the social sciences, the quantitative explosion of NGOs and their success in several instances, including the global campaign to ban landmines, and the anti–World Trade Organization demonstrations in Seattle have attracted considerable academic attention. Despite much talk about the rise of a multitrack "new diplomacy," however, there is little agreement on the definition or impact of "global civil society." As some have cautioned, "NGOs may have a right to a voice, but not necessarily a vote in global fora."[5] Under what conditions does global citizen action have an impact on international and domestic politics? How do we measure the outcomes? As Cameron puts it, "few NGOs have asked themselves what it really means to 'democratize foreign policy.'"[6] To whom is global civil society accountable? What kinds of partnerships exist between intergovernmental organizations, states, and NGOs? This study of the impact on Japan of NGO-led global campaigns against violence against women and children represents a preliminary effort to address some of these issues raised by scholars and activists of global civil society.

By examining world conferences from gender perspectives, this book has opened up several questions in the study of transnational feminist organizing. Are we seeing a process of the engendering of international organizations and norms? How do feminists deal with issues of power and representation within transnational feminist organizing? What is the relationship between gender and other social relations such as race, caste, class, and sexual orientation in representational politics? From the first World Conference on Children in 1990 to the Rio Summit on Environment in 1992, the World Conference on Human Rights in Vienna in 1993, the Cairo Conference on Population and Development in 1994, the Social Summit in Copenhagen in 1995, the Beijing Conference on Women in 1995, the Second UN Conference on Human Settlements in Istanbul (Habitat II) in 1996, and the First World Congress against Commercial Sexual Exploitation of Children in Stockholm in 1996, transnational feminist organizing has been part and parcel of the rise of global civil society in the 1990s. Yet this process has been far from trouble-free. Many feminist scholars have cautioned against the hegemonic constructions of "global sisterhood."[7] As Kaplan notes, "the discourses of 'global feminism' have naturalized and totalized categories such as 'Third World women' *and* 'First World women.'"[8] Transnational feminist politics of the 1990s have demonstrated well that global solidarity cannot be used as a subtext to erase differences among women. It is well known that CEDAW, comprehensive though it is in prohibiting discrimination against women in all its forms, never mentions race. Similarly, the outcome documents of the Beijing Conference cover issues of minority women only under the sections of violence against women and discrimination against the girl child. It was not until the World Conference against Racism that the UN began to acknowledge the intersectionality of gender and other forms of discrimination.[9] How feminists might solve the double bind of feminism—that is, the fact that the movement cannot speak without other women, but at the same time it cannot speak for other women—has emerged as one of the most challenging questions transnational feminist theorists and activists face. As Ahmed puts it, "Thinking of gender as an articulated rather than isolated category means giving up the assumption that feminism itself is inclusive, or simply speaks on behalf of all women. Sexual difference cannot be ontologised as *the* difference that matters: sexual difference exists in a complex set of inter-connections with other differences."[10]

The study of gender politics in Japan—not just its impact, but its very construction—in this book precisely attempts to address the issue of power and representation within both global feminisms and local feminisms. How can gender be mobilized strategically without reproducing an exclusive gender hierarchy? As Grewal and Kaplan caution,

> Despite an unprecedented volume of theorization and innovations in methodologies, there remains a great need for *feminist* critiques of the Western model of sisterhood in the global context. . . . Notions such as "global feminism" have failed to respond to such needs and have increasingly been subject to critique. Conventionally, "global feminism"

> has stood for a kind of Western cultural imperialism. The term "global feminism" has elided the diversity of women's agency in favor of a universalized Western model of women's liberation that celebrates individuality and modernity. Anti-imperialist movements have legitimately decried this form of "feminist" globalizing (albeit often for a continuation of their own agendas). . . . Transnational feminist practices require this kind of comparative work rather than the relativistic linking of "differences" undertaken by proponents of "global feminism"; that is, to compare multiple, overlapping, and discrete oppressions rather than to construct a theory of hegemonic oppression under a unified category of gender. . . . Feminists must continually question the narratives in which they are embedded, including but not limiting ourselves to the master narratives of mainstream feminism.[11]

This study of the Japanese movement for women's human rights in the 1990s has revealed how mainstream Japanese feminism has reproduced the unspeakable ethnic, racial, and sexual Other within its national and regional boundaries. Gender as a category of analysis therefore needs to be embedded in inclusive relational contexts. As Butler puts it, "the term 'universality' would have to be left permanently open, permanently contested, permanently contingent, in order not to foreclose in advance future claims for inclusion."[12]

Transnational Social Movements and Grassroots Education

If there has been considerable attention focused on transnational social movements, the epistemic or educational aspects that I have highlighted in this book remain relatively unknown. International relations scholars seldom link education to transnational relations. The traditional focus on the legal and political *impact* of global civil society has diverted attention away from the elaborate *educational process* that these global campaigns entail. Although there is an emergent body of research linking globalization and education, most studies focus on the impact of globalization on education.[13] Despite the rise of global networks of "advocacy educators" in the 1990s, international educationalists know little about these new actors—who they are, what they do, and whether and how they matter.[14] By analyzing the role of global and local women's as well as children's human rights epistemic networks in the production and dissemination of knowledge, this study has attempted to bring education back in as an active, rather than a passive, force in the age of globalization. First and foremost, NGOs, whether issue-specific or in coalitions, need to conduct research and educate themselves about the issue at hand. As a study of a dozen cases of transnational organizing concludes, "to be credible, effective, and accountable, global citizen action must pay attention to its own knowledge and learning strategies."[15] The corpus of expert information and knowledge concerning a particular issue—for example, the worst forms of child labor, sex crimes in war, global warming, or caste discrimination—often then becomes the cornerstone of a global campaign. Educating the movement itself is only the first step. The bulk of grassroots mobilization by NGOs involves painstaking education of the public, the media, state officials, and, very importantly, international organizations. As Jody Williams and Stephen Goose recall, in the case of the landmine ban, "it was the NGOs . . . who began to educate the public as to the degree and scope of the crisis."[16] They further add, "the French campaign also held numerous meetings with French ministries and conducted a number of seminars at government offices on the issues related to a mine ban in an attempt to move forward French landmine policy."[17] The campaign leader of the anti–World Trade Organization protests in Seattle in 1999 also acknowledges,

> As important as winning that battle was realizing that the better part of a decade of grass-roots organizing—very tedious, painstaking, district by district, small town by small town, educating rooms of people, 50 at a time—had actually come to critical mass. . . . The time of all times was to see so many Americans educated enough to take time off and come to Seattle on their own dollar, with all of the chaos and confusion of trying to find a place to stay, simply to have their own word.[18]

This study has shown how feminist and human rights education is used as an important political strategy in Japan, where extrainstitutional protests are rare.

Reconstructing Japanese Political Culture from a Globalization Perspective

A study of the impact of global human rights standards on domestic political change would not be complete without looking at how those norms are contested locally. In this last section, I conclude by discussing some debates involved in the interpretations of human rights norms within Japan and addressing the implications of globalization on four key assumptions—concerning group orientation, harmony, hierarchical social organization, and national citizenship—in Japanese political culture.

Despite the entry of human rights into Japanese discourse in the past few years, there is little consensus within the country on the definitions of "women's human rights," "gender," "empowerment," and "children's human rights." Not only do representatives of the government and NGOs disagree, but even members of domestic networks argue over the meanings of these imported terms.

Although many feminist activists in Japan believe that an integrated human rights approach offers great potential to link and strengthen the separate human rights movements within Japan,[19] feminist scholars are divided about the (premature) marriage of human rights and feminism. In fact, a feminist human rights debate has emerged since the early 1990s. Ueno cautions that because of the way the concept of "human rights" developed in the West and was adopted in Japan as universal, bourgeois, and patriarchal, it is "dangerous" to use it as a conceptual base for feminism.[20] Ogoshi, however, argues that despite its abstraction, ambivalence, and lack of rootedness in Japan, a human rights perspective offers an important potential to overcome some even more dangerous "indigenous" Japanese ideas that are prevalent among many intellectuals (for example, the emphasis on "group harmony").[21]

A particularly thorny issue is the application of a human rights framework to sexuality. A debate regarding the ethics of the commodification of sex emerged in Japan in the early 1990s with the rise of "*enjo kōsai.*"[22] Some Japanese have argued that "assisted entertainment of teenagers" in Japan is somewhat different from child prostitution in other, especially developing, countries, since these girls voluntarily choose to provide sex services.[23] Several sex educators have attributed "*enjo kōsai*" to a lack of understanding, among Japanese children and adults alike, of the concept of the right to sexual self-determination (that one's body should not be controlled by others).[24] Since the 1994 Cairo Conference on Population and Development, however, the term "*seiteki jiko ketteiken*" (right to sexual self-determination) has gained increasing salience in Japan. As a feminist activist in reproductive technology notes,

> As I continue, in the various groups in which I am involved, to debate and rethink the issues of women's self-determination and abortion rights, I am developing an overwhelming sense that, whether from the perspective of women's emancipation or human rights, this process of discovery of self-consciousness is likely to produce a Copernican revolution. That is to say, in a society where women are denied the right to self-determination, and the choice to give birth or not, the term "human" is essentially a designation for men only. Even if the law speaks of "human rights," it focuses on the rights of men. With the notion of "agency over one's own body" that is at the foundation of women's demand for the right to choose, we are moving, for the first time, toward a new horizon, a way of thinking grounded in individual rights rather than the rights of men.[25]

Yamamoto urges for a sex education approach based on human rights: sex education for human rights (for the rights to sexual self-determination), sex education as human rights (the right to learn about sexuality), sex education through human rights (emphasizing children's participation), and sex education about human rights (focusing on sexuality rights).[26]

If Japanese feminists are split about the desirability of a human rights approach, child rights advocates are even more so. There is no consensus among members of the children's human rights epistemic network on how to interpret and teach the Convention on the Rights of the Child (CRC). The recent salience of a "children's human rights" discourse has in fact produced some backlash responses. In a country where teachers and parents are supposed to be in control, the teaching of children's rights is seen by many as subversive. Kawakami, for example, in his book *Gakko Hōkai* (School breakdown), attributes the long list of school troubles, including violence, dropouts, and lack of discipline, to the rise of children's human rights advocates (*jinkenha*). He argues that "it is becoming popular to believe that if we let children grow freely, they would naturally become good. Education has regressed. Students and teachers are the same human beings. As a result, students do not listen to teachers any more. Schools are just like the streets; anything goes."[27] Right-wing conservative religious groups such as Toitsu Kyōkai (United Church) have also been distributing newsletters in schools denouncing the CRC.[28] A key challenge for child rights advocates is not only to deal with the rise of an oppositional movement, but also to find innovative ways to implement children's rights in a country where children have traditionally been conceived as minors that need to be protected. The promotion of children's voice/participation as a right to self expression, stipulated in Article 12 of the CRC, represents a daunting task in an environment in which children have long been taught to follow rules rather than assert themselves.[29]

The simultaneous emergence in Japan of human rights discourses for both women and children has also raised the question of the compatibility of the two. Until the issue of sexual violence entered the mainstream in the late 1990s, the women's movement and the children's rights movement had largely been separate. The Japan Federation of Bar Associations (Nichibenren), one of the most active human rights groups in Japan, for example, has long had two rather disconnected subcommittees, one on women's rights and the other on children's rights. In 1997, out of an awareness that violence against women is intimately connected to child abuse, it created the joint Family and Violence Study Group. At their 1998 annual human rights symposium, one of the sessions, "Family and Violence: Towards the Elimination of Violence against Wives and Child Abuse," culminated in a pioneering volume analyzing the structural connections between violence against women and violence against children in Japan.[30] One of the main reasons why the two subcommittees on women's rights and children's rights had, until then, rarely joined forces was the difference in their opinions concerning the family. The former leans toward the dissolution of the family (since this is an important way that abused women can achieve independence), while the latter tries to prevent the breakup of the family at all costs (since keeping families intact is assumed to be important for the upbringing of children).[31] As one member of the Children's Rights Sub-Committee explains the problem, "a key pattern for helping children is to turn to the mothers; that is why, for members of this committee, a major issue has been the independence of women." Another committee member concurs that although it is important to consider the rights of working mothers, it is unclear how their rights could be reconciled with the rights of the child. A member of the Gender Equality Sub-Committee, however, responds that "most cases of child abuse are related to the fact that the mothers are battered. Being concerned only with saving children does not address the root cause of the problem."[32] The appropriation of various global human rights discourses within Japan is far from being unanimous.[33]

Looking at Japan from a globalization and gender perspective also forces us to reconsider four predominant notions in Japanese political culture: group orientation, harmony or nonlegalism, hierarchical social organization, and homogeneity / national citizenship. The 1990s represented a soul-searching period for Japan. After decades of sustained high economic growth, Japan found itself mired in crisis after crisis, economic, political, and social. The profound sense of malaise among the elite is reflected in a highly symbolic report by the Prime Minister's Commission on Japan's Goals in the 21st Century in January 2000:

> We Japanese have not engaged in discussion and debate on national aspirations for a long time. . . . Over a long history in a meager and harsh environment, we cultivated ethical norms extolling social and organizational harmony. Socioeconomic affluence and internationalization, however, made it difficult to sustain such ethical norms unchanged. And in the 1990s, before a national consensus on the ethical framework appropriate to an affluent society could be reached, Japan experienced a major setback and slid into the age of globalization. There was also the shock of the January 1995 Great Hanshin-Awaji Earthquake. Government (both central and local) ineptitude at crisis management, inefficiency, and lack of accountability made the public deeply anxious about the government's ability to protect citizens' lives and property. A series of unnerving incidents followed, including the Aum Shinrikyō nerve-gas attack on Tokyo subways in March 1995 and a 14-year-old boy's murder of a younger boy and assaults on several other children (one fatal) in 1997. All this left people with the impression that core attributes of Japanese society on which they had prided themselves—family solidarity, the quality of education (especially primary and lower secondary education), and social stability and safety—were crumbling. It could be said that these episodes revealed a brittleness and inflexibility of Japan's economy and society that had been building up

gradually. Perhaps all this represented the price of success. . . . Japan must now seek a better model.[34]

A longstanding characteristic of Japanese society to which the society's success is often attributed is its group orientation.[35] In particular, the primacy of the *ie* (family) has been regarded as a defining characteristic of Japanese culture.[36] Since the late 1980s, however, feminist scholars have challenged the gender assumptions in the construction of the *ie* ideology and have even argued that the contemporary family is dead.[37] The Prime Minister's Report on Japan's Goals in the 21st Century emphasizes the shift toward more individualism.

In the world of the twenty-first century individuals will possess incomparably more power than ever before. The Internet gives ordinary citizens easy access to the world. In addition, nonprofit-organization and volunteer activities have expanded people's scope of action. Varied networks are enhancing individual power. "Empowerment" is spreading. Exercising such power to the fullest is critical. . . . The other essential change is to redefine and rebuild the relationship between private and public space in civil society. This means first and foremost promoting individuality and individual initiatives: unleashing sturdy individuals who are free, self-reliant, and responsible, individuals whose ability to empathize with others makes them inclusive. Building a new system of governance, empowering the individual, and creating a new public space require the fostering of a spirit of self-reliance and a spirit of tolerance, neither of which has been allowed sufficient latitude for expression in Japanese society so far.[38]

It is unclear how the tension between individualism and a group orientation will unfold in Japan in the twenty-first century. The protracted economic and political crisis of the 1990s seems to have opened up some space for the discourse on the role of the individual, even if it is not necessarily based on a rights perspective.

Another predominant characteristic of Japanese political culture is harmony, or nonlegalism.[39] Many argue that Japan maintains a unique way of managing social conflicts.[40] The drastic legal changes in the late 1990s concerning not only women's and children's human rights but nonprofit organizations in general have put the traditional view of Japanese social management in question. As one of my interviewees, a lawyer and member of the Japan Civil Liberties Union, told me, "it is true that the law has been for a long time marginalized in Japan. But a major change has occurred since the late 1980s. As the bureaucracy has become more and more criticized, there has been an increasing reliance on and control by the law."[41] In fact, many of my interviewees from the Japanese bureaucracy acknowledged the importance of domestic laws. As the director of the Council for Gender Equality explained,

The Basic Law on Gender Equality is a very important milestone in gender equality in Japan. In 1985, when we ratified CEDAW, we were not sure whether we needed a comprehensive basic law. By the time the Plan for Gender Equality was adopted in 1996, it was clear that there should be a review about the need for a basic law. Prime Minister Hashimoto was personally committed; he said, "I will do it." Until now, we have only responded to UN pressures. But with a national Basic Law, even if the UN collapses, we will still have to do it![42]

The deputy manager of the Women's Assistance Unit of the Ministry of Welfare lamented the lack of a legal mandate for a coherent policy on domestic violence before the Anti–Domestic Violence Law was finally passed in March 2001.[43] A program officer on sexual violence at a publicly funded women's center, Tokyo Women Foundation, also complained about the lack of support for her work and its minimal impact. As she explained, "when there is no law, it is difficult to make real change."[44]

The question of legal necessity and effectiveness is hotly debated among Japanese activists. As a lawyer who is active in the domestic violence movement in Japan claims, "the law clearly defines the boundary and sends a big message to both the abusers, the victims, and the law-enforcing agencies. But the law is not enough. We need to change also people's consciousness. It is especially important to encourage victims to speak out, train civil servants, and be involved in the movement."[45] A female politician and lawyer adds, "the law might be weak, so we also need administrative guidance."[46] Some activists are also skeptical about the use of the court. As a veteran CRC activist puts it, "although I am a CRC ombudsperson, I am not advocating legalism. There is the question of desirability, especially for children, of using the court. There is also the issue of time (you know how protracted legal proceedings can be in this country). After all, Japan does not have a strong legal tradition."[47] Yet another issue is that even lawyers still have little consciousness about women's and children's human rights in Japan.[48] Many agree that legal change is only the first crucial step. As an active member of the Japanese Association of Women's Human Rights cautions, "the government can easily say '*yarimashita*' (yes, we have passed the law) and then does not do much. NGOs play an important role in making sure that the law is actually implemented and is changing people's consciousness."[49]

A third core notion in Japanese political culture is a hierarchical social organization that is inherited from Tokugawa Japan (1600–1868).[50] The 1980s and 1990s, however, saw not only a proliferation of voluntary organizations in Japan, but also the emergence of a new discourse as well as new practices in horizontal networking. The 1995 earthquake in Kobe helped cause the question of the role of public and social interest organizations in Japan to surface.[51] In its

Plan for Gender Equality 2000, passed in 1996, the Japanese government acknowledges the importance of forming a network with NGOs.[52] In 1998, the Japanese government passed the ground-breaking NPO law, which not only formally recognized their existence but also put the idea of networking to a test. Although the concept of "*nettowākingu*" (networking) became a buzzword in the nonprofit and nongovernmental communities in the 1990s, there is little consensus on what it means. As a veteran human rights activist puts it,

> There has been increasing networking among NGOs on an individual, rather than institutional, basis. But networking among human rights NGOs in Japan is anything but easy. There is no consensus about the definition of human rights. Discrimination issues in Japan are treated as many different things, with the exception of human rights issues, by various bureaucratic agencies. NGO networks, although nascent, are the most active. Networks among local government bodies start to emerge, but the gap between active and passive ones is huge. I think the central government is the most behind when it comes to networking.[53]

Many activists remain ambivalent about their relationship with the Japanese government. "Surely, the keyword is partnership. But if partnership excludes the possibility of confrontation, I am not sure it is a good thing. NGOs should be independent from the government."[54] As another cautions,

> Now we can attend official report gatherings at the Ministry of Foreign Affairs, for example, after the CSW [Commission on the Status of Women] meeting, and NGOs can give opinions. Whether they are listened to or not is a separate issue. The Council for Gender Equality has also created a network called Egalité, but they only invite one established NGO network! One has the impression it is all appearance. They say that they hear our opinions, but there is not a single time when we can discuss issues together. We can't speak of any form of real partnership yet![55]

Finally, the changes described in this book related to the issues of the Ainu people, Okinawans, wartime sexual slavery, Korean resident rights, and migrant labor beg us to reconsider the thesis that Japanese culture is homogeneous. The human rights movement of the 1990s has put the issue of discrimination against ethnic, racial, and sexual minorities at the forefront. Although still relatively invisible and marginalized, a gay, lesbian, transgender, and transsexual movement, for example, has emerged in Japan since the early 1990s. In 1990 the gay and lesbian group Ugoku Gei to Rezubian no Kai (Gay and Lesbian Action Group) brought a case to a Tokyo district court after the group was denied access to a public facility in the Tokyo metropolitan area because of the sexual orientation of its members. In 1997, the Tokyo Supreme Court ruled in favor of the group.[56] This precedent-setting case largely galvanized the gay and lesbian movement in Japan. In 1992, the first lesbian and gay festival was organized in

Tokyo. In 1994, Japan's first lesbian and gay parade took place, also in Tokyo. As of 1999, according to the "Transgender Self-Help Groups National Exchange Booklet," published by the Transsexual and Transgender Support Group, there were approximately thirty-five gay, lesbian, transgender, and transsexual groups in Japan. In November 2000, the decision by the Tokyo metropolitan government not to include sexual orientation in its human rights program was reversed largely because of the mobilization of gay and lesbian groups.

> The Japan Association for the Lesbian and Gay Movement (OCCUR) called to the international community for assistance. . . . According to the International Gay and Lesbian Human Rights Commission, the Tokyo Metropolitan Government (TMG) has set a significant precedent as the first city or country within Asia to provide anti-discrimination protection on the basis of sexual orientation.[57]

With an increasing number of overstayers taking up permanent residence in Japan, the issue of how Japan treats its migrant workers is unlikely to fade. The founder and president of the Asian People's Friendship Society, an active NGO promoting migrants' rights in Japan, Yoshinari Katsuo, points out, "Japanese society still has fantasies about our pure blood, and about the ability of Japanese people to understand each other better than others. . . . Even if the government or the business community accepts more foreigners, without much more effort on our side, these feelings of rejection toward foreigners will remain strong."[58] Ogata Sadako, the former UN High Commissioner for Refugees, urges her country to consider globalization in terms of cultural openness and says, "we live under the illusion of one ethnic race, one culture. A monoethnic island of prosperity won't survive in the twenty-first century."[59] The 2000 report of the Prime Minister's Commission on Japan's Goals in the 21st Century also concludes:

> What we can say with certainty is that the age ahead will be one in which the whole range of issues like trade, finance, population growth, poverty, food, and environmental protection will transcend the level of single nations or regions and will demand world-scale attention and responses. It will not be possible to handle such issues with the resources of a single country or at the level of the state. In such an age, it will not be sufficient for the state and its bureaucratic apparatus alone to handle international relations; broader involvement of the general public will be required. This should primarily be civilian in nature, and we should fully bring the private sector, both organizations and individuals, into play. This means providing active support for international governance and getting people actively involved in the global "public space"—in other words, in the creation of global public goods.[60]

The question of how Japan grapples with the demands of globalization is reflected in the debate on the desirability of adopting English as a second official language in Japan, recently renewed as a result of a Singaporean politician's criticism that the Japanese speak poor English and lack "global literacy." Back in the 1870s, Japan's first education minister, Mori Arinori, already advocated the adoption of English as Japan's first language in order to facilitate learning about science and technology from the West.[61] Many, however, continue to fear that English would threaten Japanese national identity and culture. Tokuoka Takao, a seventy-year-old journalist who once served as a foreign correspondent with Mainichi Shimbun, for example, is not hesitant to voice his reservation: "I believe that the proposal to make English an official language is wrong because such a policy would only end up producing Japanese who do not understand their own culture. It could create people who do not have their own national identity."[62] In April 2003, the National Institute for Japanese Language, affiliated with the Education, Culture, Sports, Science, and Technology Ministry, announced the prohibition of fifty-nine English words in the Japanese language, including "informed consent," "delivery," "second opinion," "barrier-free," and "lifeline." The tug of war between the conservationists and the internationalists, if reminiscent of the Meiji era, continues to play out in Japan's cautious march toward postnational citizenship.

If NGOs were largely able to to politicize the issues of racism and forge alliances with transnational advocacy networks in Durban, follow-up efforts in Japan included targeting key politicians to support the enactment of an anti-discrimination bill. Bringing Durban home also translates into several issues for advocacy NGOs in Japan. Many human rights NGOs remain small and are in dire need of capacity building, or, in their own words, "professionalization," in terms of both creating partnerships domestically and networking internationally.[63] The idea of multiple discrimination against minority women has also pushed NGOs toward more coherent cross-convention human rights work in Japan, and the government toward better cross-agency coordination of human rights protection.[64] With the current conjuncture of prolonged economic recession and the post–September 11th anti-terrorism climate, it remains uncertain how the newly reframed anti-racism movement will translate politically. One thing is certain, however: there is increasing pressure, from both inside Japan and out, for Japan to move from "*tanitsu minzoku*" (a monoethnic nation) to "*tabunkashakai*" (a multicultural society).

APPENDIXES

APPENDIX A

Interviewees

Nongovernmental Organizations (55)

"VIOLENCE AGAINST WOMEN" GROUPS (18)

Abused Women Shelter (AWS)
Association against Sexual Violence
Bona Date Rape Group
Campus Sexual Harassment Network
Domestic Violence Action and Research Group
FTC Shelter
Fund for Female Genital Mutilation
Japan Anti-Prostitution Association (JAPA)
Korean Council for Women Drafted for Military Sexual Slavery by Japan
No! Sexual Harassment Group
Rape Crisis Survivors Net Kansai
SARA Shelter
Taiwanese Comfort Women Trial Support Group
Tokyo Rape Crisis Center
Uli Yosong Network on Comfort Women (now-defunct Korean resident group)
Video-Juku (comfort women testimonies)
Violence against Women in War (VAWW)–Net Japan
Women's Health and Safety Education Center

OTHER WOMEN'S GROUPS (11)

Beijing Japan Accountability Caucus
Femix (feminist counseling and publishing)
Forum on Sex Issues (sex education)
Group to Create Alternative Report for Beijing-Plus-Five
Japan Women's Congress
Japanese Association for International Women's Rights
Japanese Association of Sex Education

Japanese Women Democratic Club
Kanagawa Women's Council
International Women's Year Liaison Group Japan (fifty-one groups)
OYKOT (sex education)

MEN'S GROUPS (4)

DV Prevention Project for Batterers
Men's Lib Kanagawa
Men's Lib Tokyo
Mental Service Center (counseling programs for batterers)

OTHER HUMAN RIGHTS GROUPS (22)

Action for the Rights of the Child (ARC)
Amnesty International—Women's Human Rights Team
Children and Textbooks Japan Net 21
Children's Human Rights Net
Citizen Diplomatic Center
Citizen's Council for the Legislation of Survey on War Victims Convention of the Rights of the Child Network
Empowerment Center (CAP group)
End Child Prostitution in Asian Tourism (ECPAT) / Stop Japan
Forum 2001 (environment)
HIV and Human Rights Info Center
Human Rights Forum 21
Human Rights Info Center (Hurights) Osaka
International Human Rights NGO Network
International Movement against Discrimination and Racism (IMADR)
Japan Civil Liberties Union
Korean Democratic Women's Club
Okinawa Citizen Information Center
Setagaya Education Forum
Solidarity Network with Migrant Workers / Japan
Stop Child Sexual Abuse (SCSA)
Videodoc CAP Project

Professional Organizations (4)

LAWYERS

Japanese Federation of Bar Associations, Sub-Committee on Gender Equality

UNIONS

Federation of Japanese Unions, Gender Equality Policy Section
Japanese Teachers Union

BUSINESS

Japan's Federation of Employers Associations (Nikkeiren)

Central Government (11)

Environment Agency of Japan, Global Environment Information Centre
Former Japanese Ambassador to the UN
Ministry of Education
  National Women's Education Center
  Lifelong Education Division, Social Education Section
  Lifelong Education Division, Gender Equality Education Section
Ministry of Foreign Affairs, Human Rights and Refugee Section, CEDAW
Ministry of Health and Welfare, Family Assistance Division, Women's Assistance Section
Ministry of Justice, Human Rights Protection Bureau
Ministry of Labor, Women's Policy Section
National Police Agency, Crime Victim Policy Bureau
Prime Minister's Office, Office for Gender Equality

Local Government (9)

Kanagawa Women's Center, researcher
Kiyose City Center for Gender Equality, vice-director and counselor
Osaka Dawn Center, program coordinator
Shinjuku Women's Center, counselor
Sumida-Ward Women's Center, vice-director
Tokyo Metropolitan Government, Women's Planning Section
Tokyo Metropolitan Government, Women's Labor Section
Tokyo Women's Plaza, program coordinator
Yokohama Women's Center, counseling section chief

Politicians (5)

LIBERAL DEMOCRATIC PARTY

Moriyama Mayumi

DEMOCRATIC PARTY

Kawahashi Yukiko

SOCIAL DEMOCRATIC PARTY

Owaki Masako
Shimizu Sumiko
Fukushima Mizuho

Mass Media (3)

Asahi Evening News
NHK
Nikkei Shimbun

Academia (5)

President of Waseda Sexual Harassment Prevention Commission
Hashimoto Hiroko, Jumonji Women's College (women's studies)
Professor in moral education, Gakuin Daigaku
Kita Akihito, Waseda University (children's rights expert)
Kaino Tamie, Ochanomizu University (feminist legal scholar)

Corporations (2)

Dentsu
Hakuhodo

School Visit & Interviews (1)

Tamagawa Junior High School

Individuals (2)

Japanese survivor of domestic violence
Korean former comfort women in China

APPENDIX B

Human Rights Symposia, Seminars, and Training Workshops Attended, September 1999 to December 2001

October 1, 1999. Don't Sexually Harass and Don't Be Sexually Harassed. Panel discussion, Tokyo Women's Foundation.

October 11, 1999. Symposium on Violence against Women, Prime Minister's Office.

October 29, 1999. "Stop the Sexual Harassment": Training of Local Government Staff by Chuo Ward Government, Tokyo.

November 4, 1999. Towards a Society without Violence against Women. Symposium, Asian Women's Fund.

November 5, 1999. UNIFEM Violence against Women. Video showing, Tokyo Women's Foundation.

November 5, 1999. Let's Create a Domestic Violence Ordinance. Workshop, Femin Net.

November 6, 1999. Orientation to a Shelter, HELP.

November 8, 1999. Basic Training Course on the Basic Law on Gender Equality. Tokyo Women's Foundation.

November 9, 1999. Creating Women's Centers of the Future. Tokyo Women's Foundation.

November 15, 1999. Women and Labor. Monthly study meeting, Beijing Japan Accountability Caucus (Beijing JAC).

November 15, 1999. Domestic Violence. Panel discussion, Tokyo metropolitan government.

November 16, 1999. Establishing a Human Rights Policy for the Elimination of Discrimination against Buraku People. Annual symposium of Buraku Liberation League, Tokyo branch.

November 25, 1999. School visit, Tamagawa Junior High School.

November 25–27, 1999. Empowerment Is the Password to the Twenty-First Century: Towards a New Relationship of Sharing the Joy of Living. National Women's Education Center.

November 27–28, 1999. Respond to Children's SOS. Annual Convention of Rights of the Child Forum 99. CRC Net and International Children's Rights Center.

December 2, 1999. Children's Human Rights under Armed Conflict. Women's Human Rights under Armed Conflicts: The 13th Study Group Meeting. Asian Women's Fund.

January 15, 2000. T-shirt Campaign against Domestic Violence. Women's Human Rights Sub-Committee, Human Rights Student Group, Waseda University.

January 17, 2000. Domestic Violence Prevention Law Project Team Interim Report. Japan Civil Liberties Union.

January 17–19, 2000. Workshop on National Plans of Action for Human Rights Education in the Asia-Pacific Region. Office of the UN High Commissioner for Human Rights.

January 20, 2000. Asia-Pacific Symposium on Trafficking in Persons. Japanese Ministry of Foreign Affairs.

January 28, 2000. Global Warming and Bio-Diversity: From a Perspective of Marine Life. Bio-Diversity Japan and GENKI (Women's Network for a Global Environment).

January 29, 2000. Violence against Women Campaign Meeting. Women's Human Rights Team, Amnesty International Japan.

February 16, 2000. Founding Meeting. Association to Examine Domestic Violence in the Tama Area.

February 18, 2000. Domestic Violence. Association of 6PM.

February 19, 2000. Work, Marriage, Child Rearing, and Caring: Reflections from the Beijing Conference Experience. For a gender-equal society seminar, Women's Overseas Tours Association in Tokyo (15th Group).

February 19, 2000. Consciousness Raising on Self-Image. Kanagawa Men's Lib Group.

March 4, 2000. The Testimony of a Taiwanese Comfort Woman. Video showing and discussion, Association on Women's Issues in Shinjuku-Ward in Tokyo.

March 5, 2000. Female Genital Mutilation Movement Today. Meeting, Association for the Elimination of FGM.

March 6, 2000. Future Issues Concerning the Support of Foreign Workers in Japan: The Role of NPOs in Japan. Japan Foundation.

March 8, 2000. University Sexual Harassment Study Meeting. Sexual Harassment Association at Ochanomizu University.

March 16, 2000. A Gathering of Students Concerned with Sexual Harassment: Have Workplaces and Universities Changed with Guidelines? Sexual Harassment Association at Ochanomizu University and Campus Sexual Harassment Network.

March 16, 2000. Domestic Violence and Child Abuse from a Legal Perspective. Association of 6PM.

March 27, 2000. Domestic Violence Prevention Law Expert Hearing. Female Diet members of the Social Democratic Party.

March 30–April 1, 2000. International Symposium on Chinese Comfort Women, Shanghai. Chinese Comfort Women Research Center, Shanghai Teachers College, Historical Research Journal Association, and Anti-Japanese War Journal Association.

April 4, 2000. Violence against Women Prevention Law Caucus Study Meeting. Beijing Japan Accountability Caucus.

April 11, 2000. Criminal Law Responses to Domestic Violence and Child Abuse: Measures in the U.S.-Japan Police Policy Research Center.

April 13, 2000. Contested Historiography—Feminist Perspectives on World War II. Deutsche Institut für Japanstudien.

April 27, 2000. 4th International Follow-up Seminar in Tokyo of the World Congress against Commercial Sexual Exploitation of Children in Stockholm, 1996. Embassy of Sweden, Japan Committee for UNICEF, and ECPAT/Stop (Japan).

June 5–9, 2000. UN Beijing-Plus-Five Conference, New York.

June 5–9, 2000. Presentations by Japanese nongovernmental groups at the Beijing-Plus-Five Feminist Symposia at the City University of New York.

December 8–12, 2000. Women's International War Crimes Tribunal on Japan's Military Sexual Slavery, Tokyo. Violence Against Women in War–Japan, Asian Center for Women's Human Rights, Korean Council for Women Drafted for Military Sexual Slavery by Japan.

December 8–12, 2000. Public Hearing on Current War Crimes against Women, Tokyo. Women's Caucus for Gender Justice.

August 23–September 7, 2001. NGO Forum and Intergovernmental World Conference against Racism, Durban. United Nations High Commissioner for Human Rights.

December 17–20, 2001. Second World Congress against Commercial Sexual Exploitation of Children, Yokohama. ECPAT and UNICEF.

Notes

Chapter 1

1. For a self-respect checklist used in assertiveness training, see Kawamura 1999. See also Inoue 1998.

2. The Okinawans have been categorically omitted in all of Japan's periodic reports to the UN Human Rights Committee and CERD (Committee on the Elimination of All Forms of Racial Discrimination) after Japan ratified the International Covenant on Civil and Political Rights in 1979 and ICERD in 1994.

3. For a discussion on Japan's low profile in promoting human rights regionally or internationally, see Onuma 1997. Onuma attributes five reasons for a weak human rights policy: "First, the notion of proselytizing for a high cause has been somewhat alien to Japan. In Japanese culture, the virtue of modesty is highly appreciated.... Second, legalistic thinking has been rather foreign to many Japanese.... Third, for the Japanese government the term 'diplomacy' meant, for most of the postwar period, nothing more than bilateral diplomacy.... International protection of human rights was regarded within this general or multilateral area, and as such, something to be handled by the United States and Western European nations.... Fourth, as in many other countries, the business circle in Japan has not been very interested in the human rights situation in developing countries.... Finally, the failure of Japan to confront the problem of war responsibility and colonial guilt prevented Japan from taking a leading role in Asia" (pp.54–55).

4. Keck and Sikkink 1998.

5. According to Peter Haas (1992), an epistemic community is a network of professionals with recognized expertise and competence in a particular domain and an authoritative claim to policy-relevant knowledge within that domain or issue-area.

6. For a comprehensive introduction and discussion, see Schwartz and Pharr 2003.

7. Sakai, quoted in Chow 1993.

8. For a further discussion, see Mackie 2002.

9. See Ramirez 2001, 356–74.

10. For a discussion on gendered exclusions in national histories in the case of military prostitution in Japan, see Mackie 2000.

11. Mackie 2001, 180–206.

12. Personal interview with Kyoko Akamatsu, former Japanese ambassador to the UN, May 2, 2000.

13. Quoted in Kajiyama 1999, 65.

Chapter 2

1. Johnson 1982.
2. Upham 1987, 12.
3. Pempel 1990.
4. Curtis 1999, 16.
5. Kohno 1997.
6. Calder 1987.
7. "Examining the more formal political realm and how it was influenced by postwar affluence, one finds that interest groups expanded in close conjunction with economic growth through at least the late 1960s" (Allinson 1993).
8. Okimoto 1989, 145.
9. Van Wolferen 1989.
10. McKean 1981.
11. Broadbent 1998.
12. Apter and Sawa 1984, 226.
13. LeBlanc 1999, 8.
14. Gerda 1979. Examples of "housewife studies" include LeBlanc 1999; Imamura 1978, 1987; Allison 1991; Harris and Long 1993.
15. See, for example, McCarthy and Zald 1977; McAdam 1982; Snow and Benford 1988; Tarrow 1983.
16. McAdam, Tarrow, and Tilly 1994, 22.
17. Ibid., 31.
18. Meyer et al. 1997.
19. The creation of a central world organizational frame at the end of World War II sped the development of world society. In the UN system, subjects related to an ever-broader range of social life are seen as legitimate topics to be discussed, rationalized, and organized: political structure, education, medicine and health, science, sexuality, population, natural resources, and children. The number of intergovernmental and nongovernmental organizations covering this broad range of activities has mushroomed since 1945. Boli and Thomas 1997.
20. See, for example, Wendt 1999.
21. Ruggie 1998, 33.
22. Keck and Sikkink 1998, 2.
23. Ibid.
24. Finnemore 1996, 136.
25. Risse-Kappen, 1995, 4–6.
26. Schreurs 1997, 156.
27. Gurowitz 1999, 414.
28. Okimoto 1989, 145.

Chapter 3

1. Rupp 1997; Miller 1991.

2. Rupp 1997, 14.

3. Miller 1991, 82.

4. "Another powerful argument for gender difference targeted wartime sexual violence as a stark boundary separating women from men. The International Council for Women Peace Committee protested in 1913 against 'the horrible violation of womanhood that attends all war,' and the quinquennial congress the following year appealed to the next international peace congress to take up the protection of women from rape in wartime" (Rupp 1997, 86).

5. "Organizationally, these first-wave women's organizations are formally structured with hierarchical officers and procedures that often reflect *Robert's Rules of Order*. Although these groups now have members from around the world, their leaders are drawn from the elite; their headquarters, and some would say orientation, are in the North. Most would consider women to have similar concerns everywhere for civil rights, education, and fair working conditions and so assume that there is one international women's movement. Second-wave women's organizations have discarded tight structures in favor of more egalitarian forms and have preferred networks or coalitions to formal international organizations. These groups tend to be more active in outreach to the poor or disadvantaged" (Tinker 1999).

6. For a detailed analysis, see Gaer 1998.

7. Prugl and Meyer 1999; Fitzpatrick 1994.

8. Joachim 1999, 144.

9. "When several Northern women's organizations condemned the operation as 'a barbaric practice imposed on women by male-dominated primitive societies' (Toubia 1995, 232), several Southern women's organizations defended it as a cultural practice and took the criticism of Northern women's groups as yet another expression of 'Western imperialism' " (quoted in Joachim 1999, 144).

10. "[Article] 140f calls on UN member states to improve the physical and mental health of all members of society through . . . the development of policies and programs aimed at the elimination of all forms of violence against women and children and the protection of women of all ages from the physical and mental abuse resulting from domestic violence, sexual assault, sexual exploitation, and any other form of abuse (United Nations 1980, 31)." Quoted in Joachim 1999, 159.

11. Charlotte Bunch, quoted in Joachim 1999, 146.

12. "Violence Against Women exists in various forms in everyday life in all societies. Women are beaten, mutilated, burned, sexually abused and raped. Such violence is a major obstacle to the achievement of peace and the other objectives of the Decade and should be given special attention. Women victims of violence should be given particular attention and comprehensive assistance. To this end, legal measures should be formulated to prevent violence and to assist women victims. National machinery should be established in order to deal with the question of violence against women within the family and society. Preventive policies should be elaborated, and institutionalized forms of assistance to women victims provided" ("Nairobi Forward-Looking Strategies for the Advancement of Women," United Nations 1985, paragraph 258; prostitution and trafficking provisions are contained in the next paragraph, 259).

13. Quoted in Carrillo 1997.

14. I draw this historical information primarily from the introductory chapter, "And Never the Twain Shall Meet," in *The International Human Rights of Women: Instruments of Change* (Gaer 1998).

15. Ibid., 26.

16. Clark, Friedman, and Hochstetler 1998.

17. Martha Alter Chen, quoted in Prugl and Meyer 1999, 11.

18. "The earliest documented conference link between environmentalists and women's activists was in 1982, when the United Nations Environment Program held a special meeting in Nairobi to evaluate the achievements of Stockholm, ten years after that conference. Although the meeting was not a global conference on the scale of Stockholm or Rio, about one hundred NGOs took part. A women's caucus met twice and established a network 'to increase the involvement of women's organizations in environmental issues'" ("ELCI Global Meeting on Environment and Development for NGO-Nairobi," quoted in Clark, Friedman, and Hochstetler 1998).

19. Clark, Friedman, and Hochstetler 1998.

20. According to Prugl and Meyer (1999, 12), "perhaps the most significant outcome of international conferencing for women has been that governments and international organizations have begun to take steps to mainstream, or integrate, a gender perspective into various policies, programs, and bureaucratic procedures."

21. The quantity of IGO, state, and NGO materials on violence against women at the Beijing-Plus-Five conference was phenomenal compared to the 1993 Vienna conference. UNIFEM had compiled "Women against Violence: Breaking the Silence" (1997). WHO had compiled an extensive report on female genital mutilation (1996). Every country report included information on women's human rights. Above all, NGOs distributed their work on violence against women. Some examples include Domestic Violence and Family Life as Experienced by Turkish Immigrant Women in Germany, Women for Women's Human Rights Reports No. 3, 1996, by Women for Women's Human Rights Turkey; Conveying Concerns: Women Report on Gender-Based Violence, by the Population Reference Bureau of MEASURE Communications with funding from USAID, 1998; and ASPBAE Mid-Report on Violence against Women in the Asia-Pacific Region, June 2000, funded by Toyota Foundation.

22. Carrillo 1997.

23. "Working for Women's Sexual Rights," *New York Times*, October 2, 2000.

24. Quoted in Carrillo 1997.

25. "The ad hoc Tribunals belittled the prospects of sexual assault prosecutions, asserting that any trials would be a forced bow to 1990s political correctness and that any judgments would be fatally devoid of legal rigor" (Sellers 1999, 1–13).

26. Article 3, common to all four Geneva Conventions, applied to noninternational armed conflicts and prohibited "outrages upon personal dignity." In addition, Article 27 of the Fourth Geneva Convention, relating to the protection of civilians in time of war, stipulates that "women shall be especially protected against any attack on their honour, in particular against rape, enforced prostitution, or any form of indecent assault."

27. See, for example, the historic judgment of The Prosecutor v. Jean-Paul Akayesu by the ICTR (ICTR-96-4-T), September 1998, and the judgment of The Prosecutor v. Anto Furundzija by the ICTY (IT-95-17/1-T), December 1998.

28. The information in this section is based on two summary leaflets, "Treatment of Sexual Violence in International Law" and "Gender Integration in the Statute of the International Criminal Court," by the Women's Caucus for Gender Justice.

29. The United Nations web site on the UN Convention against Transnational Organized Crime, www.undcp.org/crime_cicp_convention.html (accessed on May 12, 2002).

30. From the "Yokohama Global Commitment 2001," part II, adopted at the conclusion of the Second World Congress.

31. There were strong pressures from the United States and the United Kingdom for UNESCO to be intergovernmental, and programming principles were "put in place before any consideration had been given to the nature of UNESCO activities themselves" (Jones 1990, 46).

32. In 1953 UNESCO created the Associated School Project, which formed a network of high schools in different countries that experimented with applying UNESCO education initiatives. The first major recommendation, which concerned promoting international understanding, cooperation, and peace, was passed only in 1974. Soon the First International Congress on the Teaching of Human Rights was organized in 1978, and the First Meeting of Experts on the Teaching of Human Rights was convened in 1982. Little is known about what came out of these meetings.

33. For examples of efforts undertaken by various UN agencies, including UNDP, UNHCR, UNICEF, and WHO, see Office of the High Commissioner for Human Rights 1998.

34. As of 1998, countries that had set up national committees for human rights education included France, Argentina, the Philippines, Tunisia, and Uzbekistan, among others. For a complete list, see ibid. For a full report on the mid-decade evaluation by the Office of the High Commissioner for Human Rights, see www.unhchr.ch/Huridocda/Huridoca.nsf/(Symbol)/A.55.360.En?Opendocument.

35. West 1999, 187.

36. Al-Azhar, quoted in West 1999, 188.

37. Robin Morgan, quoted in West 1999, 188.

38. Druelle 2000.

39. "'In terms of sex education we have been adamant that abstinence be included as the strongest choice,' a U.S. official told reporters. 'Abstinence is the solution to the problems we are discussing at this conference. All the other forms of sex education are dealing with the side effects'" (Doug Saunders, "Compromise Saves UN Deal," *Globe and Mail*, May 11, 2002).

40. For more details of the final document, see the special session web site at www.unicef.org/specialsession/index.html.

41. Wolfrum 2001, 26.

42. Ibid.

43. Wolfrum 2001.

44. Center for Women's Global Leadership pamphlet, "A Women's Human Rights Approach to the World Conference against Racism."

45. Gallagher 1997.

46. Ibid.

47. Crenshaw 2000, 7, 11.

48. Author's observation in the WCAR drafting committees, September 7, 2001.

49. This footnote has its origins in the intense negotiations regarding the term "gender" during the Beijing Conference. In the UN Report of the Fourth World Conference on Women, the different interpretations and reservations by various states about the term "gender" are reported. See a discussion in Druelle 2001.

50. Author's observation in the WCAR drafting committee on the final Programme of Action, September 6, 2001.

51. For a detailed analysis of feminist mobilization at WCAR, see Chan-Tiberghien forthcoming.

52. Deborah Stienstra, quoted in Meyer and Prugl, 1999, 13.

53. Jean Bethke Elshtain, quoted in ibid., 13.

Chapter 4

1. *Asahi Evening News*, December 21, 1999.

2. "If men did not face any punishment for raping women, then all men—including myself—would be rapists" (ibid.).

3. Matsui 1997.

4. Shiga-Fujime 1993.

5. Personal interviews with the vice-director of the Christian Women Temperance Union (February 10, 2000) and the personal assistant of the late Fusae Ichikawa (April 7, 2000).

6. In the 1970s, because of the rapid economic growth, many Japanese men went on organized sex tours in Korea, Taiwan, Thailand, and the Philippines. For detailed analyses, see Matsui 1996.

7. Kawashima 1999, 7–8; Kanai 1994.

8. *Shasei sangyō* refers to a diverse range of pleasure businesses that offer sex services to stimulate ejaculation with the condition that there is no penetration.

9. "I don't think I am guilty of denying the self-determination of these women. I do, however, insist that Japanese women recognize their own complicity in the economic and political structures that create the poverty underlying the limited range of options available to these women. When you stop to ask how Japan maintains its present level of prosperity, you are confronted with the reality of the lives of the peoples of the Asia region. The economic hardships faced by the Filipino women are intimately linked with the profits Japanese corporations send back to their head offices from their overseas operations. Japanese women both support and benefit from this economic system. . . . One Japanese feminist commented on this position of mine in a recent article. She argued that it was not realistic for me to expect Japanese women to deal with the liberation of the women of Asia when so many of us still don't have even the most basic understanding of our own status and rights. This is the old 'help those in your own backyard first' approach, and I cannot accept it. The problem arises from a willingness to separate the lack of politicization and self-awareness among Japanese women and Japan's role in the Asian region. The existing patriarchal structures have colonized women's bodies, Japanese and Filipino alike, just as they have colonized this entire geographic region" (Matsui 1997, 137–38).

10. The Tokyo metropolitan government in 1997 conducted the first public survey

on domestic violence in Japan, and the prime minister's office conducted the first national survey on the same issue in 1999.

11. The Council for Gender Equality organized the first public symposium on violence against women in 1998, a symposium that has since become an annual event. Meanwhile, lectures, seminars, and workshops on various issues related to violence against women organized by public women's centers have dramatically expanded in the past few years. This will be further discussed in chapter 6 on education and training concerning violence against women.

12 Yamashita 1993.

13. "The [National] Plan [of Action] states government commitment to strive to end all forms of violence against women as one of the measures to attain peace in the National Report of the Government of Japan for the Fourth World Conference on Women by the Council for Gender Equality, the Prime Minister's Office (1994, 42)."

14. Personal interview with a staff member of the Policy Section, Women's Bureau, Ministry of Labor, March 27, 2000.

15. Figures quoted in Kuninobu 2000.

16. According to Masao Kaneko, counselor and expert on sexual harassment in the Labor Bureau of the Tokyo metropolitan government (personal interview, March 14, 2000).

17. Personal interview, March 19, 2000.

18. Personal interview, March 24, 2000.

19. Okuyama 1999.

20. Campus Sexual Harassment Network 1999.

21. According to Masao Kaneko, counselor and expert on sexual harassment in the Labor Bureau of Tokyo metropolitan government (personal interview, March 14, 2000).

22. No national survey has yet been conducted. The latest regional survey in northern and eastern Japan conducted by the Campus Sexual Harassment Network in March 2000 found that out of a sample of forty-eight universities, forty-six had either planned or put into place a sexual harassment policy (more precisely, five had established a sexual harassment policy before the Ministry of Education guidelines took effect in March 1999; fifteen introduced a policy after the Ministry of Education guidelines took effect; and sixteen had concrete plans for a sexual harassment policy from April 2000) (Campus Sexual Harassment Network Northern and Eastern Japan Bloc meeting, March 2000).

23. The system was almost scrapped (made voluntary rather than mandatory) under the decentralization reforms of Hashimoto in 1996 and was saved only after serious protests by counselors and women's groups.

24. Personal interview with a women counselor of Kiyose City Women's Center, Tokyo, February 16, 2000.

25. Harada 1998.

26. Communication No. 514 from the Child Family Bureau Chief of the Ministry of Health and Welfare to all mayors and governors.

27. Personal interview with the deputy manager of the Women's Assistance Unit, Family Assistance Section, Social Protection Bureau of the Ministry of Health and Welfare, April 28, 2000. In fact, the Women's Assistance Unit is so small that it does not even figure in the organizational chart of the ministry.

28. Ibid.

29. Ibid.

30. The fourth Japanese government report to the CEDAW Committee on the implementation of CEDAW in Japan, 1998.

31. "The Present Situation of the Police-led Assistance Program for Crime Victims in Japan—Centering on the Assistance to Victims of Sex Crimes," presentation by the deputy manager in charge of sex crimes of the First Criminal Investigation Division of the National Police Agency at the Ninth International Symposium on Victimology in 1997. Document received at the personal interview with the deputy manager on May 2, 2000.

32. Ibid.

33. "*Gaman*" means to bear with the situation, an act that is often considered a virtue in Japan. Personal interview with a staff member of Josei no Ie, SARA (a four-room shelter established in 1992), March 14, 2000.

34. Personal interview with the deputy manager in charge of sex crimes, First Criminal Investigation Division of the National Police Agency, May 2, 2000.

35. By 1960, every prefecture had at least one *fujin kaikan*. In 1991, they numbered 123 throughout Japan (Fujin Dantai Rengō, 1993).

36. Ito 1999.

37. For example, in 1996, the name of the annual summer workshop organized by NWEC was changed from Women's Studies Forum to Women's Studies and Gender Research Forum. The theme of the 1999 NWEC International Forum was empowerment, and the keynote speech was "Women and Human Rights." For a detailed discussion, see Inoue, Tanaka, et al. 1999.

38. Personal interview with the specialist in the Gender Equality Learning Division, Lifelong Education Division, Ministry of Education, April 24, 2000.

39. Personal interview with the director general of the National Women's Education Center, Ministry of Education, April 21, 2000.

40. Ibid.

41. The Yokohama city government created the Jose e no Bōryoku no Sōdan Nado no Kanrenkikan Renrakukai (Network on Counseling and Other Institutions on Violence against Women) in 1998, which meets four times per year. Personal interview with the coordinator, Counseling Section, Yokohama Women's Center, March 2, 2000.

42. Ibid.

43. Dawn Center newsletter, November 1998. Telephone interview with program coordinator, Dawn Center, April 23, 2000.

44. For a table summarizing the changes before and after the revision of the law, see Pamphlet No. 17 of the Women's Bureau, Ministry of Labor, May 1999.

45. The original Japanese title of the Vision Plan, as well as Basic Law on Gender Equality (Danjo Kyōdō Sankaku) actually means "equal gender participation" and has been heavily criticized by feminist scholars and women's groups alike for its ambiguity and lack of boldness. Local ordinances, however, are named under either equal gender participation (Danjo Kyōdō Sankaku) or gender equality (Danjyo Byōdō).

46. For a critique of this law emphasizing the equal participation, rather than equality, between men and women, see Nakajima 2000.

47. International Cooperation—Adoption of the Resolution on "The Role of the United Nations Development Fund for Women in Eliminating Violence against Women" (www.sorifu.go.jp/dangjyo/women96/international/i2.html).

Chapter 5

1. Norgren 1998, 63.
2. Ashino 1999a, 86.
3. "Family planners and mainstream women's organizations stayed on the sidelines of the pill debate, and feminist groups—with the exception of a radical feminist group called Chūpiren—did not advocate pill approval. Japanese feminists took this position in part because of reports from US feminists that oral contraceptives had not been adequately tested and had dangerous side effects, fueling their suspicions that drug companies and doctors were conspiring with the government to reap profits at the expense of women's health. But Japanese feminists were also afraid that if the pill was approved, it would help justify limiting access to abortion" (Norgren 1998, 87).
4. Ashino 1999a.
5. Quoted in Ashino 1999b, 36.
6. Tsunoda 1993a, 54.
7. Ibid., 56.
8. The phrase used in Japanese is "*shokuba ni oite okonawareru seiteki na gendō*," which means "sexual words or actions at the workplace."
9. Testimony of three comfort women who brought their cases to a local court in Shimonoseki, a port city where many forced laborers and comfort women arrived from Pusan in South Korea, in 1992.
10. Yoshimi 1995.
11. Ibid.
12. The lack of attention paid to the comfort system as a crime by the American military has been criticized by many Japanese scholars including Toshiyuki Tanaka, quoted in Ueno 1998.
13. Yoshimi 1995.
14. Suzuki 1997.
15. "The Korean women's groups already saw the linkage between the comfort system and present-day sex tourism. At that time, Japanese women's groups did not pick up the issue." Personal interview with the executive director of Violence against Women in War-Net Japan and a veteran feminist involved in the sex tourism campaign in the 1970s, April 20, 2000.
16. Speech at the First Asian Solidarity Forum on Military Sexual Slavery in 1992, recorded in "Against Prostitution and Sexual Exploitation Activities in Japan," by the Japan Anti-Prostitution Association, September 1997.
17. Personal interview with the former president of the Democratic Korean Women's Club, a Korean resident club in Japan, April 21, 2000.
18. Speech at the First Asian Solidarity Forum on Military Sexual Slavery in 1992, recorded in "Against Prostitution and Sexual Exploitation Activities in Japan," by the Japan Anti-Prostitution Association, September 1997.
19. Suzuki 1997.

20. Yoshimi 1995.

21. Suzuki 1997.

22. Ueno 1998.

23. "Tokyo Vows to Solve School Book Dispute," *Financial Times*, May 2, 2001.

24. Tawara 1997.

25. Ibid., 58.

26. Quoted in Suzuki 1997, 80.

27. For details, see Tawara 1997.

28. "Textbooks from seven other publishers that are now in use include references to 'comfort women,' the euphemism for women forced to provide sex for Japanese soldiers in wartime. In the editions that will be in use beginning with the 2002 school year, three of the seven publishers make no mention of comfort women at all. . . . Representatives of the respective publishers said the references were taken out because teachers had complained of the difficulty of teaching about issues involving sex in the classroom" ("Other Texts Scale Back War References: An Excuse for Dropping the Issue of 'Comfort Women' Is That It Is Difficult to Teach Sex in the Classroom," *Asahi Shimbun*, April 5, 2001).

29. "South Korea on Tuesday formally demanded that Japan make thirty-five revisions to eight junior high history textbooks that critics say gloss over Japan's wartime atrocities and its colonial rule of the Korean Peninsula. Han Seung Soo, South Korea's foreign affairs and trade minister, summoned Japanese ambassador Terusuke Terada and handed over the written request, making the textbook issue an official diplomatic problem between the two countries" ("Seoul Seeks History Text Changes: Revision Request Turns Issue into Official Diplomatic Problem," *Japan Times*, May 9, 2001).

30. "A potentially far-reaching settlement was reached here today in a court case brought on behalf of nearly 1,000 Chinese who were forced to work in Japan in World War II. The largest general contractor in Japan, the Kajima Corporation, agreed to establish a fund with 500 million yen, or $4.6 million, to compensate wartime laborers at its Hanaoka copper mine and their survivors. The Chinese Red Cross will administer the fund. The agreement could set a precedent for dozens of similar cases here and in the United States, where Chinese, Koreans, Filipinos and Americans forced to work on behalf of the Japanese war effort are seeking compensation from corporations like Mitsubishi and Mitsui. 'This settlement is extremely significant, because companies similarly accused are likely to set up similar funds to deal with wartime compensation issues,' said Yoshitaka Takagi, head of the Association of Lawyers for Coordinating Action Seeking Postwar Compensation" ("Fund for Wartime Slaves Set Up in Japan," *New York Times*, November 30, 2000).

31. Otto (Koibito) kara no Bōryoku Survey Research Group "*Domesutikku Baiorensu*" (Domestic violence), 1999, 1.

32. Personal interview with the former Japanese ambassador to the UN, May 2, 2000.

33. Watanabe 1994.

34. For case details, see Nichibenren 2000.

35. See, for example, "Workshop to Solve Violence against Women," Forum Yokohama, 1997, and "Domestic Violence: The Legal Policies of Advanced Countries," Kanagawa Women's Center, 1996.

36. The first nongovernmental shelter for immigrant battered women, HELP, was created in 1987. Until 1993, there were only seven shelters in Japan. Thirteen more were created between 1993 and 1999.

37. HELP Asian Women's Shelter, Network News No. 33 and 35, September 1998 and May 1999.

38. Personal interviews with the founders of Men's Lib Tokyo (May 1, 2000) and Men's Lib Kanagawa (February 19, 2000).

39. According to the Report on Violence against Women Survey conducted by the Kanagawa Women's Center between January 1998 and March 1999, there were 206 media reports on the topic of domestic violence although the phrase "domestic violence" was virtually unknown before 1995.

40. For example, the public channel Nihon Hōsō Kyōkai (Japan Broadcasting) featured a program on domestic violence during prime time in December 1999.

41. Moriyama 1999.

42. According to the Summary of Activity 1992–1999 of ECPAT Japan.

43. Ibid.

Chapter 6

1. An official in the Human Rights Education Section within the Civil Liberties Bureau confirmed in a personal interview (May 1, 2000) that human rights education and, more recently, training remain the primary activity of the bureau.

2. As noted in the concluding observations of the UN Human Rights Committee concerning the Japanese government's fourth periodic report in 1998, "The Committee is of the view that the Civil Liberties Commission is not [an effective] mechanism, since it is supervised by the Ministry of Justice, and its powers are strictly limited to issuing recommendations" (Working Paper for UN Workshop on National Plans of Action for Human Rights Education in the Asia-Pacific Region, Tokyo, January 17–19, 2000, Japan Federation of Bar Associations).

3. Human Rights Forum 21, 1998.

4. Patel 1996.

5. Hara 1995.

6. Morita 1999, 40.

7. In one of the recent CRC annual sessions in Geneva, the CRC Committee asked the Japanese why women were underrepresented in their delegation.

8. Federation for the Protection of Children's Human Rights (Japan) 1997.

9. For details of local government measures, see ibid.

10. Personal interview with the founder and representative of CRC Network.

11. Preamble, National Plan of Action for HRE, 1997.

12. The specialized professions include thirteen categories: judges, those working in correctional services, immigration officers, teachers, medical professionals, welfare officers, marine security officers, labor administrators, fire fighters, police, self-defense officers, civil servants, and mass media professionals.

13. "Buraku Liberation Tokyo Symposium Report," 1999.

14. For details, see "The End of Dowa Education," *Kaiho Kyoiku*, Special Edition, December 1999.

15. See, for example, "Gender and Sexuality Education" in the Summer 1999 issue and "Gender Empowerment and Education" in the Autumn 1999 issue.

16. For example, IMADR (International Movement against All Forms of Discrimination and Racism) Japan, which has traditionally focused on Buraku issues, started a "minority women" subgroup with monthly study meetings in 1999. Personal interview with the undersecretary-general, May 10, 2000.

17. For example, the Solidarity Network with Migrant Workers Japan started projects that focused on the issues of domestic violence, trafficking, and domestic workers.

18. Clemens 1993, 755–98.

19. Forerunner of Women's Studies: Fujin Mondai Jurokko (Sixteen Lectures on Women's Problems) in 1925 by Oku Mumeo, quoted in Tokuza 1999.

20. Many scholars have noted the development of "women's studies" outside academia in Japan as a characteristic of women's studies in Japan. See Kanai 1998.

21. Personal interview with one of the founders of the Domestic Violence Prevention Project for Batterers (1998), April 18, 2000.

22. These represent some of the themes addressed by Forum on Sex Issues, a pioneering NGO focusing on sex education. See their quarterly newsletter "Anata to watashi to sei" (Let's talk about sexuality).

23. Telephone interview with the executive director of the Empowerment Center, Osaka, a pioneer CAP group in Japan, April 18, 2000.

24. Ibid.

25. "Many Youths Dissatisfied with Sex Education: Study," *Japan Times*, August 21, 2001.

26. See Freire 1970.

27. hooks 1994, 12.

28. Sattler 2000, xii, xix.

29. For example, in 1997 the Northern Kyushu Women's Center called their seminars "*enpawāmento no Joseigaku*" (women's studies for empowerment).

30. National Women's Education Center 1999, 198–203.

31. Ibid. In November 1999 I participated in a three-day conference at NWEC entitled "Empowerment Education." There was little consensus on what the term really meant and how it could be achieved.

32. See Nakamura 1998.

33. Kaku Sechiyama, quoted in Ueno 1997a.

34. Personal interview with the founder of Men's Lib Tokyo, May 1, 2000.

35. For example, Morita 1999.

36. Personal interview with a batterer counselor, April 7, 2000.

37. Personal interview with the executive director of Femix, a publishing and CR/AT training company, January 20, 2000.

38. Personal interview with the founder of ARC (Action for the Rights of Children), April 17, 2000.

39. Personal interview, April 17, 2000.

40. Personal interview with the founder and executive director of the Forum on Sex Issues, February 15, 2000.

41. "Twenty years ago, there was not much mentioning of 'comfort women' in Japanese history textbooks. Just when it has gotten better since the late 1980s, the latest resur-

gence of right-wing mobilization threatens the fruits of our long battle. Now we spend most of our energy in reversing the worsening textbook movement." Personal interview with the vice-director of Children and Textbooks Japan Net 21, May 10, 2000.

42. Personal interview with a feminist legal scholar at Ochanomizu University, March 16, 2000.

43. Rape, sexual harassment, domestic violence, shelter, reproductive rights, empowerment, women's human rights, violence against women, gender, and trafficking, respectively.

44. Office for Gender Equality newsletter, January 2000.

45. Personal interview, April 25, 2000.

46. Personal interview with Professor Kita Akito, Waseda University School of Education, April 19, 2000.

47. Only nine NGOs were present, six of which were Japanese. There were complaints among NGO participants that the Ministry of Foreign Affairs did not inform the NGO community about the workshop until a few days before it took place.

48. Japan's National Plan of Action for UN Decade for Human Rights Education, 1996.

49. Personal interview with the president of the Sexual Harassment Guideline Working Group, Waseda University, April 26, 2000.

Chapter 7

1. The First and Second Report by the Japanese government on the International Convention on the Elimination of All Forms of Racial Discrimination, June 1999.

2. Ibid.; NGO Committee for the Reporting on the ICERD 2001.

3. Herbert 1996.

4. Neary 2002.

5. Weiner 1997.

6. Ibid., 10–11.

7. Lie 2001.

8. Kerr 2000, 447–48.

9. Duus 1995.

10. Lie 2001, 107.

11. Ibid.

12. Ibid.

13. On the Burakumin, see Neary 1989; on the Ainu, Siddle 1996, 39; on Okinawans, Taira 1997; on Koreans, Fukuoka 2000; and Ryang 2001; and on foreign workers, Herbert 1996, Hingwan 1996, and Brody 2001.

14. Upham 1987; Patel 1996.

15. Neary 1997.

16. Siddle 1996.

17. "We are now editing our history, claiming our rights, understanding our identity, beginning to walk for ourselves. As we advance our work, we can gain solidarity, with the Buraku Liberation movement, the movement of Koreans in Japan, the physically handicapped, the women's movement, and various citizens' movements. Some people have indicated that the anti-nuclear movement seen from an international view-

point has close relation to us as a minority's problem." Tokuhei Narita, quoted in Siddle 1996, 39.

18. Gurowitz 1999, 413–45.

19. Lie 2001, 100.

20. Personal interview, December 19, 2001.

21. Yuki Fujime, quoted in Ueno 1997a.

22. Ogoshi 1997, 244.

23. Presentation at the international symposium Contested Historiography: Feminist Perspectives on World War II, German Institute of Japanese Studies, Tokyo, April 13–14, 2000.

24. Matsui 1997, 136. For critiques of mainstream Japanese feminism, see also Tomioka 1997; and Cho 1997. See also Matsui and Wakakuwa et al. 1996.

25. Sellek 1997.

26. Mori, quoted in Brody 2001, 41. The rationale was laid out in the monthly magazine of the LDP: "Admitting Nikkeijin legally will greatly help to ameliorate the present acute labor shortage. People who oppose the admission of the unskilled are afraid of racial discrimination against foreigners. Indeed, if Japan admitted many Asians with different cultures and customs than those of Japanese, Japan's homogeneous ethnic composition would collapse. However, if Nikkeijin were admitted, this would not be a problem. . . . Nikkeijin, as relatives of the Japanese, would be able to assimilate into Japanese society regardless of nationality and language" (Nojima, quoted in Linger 2001, 23).

27. The First and Second Report by the Japanese government on the International Convention on the Elimination of All Forms of Racial Discrimination, June 1999.

28. "Fuhō Taizai 21 Nin ga Shuttō: Zairyu Kyoka wo Mitomeru" (21 Illegal Residents Come Out: The Demand for Residency Permits), *Asahi Shimbun*, September 2, 1999.

29. Herbert 1997.

30. "Japan's Cultural Bias against Foreigners Comes Under Attack." *New York Times*, November 15, 1999; "The Fight for Equal Protection of the Law: Judgment could Deal Blow to Discrimination," *Japan Times*, November 8, 2002 and "Bathhouse Loses Racism Lawsuit: Men Barred at Otaru Bath Awarded 3 Million Yen in Damages," *Japan Times*: November 12, 2002.

31. Szymkowiak and Steinhoff 1995, 265.

32. See Cripps 1996 and Shimizu 1999.

33. NGO Committee for the Reporting on the ICERD 2001. See also Yayori Matsui. 2000. "The Governor of Tokyo Ishihara Is a Proponent of Ethnic Discrimination (Racism) and an Advocate of Sexism—We Demand His Resignation!" Asia-Japan Women's Resource Center, *Women's Asia 21: Voices from Japan*, no. 6 (Autumn).

34. Howard French, "Koizumi's Visit to War Shrine Angers Japan's Neighbors," *New York Times*, April 22, 2002.

35. For a detailed political discussion on the passage of the law, see Pekkanen 2000.

36. Peek 1992, 217–29; Yasuhiko Saito, quoted in Buhmann 1989, 10.

37. See table for note 37.

38. As Owada (1999: 359) argues, "this basic posture of Japan for scrupulous observance of the law did not basically go beyond an attitude of passive observance of the law born out of the concern that such scrupulous observance was a prerequisite for Japan to be accepted as a worthy member of the community of civilized nations."

TABLE FOR NOTE 37

Conventions	UN adoption year	Japan ratification year
Trafficking and Prostitution	1949	1956
Political Rights of Women	1952	1955
Nationality of Married Women	1957	Not ratified
Refugees	1951	1982
Racism (CERD)	1965	1995
Economic, Social, and Cultural Rights (CESCR)	1966	1979
Civil and Political (CCPR)	1966	1979
Women (CEDAW)	1979	1985
Torture (CAT)	1984	1996
Children (CRC)	1990	1994
Migrants	2003	Not ratified

Source: Buhmann 1989 and Human Rights Forum 21 1998.

39. Patel 1996. The Human Rights Committee of the United Nations (International Human Forum 21) has heavily criticized this often-invoked umbrella injunction by Japanese courts (International Human Rights NGO Network 1999).

40. Members of the NGO Liaison Group include the Japan Civil Liberties Union, Japan Human Rights Information Center, Domestic Violence Survey Research Group, and International Movement against All Forms of Discrimination and Racism. For a full list, see Ebashi and Sekai Jinken Kaigi NGO Renrakukai 1996, 196.

41. Uemura 2002.

42. Ibid.

43. Lie 1999, 47.

44. Tominaga 1999; the First and Second Report by the Japanese government on the International Convention on the Elimination of All Forms of Racial Discrimination, June 1999.

45. For a discussion, see Miyazaki 1999.

46. Tominaga 1999.

47. Onoyama 2002.

48. IMADR 2001.

49. www.hrw.org/campaigns/caste/.

50. It states, "Caste is a historically entrenched, false ideological construct which often has religious and ideological sanction, and which allows for the treatment of some people as inferior. Casteism and racism operate at personal, social and structural levels. Caste is descent and occupation based and hereditary in nature, determined by one's birth into a particular caste. Caste and descent-based discrimination affects nearly 240 million people in the Asia Pacific region, for example, Dalits in India and Nepal and Burakumin in Japan, irrespective of the faith that they practice. . . . We assert that Untouchability is a Crime against Humanity (paragraphs 26–28)" (IMADR 2001).

51. Onoyama 2002.

52. Ibid.

53. Mushakoji 2002.

54. Ibid., 14.

55. Onoyama 2002.

56. Siddle 1996.

57. Supplementary Report on the First and Second Report, submitted by Japan's government under the International Convention on the Elimination of All Forms of Racial Discrimination, Ainu Association of Hokkaido, 2001.

58. The government report wrote, "As for the question of the people of Ainu raised in relation to Article 27, while it is recognized that these people preserve their own religion and language and maintain their own culture, they are not denied enjoyment of the right mentioned above, as Japanese nationals who are guaranteed equality under the Japanese Constitution." Ibid.

59. Uemura 1999.

60. "Comprehensively viewing the above-recognized facts, we can see that for the most part the Ainu people have inhabited Hokkaido from before the extension of our country's rule. They formed their own culture and had an identity. And even after their governance was assumed by our country, even after suffering enormous social and economic devastation wrought by policies adopted by the majority, they remain a social group that has not lost this unique culture and identity. Accordingly, the definition provided above of an 'indigenous people' should certainly apply" (NGO Committee for the Reporting on the ICERD 2001). For a full analysis of the case, see Stevens 2001.

61. "Appeal to WCAR Participants on Racism and Racial Discrimination and Related Intolerance in Japan," Durban, Issho Kikaku, a member organization of Durban 2001 Japan, August 30, 2001.

62. Presentation by Luis-Enrique Chavez, chairperson of the Working Group on the Draft Declaration of the Rights of Indigenous Peoples, September 5, 2001, at WCAR.

63. Hasegawa 2002.

64. Taira 1997.

65. Kikuzato 2002.

66. Ibid.

67. Taira 1997.

68. Kikuzato 2002.

69. Taira 1997.

70. Ibid.

71. NGO Committee for the Reporting on the ICERD 2001.

72. The First and Second Report by the Japanese government on the International Convention on the Elimination of All Forms of Racial Discrimination, June 1999.

73. Okamoto 1999b.

74. Ibid.

75. Maeda 2002.

76. Author's observation in the WCAR drafting committees, September 4, 2001.

77. The First and Second Report by the Japanese government on the International Convention on the Elimination of All Forms of Racial Discrimination, June 1999.

78. NGO Committee for the Reporting on the ICERD 2001.

79. Okamoto 1999a.

80. Koyama 1999.

81. Inaba 2002; "Migration and Refugee NGO Caucus Background Document:

Contribution to the Draft Declaration," August 2001, "produced collectively by NGOs involved at various stages of the preparatory process."

82. A preamble paragraph, for example, reads, "Reaffirming that States have the duty to protect and promote the human rights and fundamental freedoms of all [indigenous peoples, people of African descent, people of Asian descent, migrants—documented and undocumented—refugees and asylum-seekers, internally displaced persons, and persons belonging to other vulnerable groups], and that they should apply a gender perspective, recognizing the multiple forms of discrimination which women can face, and that the enjoyment of their civil, political, economic, social and cultural rights is essential for the development of societies throughout the world . . ."

83. This represented a step backward for the Migration and Refugees Caucus, which had emphasized that it was "extremely important for 'undocumented' to be mentioned, as they are in a particularly vulnerable situation. Reference to 'undocumented' was already included in the 1978 and 1983 world conferences against racism, in paras. 24 and 26 respectively. It is unacceptable that the twenty-first-century World Conference against Racism should settle for anything less than what was recognized twenty years ago." "Migration and Refugee NGO Caucus Background Document: Contribution to the Draft Declaration," August 2001.

84. Author's observation in the WCAR drafting committees, September 5, 2001.

85. Ibid.

86. Takeuchi 2002. See also Okuda 1997.

87. Hasegawa 2002.

88. Yui 1997.

89. IMADR, Comments on the Japanese Fourth and Fifth Government Reports to CEDAW (December 27, 2002).

90. Ito 2002.

91. For a full report of the twelve meetings of the Research Group on Multiple Discrimination against Minority Women between 1999 and 2000, see IMADR 2002.

92. One state representative from the OIC (Organization of Islamic Countries) protested the frequent use of the term "gender-sensitive," arguing that it "made no sense in Arabic," while many Asian, African, and Islamic states as well as the Holy See were against adding gender in the racism conference for fear of "diluting" it, and were vehemently opposed to any mention of sexual orientation in the outcome texts. For a detailed analysis of feminist mobilization at WCAR, see Chan-Tiberghien forthcoming.

93. See in the Declaration, paragraphs 2, 54a, and 69, and in the Programme of Action, paragraphs 14, 18, 31, 49, 79, 104c, 172, and 212.

94. Paragraph 8 states that "women belonging to these minority groups, whether Japanese or non-Japanese, are often excluded from the planned beneficiaries of (or benefit little from) the measures that the government claims to have taken in its reports to CEDAW for the empowerment of women (Article 3), gender equality (Article 10), participation of women in public life (Article 7), a better choice of jobs and vocational training (Article 11), health care and other services (Articles 11 and 12), and protection from domestic violence and remedies (Article 16)."

Chapter 8

1. Nearly one hundred sexual harassment cases alone were filed between 1989 and 1999, and almost all the plaintiffs won (personal interview with a sexual harassment expert lawyer, April 13, 2001). In the case of comfort women, "since the 1980s, victims around the region like the sex slaves, or 'comfort women,' have launched more than 50 legal battles to force Japan to unequivocally apologize and pay compensation to individuals for wartime atrocities" ("Sorry Is the Hardest Word: The Failure of Japanese Leaders to Come to Terms with the Country's Wartime Past Mystifies Many," *Far East Economic Review*, March 8, 2001). In May 2001, a Tokyo High Court judge was arrested on suspicion of having sex with a fourteen-year-old girl, and a Yokohama man was arrested on suspicion of putting pornographic images of young girls on a web site in violation of the national law banning child prostitution, which covers child pornography. The pornography on the web site run by Naotaka Sekino, a twenty-four-year-old company employee, was discovered by investigative authorities in Denmark, who notified their Japanese counterparts ("Yokohama Man Held for Child Porn," *Japan Times*, May 20, 2001; and "Judge Held over Sex with Girl, 14," *Asahi Shimbun*, May 21, 2001).

2. Narita 1999.

3. Curtis 1999.

4. Osawa 2000.

5. The formal coalition ended in November 1996, but cooperation between the three parties in the Diet continued until mid-1998.

6. "Why is Japanese abortion policy liberal, whereas contraception policy is conservative? The government legalized late-term abortions in 1948 but has not yet approved oral contraception (the pill). This paper argues that the contradictory policies are products of very different interest group configurations and historical circumstances. Doctors and family planners used a small window of opportunity to legalize abortion; afterward, doctors and women battled religious groups to uphold the law. The pill first appeared at a historically inauspicious time, and the pharmaceutical industry was its lone champion: until recently, doctors, midwives, family planners, and women opposed the pill as a threat to their livelihoods, abortion rights, and women's health" (Norgren 1998, 59).

7. "It is widely believed, however, that the real reason the pill ban has not been lifted is that bureaucrats fear pill use would further lower Japan's already low birth rate—an idea first planted in their minds 30 years ago by the same groups that now advocate approval. And so far, [the Ministry of Health and Welfare] has held firm in the face of sustained lobbying by doctors, family planners, pharmaceutical companies, and concerned politicians, aided in maintaining its anti-pill position by the fact that the majority of ordinary Japanese women, as well as midwives, female *hyoronka* (social commentators), and most feminists, view the pill with suspicion and express little interest in using it. Over the last decade, only 13 percent of Japanese women at most have said they would want to use the pill if it was approved" (Ashino 1999a, 90).

8. As a specialist in the Office of Labor Law of Nikkeiren told me, "Since the Japanese government has taken up the issue, we follow" (personal interview, April 20, 2000).

9. "It's sad to say, but the offices of conservative Diet members are swarming with nationalists," says Akira Yamada, a history professor at Meiji University in Tokyo, who

has written extensively about Japanese war guilt. Cemented at the turn of the 19th century, conservative politicians' ties to the far right have proved remarkably resilient. Today, the bulk of the LDP's leadership relies on right-wing thugs as fixers. What is more, as a weak economy has cut into campaign donations, the entire party has grown more dependent on money from single-issue religious groups dedicated to glorifying Japan's military past. . . . In any case, LDP links to right-wing extremists are arguably less disconcerting than its links to nationalist religious groups. Of these, one of the most powerful is the million-strong Japan Association of the Bereaved Families of the War Dead. [. . .] 'It's simple,' says Nobunao Tanaka, the co-author of a stinging critique of the association's influence on images of the war in school textbooks and daily discourse. 'The War Bereaved Association gets out the vote for the LDP and gives it money, and in exchange the LDP has to swallow the association's idea'" ("Sorry Is the Hardest Word: The Failure of Japanese Leaders to Come to Terms with the Country's Wartime Past Mystifies Many," *Far East Economic Review*, March 8, 2001).

10. These veterans included Yuri Morita and Tokiko Tagami. See Morita 1999.

11. Personal interview with a board member of the DV Survey Research Group, February 13, 2000.

12. The word "shelter" did not exist in Japanese until the early 1990s. The word "*kakegomidera*" was used until recently, but it referred specifically to refuge for prostitutes.

13. "We, Filipino women got to know of the existence of 'comfort women' during the Asian Conference on Women in Seoul last December 1991. Public attention was then given to three Korean women who came out in the open to tell their stories and to sue the Japanese government for the inhumanity of forcing the women to serve as sex slaves during World War II. Our sisters from Korea reported that 70,000–200,000 Korean women were forced to become sex slaves by the Japanese Imperial Army and herded to occupied countries in Asia. On March 10, 1992, a news article in a Philippine newspaper reported that among the thousands of 'comfort women' during World War II were Filipino women" (Nelia Sancho 1998, 7).

14. "I consider the suppression of the shame of sexual violence victims itself an intolerable act of sexual violence" (Yumiko Ehara, quoted in Ueno 1998, 106).

15. Personal interview, April 21, 2000.

16. Personal interview with a board member of Femin, Women's Democratic Club, March 13, 2000.

17. Only sixteen Japanese NGOs participated in the World Conference on Human Rights in Vienna in 1993, and only a few hundred Japanese participated in the Cairo Conference on Population and Development. In great contrast, hundreds of Japanese NGOs and about six thousand Japanese went to Beijing in 1995.

18. Personal interview with the counseling director, Forum Yokohama, March 24, 2000.

19. Personal interview with a Korean resident feminist activist, board member of VAWW-Net Japan, April 2, 2000.

20. Ashino 1999a.

21. The eleven founding members of Japan's Network for Women and Health were Makiko Arima, Yuriko Ashino, Akiko Domoto, Kuniko Funabashi, Hiroko Hara, Keiko

Higuchi, Kiyoko Ikegami, Yuriko Marumoto, Yoriko Meguro, Masako Owaki, and Yumiko Jansson-Yanagisawa (Japan's Network for Women and Health 1995).

22. Ibid., 5.

23. Newsletter "Akiko Network," Winter 1999.

24. Ashino 1999a, 87–88.

25. Moriyama 1999.

26. ECPAT International home page, www.ecpat.net/ecpat1/index2.htm.

27. The LDP preferred sixteen to eighteen as age below which prostitution is prohibited, to emphasize the children's "well-being" rather than their human rights, and to exclude the possession of pornographic materials for personal consumption from the mandate of the law.

28. Ever since the Convention on the Rights of the Child (CRC) became an issue in Japan in the early 1990s, the terms used to refer to children have become the subject of a political debate. In Japanese, there are several words for "children," including "*jidō*," "*kodomo*," and "*shōnen*." When the Japanese government officially translated the CRC, it used "*jidō*," which is the term used in other child welfare laws and policies. However, nongovernmental groups and some politicians have urged the use of the more neutral "*kodomo*" instead of "*jidō*," which connotes protection. The term "*jidō*," proposed by the coalition, is used in the current law. The second point of contention relates to the definition and scope of child prostitution. The coalition preferred a broader definition that included "sexual intercourse and/or similar acts performed," while the opposition wanted strictly "sexual intercourse." The former is now incorporated in the law. The third argument is whether pornography should be defined as consisting of the "naked or half-naked bodies of children" or the more restrictive "sexual organs of children." The former, proposed in the coalition bill, was kept. The fourth argument is over the duration of the penalty. The lighter sentence of three years, proposed by the opposition, was finally adopted over a penalty of five years. Lastly, the issue of personal possession of pornographic materials was shelved, as proposed by the opposition.

29. Newsletter "Akiko Network," Winter 1998.

30. Speech during the Asia-Pacific Symposium on the Trafficking in Persons, January 20, 2000.

31. Personal interview with Mayumi Moriyama, a member of LDP and chair of the Child Prostitution and Pornography Prohibition Law Coalition Team, March 27, 2000.

32. Presentation by Sumiko Shimizu, member of the Social Democratic Party and head of the official delegation to the First World Congress against Commercial Sexual Exploitation of Children in Stockholm, during the 4th International Follow-Up Seminar on the First World Congress, Tokyo, April 27, 2000.

33. Personal conversation with an ECPAT Japan representative at the Women's International War Crimes Tribunal: Japanese Military Sexual Slavery, December 9, 2000.

34. Akiko Domoto, a prominent member of the Lower House, iterated that an anti–domestic violence law in Japan might take up to ten years to pass.

35. Female politicians were split on this issue. The very same politician who was behind the revision of the Equal Employment Opportunity Law, the legalization of the pill, and the passage of the Child Prostitution and Pornography Prohibition Law and the Domestic Violence Prevention Law, Sumiko Shimizu, a member of the Social Democratic Party of Japan in the ruling coalition between 1994 and 1996, supported the creation

of the private Asian Women's Fund in 1995. Personal interview with Sumiko Shimizu, April 13, 2000.

36. All the lawsuits filed by the comfort women in Japan were unsuccessful, except for one. In 1998 a district court in Yamaguchi Prefecture recognized that the three Korean plaintiffs were forced to serve at the stations and ordered the Japanese government to pay them 300,000 yen (about $3,000) each.

37. The account below of UN developments concerning the comfort women issue is drawn from Suzuki 1997 and Kim 1996.

38. *Asahi Shimbun*, November 23, 1994.

39. Soh 2000.

40. Keynote address by Gay McDougall, "How to End Violence against Women in War and Armed Conflict Situations: Japan's Military Sexual Slavery Viewed from International Law," June 1, 1999, Tokyo.

41. "Report on the Mission to the Democratic People's Republic of Korea, the Republic of Korea, and Japan on the Issue of Military Sexual Slavery in Wartime," by the special rapporteur on violence against women, 1996.

42. Yeong-ae Yamashita, quoted in Ueno 1998, 129.

43. Suzuki 1997; Ueno 1997.

Chapter 9

1. All of the above-mentioned politicians are well-traveled women who speak English fluently and who have strong connections to international organizations. Domoto, for example, the regional councilor and vice president of the IUCN (and the World Conservation Union), has been a main force in introducing international environmental norms to Japan.

2. Shimizu, Tsujimoto, and Fukushima were closely connected to Japanese grassroots movements even before they became lawmakers, and they continue to serve as board members of many NGOs. Domoto has founded her own nongovernmental group on environmental issues in Japan. Owaki also founded an NGO group on domestic violence, DV Prevention Center, and is also a representative of the Lawyers Association for Foreigners' Labor Rights. Personal interviews with Fukushima (April 13, 2000) and Owaki (April 11, 2000). Personal conversation with Akiko Domoto (April 15, 2000).

3. The issue of domestic violence has garnered so little political support that an influential politician behind the passage of the revised Equal Employment Opportunity Law, the legalization of the pill, the Child Prostitution and Pornography Prohibition Law, and the Anti-Stalking Law exclaimed at a March 2000 expert hearing on domestic violence at the Diet that "the law might take up to ten years to realize."

4. Personal interview with the director of the Office for Gender Equality, May 1, 2000.

5. Edwards and Gaventa 2001, "Introduction."

6. Maxwell Cameron, quoted in Scott 2001, 124.

7. "The claiming of a world space for women raises temporal questions as well as spatial considerations, questions of history as well as of place. Can such claims be imagined outside the conceptual parameters of modernity? Can worlds be claimed in categories such as "woman" in all innocence and benevolence, or do these gestures mark the

revival of a form of feminist cultural imperialism?" Kaplan 1994, 137. See also a discussion in Mackie 2001.

8. Kaplan 1994, 137.

9. Thirty-seven out of 473 provisions in the final NGO outcome documents mention gender in conjunction with the themes of slavery, peoples of Asian descent, caste, criminal justice, minorities, environmental racism, health, HIV, labor, trafficking, migration, refugees, sexual orientation, and the girl child. As paragraph 119 of the NGO Declaration defines, "an intersectional approach to discrimination acknowledges that every person be it man or woman exists in a framework of multiple identities, with factors such as race, class, ethnicity, religion, sexual orientation, gender identity, age, disability, citizenship, national identity, geo-political context, health, including HIV/AIDS status, and any other status all determinants in one's experiences of racism, racial discrimination, xenophobia and related intolerances." Paragraph 212 of the intergovernmental Platform for Action "urges States to establish and strengthen effective partnerships with and provide support, as appropriate, to all relevant actors of civil society, including non-governmental organizations working to promote gender equality and the advancement of women, particularly women subject to multiple discrimination, and to promote an integrated and holistic approach to the elimination of all forms of discrimination against women and girls." Workshops organized by feminist NGOs emphasizing the multiplicity of gender discrimination included the World Court of Women; Women at the Intersection of Racism and Other Oppressions: A Human Rights Hearing; Women of Dalit Communities: Breaking the Culture of Silence; Voices of Indigenous Women; Refugee Roundtable focusing on refugee women; and the picket for Gay and Lesbian Equality and Human Rights for All.

10. Ahmed 1998, 16.

11. Grewal and Kaplan 1994, 3, 17–18.

12. Butler 1992, 8.

13. See, for example, Stromquist and Monkman 2000; Burbules and Torres 2000; and Arnove and Torres 1999.

14. For a discussion of emerging transnational advocacy networks in education, see Mundy and Murphy 2001.

15. Edwards and Gaventa 2001, 283.

16. Jody Williams and Stephen Goose, "The International Campaign to Ban Landmines," in Cameron, Lawson, and Tomlin 1998, 21.

17. Ibid., 28.

18. "An Interview with Lorl Wallach," *Foreign Policy* (Spring 2000): 32.

19. "One of the major reasons why human rights protection is weak in Japan is that we do not have a Civil Rights Act like in the United States. I think the women's movement should link with the Buraku struggle and the handicapped people's movement. Women's groups should encourage these minority women to speak up. And at the same time these minority groups should encourage women within their groups to become visible." Personal interview with a veteran member of the Japan Civil Liberties Union (1947), one of the oldest NGOs in Japan, March 23, 2000.

20. Cited in Kano 1997.

21. See a discussion of Ogoshi's critique of Ueno in Aiko Ogoshi, quoted in Kano 1997.

22. See Ehara, ed. 1992. The volume is in part a response to an article written by Daisaburo Hashizume in 1992, "What Is Bad about Prostitution?" Daisaburo Hashizume argues that "if prostitution is voluntary, it cannot be regarded as a human rights violation." He adds that "the objectification and commodification of relations is a feature of contemporary society. We can't say that the commodification of women/their bodies is a violation of human rights." Quoted in Ehara 1995, 290. In *Feminizumu no Shuchō*, several feminist scholars challenge his position. Chie Asano, for example, argues that it is impossible to distinguish between freedom and coercion and that the false dichotomy between freedom and coercion has created another false divide between sex workers and other workers. She insists that one cannot fully understand the commodification of sex without addressing its gender aspects, that is, how it disproportionately affects women. Tomoko Kawabata argues that one cannot ignore the possibility that prostitution is a violation of women's human rights even when it is voluntary, since it is difficult to understand one's victimhood. The "prostitute" label is problematic because it implies that sexual workers give up their sexual rights entirely. She further argues that instead of treating prostitution as a violation of the sex workers' human rights, it should be viewed as a sexual slavery system that concerns all women.

23. Nagata 1995, 5.

24. Yamamoto 1998, 298; personal interview with the founder of the Forum on Sex Issues, February 15, 2000.

25. Kanazumi 1997, 83.

26. Yamamoto 1998, 256.

27. Ryōichi Kawakami, quoted in Morita 1999, 50.

28. Personal interview with the founder of the Forum on Sex Issues, February 15, 2000. See also the brief description in Yamamoto 1998, 142–56.

29. Some local education commissions have taken measures to promote the convention and children's participation through white papers, action programs, children's rights consciousness surveys, children's congresses, and children's human rights forums. For details of local government measures, see Federation for the Protection of Children's Human Rights (Japan) 1997.

30. Japan Federation of Bar Associations 1998.

31. Ibid., 256.

32. Ibid., 259.

33. See, for example, Hayashi 1999.

34. Prime Minister's Commission on Japan's Goals in the 21st Century 2000.

35. See, for example, Nakane 1970.

36. Ehara et al. 1985, 68.

37. For example, Ochiai 1988 and Ueno 1994.

38. Prime Minister's Commission on Japan's Goals in the 21st Century 2000.

39. See, for example Pharr 1990, 17: "Japan has been widely recognized as a country with manageable levels of social conflict. Two major explanations address that phenomenon. The first explanation sees the key to the lack of social strife in the nature of Japanese political culture, the basic values and beliefs of which not only affect would-be protesters themselves, their potential allies, and the watching public, but also work to prevent a protest from emerging in the first place, or at least from winning support if its emergence is unavoidable. The second explanation emphasizes the role of authorities in

responding to protest when it arises. Even if Japan today provides a relatively free environment from the standpoint of coercive or legal methods of protest control, the role exercised historically by authorities in relation to protest was highly repressive; not until quite recently—that is, until the end of World War II—did this situation change."

40. Campbell, for example, argues that Japanese authority figures "carry around a distinctively Japanese 'implicit theory' of decision-making and conflict resolution," which sees the consensus model as producing the most satisfactory solution to a problem. Cited in Pharr 1990, 208.

41. Personal interview, March 23, 2000.

42. Personal interview with the director of the Council for Gender Equality, May 1, 2000.

43. "We are having a terrible time. Everybody criticizes us these days, but it should not be us who have to do everything. Without a clear legal provision, we have no mandate." Personal interview, April 28, 2000.

44. Personal interview, April 14, 2000.

45. Personal interview with a member of the Tokyo Lawyers Association and a founding member of the DV Prevention Project for Batterers, April 18, 2000.

46. Personal interview with a member of the Diet, Mizuho Fukushima, April 13, 2000.

47. Personal interview with the founder and executive director of Setagaya Education Forum, January 30, 2001.

48. Personal interview with a member of the Gender Equality Sub-Commission of the Japan Federation of Law Associations, April 10, 2000.

49. Personal interview, April 17, 2000.

50. "The new constitution that brought the Imperial Diet into being carried forward Tokugawa social principles by stating subjects' duties while failing to guarantee their rights. The basic values that in Tokugawa Japan had defined the boundaries of obligation and responsibility in human relationships continued to be based on hierarchy and natural inequality in social relations. Indeed, in the Meiji-era 'samurization' of society sponsored by the ex-samurai elite who led the country, a warrior-caste ideal of duty to superiors became a part of national ideology. The newly created public education system affirmed, through its 'morals' course, a hierarchical social order in which superiors exercised authority on behalf of their inferiors and inferiors showed them deference; final authority, of course, was vested in the emperor at the top of the social pyramid" (Pharr 1990, 24).

51. For a discussion on public interest and civil society, see, for example, Yoshida 1999.

52. It emphasized the necessity of forming "a network centered around the national machinery that enables the mutual provision of information on trends in national and local government policy and international conferences, as well as the daily activities of NGOs and information on pioneering action, considering the extremely large role NGOs play toward the creation of a gender-equal society by offering a unique perspective in carrying out volunteer activities in various areas, in order to establish equal cooperative relations among the national government, local government, and NGOs" (Headquarters for the Promotion of Gender Equality 1996, 73).

53. Personal interview with the executive director of the Human Rights Forum, April 17, 2001.

54. Personal interview with the executive director of Asia-Pacific Women's Resource Center and Violence against Women in War-Net Japan, April 20, 2000.

55. Personal interview with a board member of Japan Women's Congress (a national women's organization of more than thirty thousand members, established in 1962), April 12, 2000.

56. "Gay: Dansei Dosei Ai" (Gay Homosexuality), *Men's Net Newsletter*, September–October 1998, 19. See also a description of discrimination against homosexuals in Japan in Yukiko Tsunoda 1993b, 199–218.

57. Barbara Dozetos, "Tokyo government reinstates protections for gays and lesbians," Gay.Com Network, December 12, 2000.

58. Ibid.

59. "Japan's Cultural Bias against Foreigners Comes under Attack," *New York Times*, November 15, 1999.

60. Prime Minister's Commission on Japan's Goals in the 21st Century 2000.

61. Toshio Jo and Kishiko Hisada, "Poor Communication Japan's No. 1 Enemy Abroad. Language Debate Dates Back to Meiji Era," *Asahi Evening News*, March 1, 2000.

62. Ibid.

63. Risa Kumamoto, "NGO no Fuoroappu Katsudō" (Follow-up activities of NGOs), in IMADR 2001.

64. Ibid.

References

Ahmed, Sara. 1998. *Differences That Matter: Feminist Theory and Postmodernism.* Cambridge: Cambridge University Press.

Allinson, Gary. 1993. "Citizenship, Fragmentation, and the Negotiated Polity." In Gary Allinson and Yasunori Sone, eds., *Political Dynamics in Contemporary Japan.* Ithaca, N.Y.: Cornell University Press.

Allison, Anne. 1991. "Japanese Mothers and Obentos: The Lunchbox as Ideological State Apparatus." *Anthropological Quarterly* 65, no. 1: 41–66.

Apter, David, and Nagayo Sawa. 1984. *Against the State.* Cambridge, Mass.: Harvard University Press.

Arnove, Robert, and Carlos Torres, eds. 1999. *Comparative Education: The Dialectic of the Global and the Local.* Boulder, Colo.: Rowman and Littlefield.

Asano, Chie. 1995. "Senzaiteki Shohintoshite no Shintai to Sesshoku Shōgai" (Anorexia and the subconscious commodification of the body). In Ehara Yumiko, ed., *Sei no Shōhinka* (The commodification of sex). Tokyo: Keiso Shobo.

Ashino, Yuriko. 1999a. "Long Wait for Birth Control Pills." *Japan Quarterly* Vol. 46, Issue 4: 86.

———. 1999b. *Piru no Koto wo Shiritai* (I want to know more about the pill). Tokyo: Iwanami.

Baxi, Uprenda. 1997. "Human Rights Education: The Promise of the Third Millennium?" In George Andreopoulous and Richard Claude, eds., *Human Rights Education for the Twenty-First Century*. Philadelphia: University of Pennsylvania Press.

Boli, John, and George Thomas. 1997. "World Culture in the World Polity: A Century of International Non-Governmental Organization." *American Sociological Review* 62: 171–90.

Broadbent, Jeffrey. 1998. *Environmental Politics in Japan: Networks of Power and Protest.* Cambridge: Cambridge University Press.

Brody, Betsy. 2001. *Opening the Door: Immigration, Ethnicity and Globalization in Japan.* London: Routledge.

Buhmann, Karin. 1989. *Civil and Political Rights in Japan: International and Constitutional Standards and National Practice.* Copenhagen: Danish Center of Human Rights.

Burbules, Nicholas, and Carlos Torres, eds. 2000. *Globalization and Education: Critical Perspectives*. New York: Routledge.

Butler, Judith. 1992. "Contingent Foundations: Feminism and the Question of Postmodernism." In Judith Butler and Joan Scott, eds., *Feminists Theorize the Political*. New York: Routledge.

Calder, Kent. 1987. *Crisis and Compensation*. Princeton, N.J.: Princeton University Press.

Cameron, Maxwell, Robert Lawson, and Brian Tomlin, eds. 1998. *To Walk Without Fear: The Global Movement to Ban Landmines*. Oxford: Oxford University Press.

Campus Sexual Harassment Network. 1999. *Gaidolain no Tebiki: Kyanpasu Sekushyaru Harasumento* (Campus sexual harassment guideline). Tokyo.

Carrillo, Roxanna. 1997. "Violence Against Women: An Introduction." In Ana Maria Brasiliero, ed., *Women Against Violence: Breaking the Silence*. New York: UNIFEM.

Chan-Tiberghien, Jennifer. "Gender-Skepticism or Gender-Boom: Poststructural Feminisms, Transnational Feminisms, and the World Conference against Racism." Forthcoming in *International Journal of Feminist Politics*.

Chen, Martha Alter. 1996. "Engendering World Conferences: The International Women's Movement and the UN." In Thomas Weiss and Leon Gordenker, eds., *NGOs, the UN and Global Governance*. Boulder, Colo.: Lynne Rienner.

Cho, Yon-Em. 1997. "Feminizumu no naka no Reshizumu" (Racism in feminism). In Ehara Yumiko and Yoshiko Kanai, eds., *Feminizumu* (Feminism). Tokyo: Shinyosha.

Chow, Rey. 1993. *Writing Diaspora: Tactics of Intervention in Contemporary Cultural Studies*. Bloomington: Indiana University Press.

Clark, Ann Marie, Elisabeth J. Friedman, and Kathryn Hochstetler. 1998. "The Sovereign Limits of Global Civil Society: A Comparison of NGO Participation in UN World Conferences on the Environment, Human Rights, and Women." *World Politics* 51 (Oct.): 1–35.

Clemens, Elisabeth. 1993. "Organizational Repertoires and Institutional Change: Women's Groups and the Transformation of US Politics, 1890–1920." *American Journal of Sociology* 98, no. 4: 755–98.

Crenshaw, Kimberlé. 2000. "Gender-Related Aspects of Race Discrimination." Paper presented at the Expert Group Meeting on Gender and Racial Discrimination, Nov. 21–24, 2000, Zagreb, Croatia.

Cripps, Denise. 1996. "Flags and Fanfares: The Hinomaru Flag and Kimigayo Anthem." In Roger Goodman and Ian Neary, eds., *Case Studies on Human Rights in Japan*. Surrey: Japan Library.

Curtis, Gerald. 1999. *The Logic of Japanese Politics: Leaders, Institutions, and the Limits of Change*. New York: Columbia University Press.

Druelle, Anick. May 2000. "La Presence des groupes de droite anti-feministes aux Nations Unies, Institut de recherches et d'etudes feministes." Université du Québec à Montréal, http://netfemmes.cdeacf.ca/documents/Anti-Feminist% 20Groups-USLetter. pdf.

———. 2001. "Mouvements de femmes et mondialisation capitaliste: pratiques et discours au sein des conférences mondiales des Nations Unies sur les femmes, 1975–1995." Ph.D. diss., Université du Québec, Montréal.

Duus, Peter. 1995. *The Abacus and the Sword: The Japanese Penetration of Korea, 1895–1910.* Berkeley: University of California Press.

Ebashi Takashi and Sekai Jinken Kaigi NGO Renrakukai. 1996. *NGO ga Tsukuru Sekai no Jinken: Wiin Sengen no Tsukaikata* (World human rights by NGOs: How to use the Vienna Declaration). Tokyo: Akashi Shoten.

Edwards, Michael, and John Gaventa, eds. 2001. *Global Citizen Action.* Boulder, Colo.: Lynne Rienner.

———. 1995. "Shohintoshite no Sei." In Ehara Yumiko, ed., *Sei no Shōhinka* (The commodification of sex). Tokyo: Keiso Shobo.

Ehara, Yumiko, ed. 1992. *Feminizumu no Shuchō* (The claims of feminism). Tokyo: Keiso Shobo.

Ehara, Yumiko, et al., eds. 1985. *Jendā to Shakaigaku* (Gender and sociology). Tokyo: Shinyosha.

Ehara, Yumiko, and Yoshiko Kanai, eds. 1997. *Feminizumu* (Feminism). Tokyo: Shinyosha.

Federation for the Protection of Children's Human Rights (Japan), ed. 1997. *Jijitai de Torikumu Kodomo no Kenri Jōyaku* (Local government's measures on the Convention of the Rights of the Child). Tokyo: Akiishi Shoten.

Finnemore, Martha. 1996. *National Interests in International Society.* Ithaca, N.Y.: Cornell University Press.

Fitzpatrick, Joan. 1994. "The Use of International Human Rights Norms to Combat Violence Against Women." In Rebecca Cook, ed., *Human Rights of Women: National and International Perspectives.* Philadelphia: University of Pennsylvania Press.

Freire, Paulo. 1970. *Pedagogy of the Oppressed.* New York: Continuum.

Fukuoka, Yasunori. 2000. *Lives of Young Koreans in Japan.* Melbourne: Trans Pacific Press.

Gaer, Felice. 1998. "And Never the Twain Shall Meet." In Carol Elizabeth Lockwood et al., eds., *The International Human Rights of Women: Instruments of Change.* Washington, D.C.: American Bar Association, Section of International Law and Practice.

Gallagher, Anne. 1997. "Ending the Marginalization: Strategies for Incorporating Women into the United Nations Human Rights System." *Human Rights Quarterly* 19, no. 2: 283–333.

Grewal, Inderpal, and Caren Kaplan, eds. 1994. *Scattered Hegemonies: Postmodernity and Transnational Feminist Practices.* Minneapolis: University of Minnesota Press.

Gurowitz, Amy. 1999. "Mobilizing International Norms: Domestic Actors, Immigrants, and the Japanese State." *World Politics* 51 (Apr.): 413–45.

Haas, Peter. 1992. "Epistemic Communities and International Policy Coordination." *International Organization* 46: 1–35.

Hara, Kimi. 1995. "Challenges to Education for Girls and Women." In Kumiko Fujimura-Fanselow and Atsuko Kameda, eds., *Japanese Women: New Feminist Perspectives on the Past, Present, and Future.* New York: The Feminist Press.

Harada, Eriko. 1998. "Shihō Kainyū to Kazoku Keā" (Legal intervention and family care). In Nichibenren, ed., *Kazoku, Bōryoku, Gyakutai no kōzō* (The structure of family, violence, and abuse). Tokyo: Yomiuri Shimbun.

Harris, Phyllis Braudy, and Susan Long. 1993. "Daughter-in-law's Burden: An Exploratory Study of Caregiving in Japan." *Journal of Cross-Cultural Gerontology* 8 (June): 97–118.

Hasegawa, Yuki. 2002. "Kaigi ni Okeru Senjū Minzoku no Kenri Kaifuku Undō" (The movement for the restoration of indigenous people's rights in WCAR). In IMADR, ed., *Mainoriti Josei ga Sekai wo Kaeru!* (Minority women change the world!). Tokyo: Kaihō Shuppansha.

Hayashi, Michiyoshi. 1999. *Feminizumu no Dokugai* (The poison of feminism). Tokyo: Soshisha.

Headquarters for the Promotion of Gender Equality. 1996. *Plan for Gender Equality 2000*. Tokyo: Prime Minister's Office.

Herbert, Wolfgang. 1996. *Foreign Workers and Law Enforcement in Japan*. London: Kegan Paul International.

Hingwan, Kathianne. 1996. "Identity, Otherness and Migrant Labour in Japan." In Roger Goodman and Ian Neary, eds., *Case Studies on Human Rights in Japan*. Surrey: Japan Library.

hooks, bell. 1994. *Teaching to Transgress: Education as the Practice of Freedom*. New York: Routledge.

Human Rights Forum 21. 1998. *Nihon no Jinken Hakusho* (White paper on human rights in Japan). Tokyo: Kaihō Shuppansha.

IMADR, 2001. *Kokuren Kara Mita Nihon no Jinshu Sabetsu* (Racial discrimination in Japan from UN perspectives). Tokyo: IMADR.

———. ed. 2002. *Mainoriti Josei ga Sekai wo Kaeru!* (Minority women change the world!). Tokyo: Kaihō Shuppansha.

Imamura, Anne. 1978. "The Active Urban Housewife: Structurally Induced Motivation for Increased Community Participation." In Merry White and Barbara Molony, eds., *Proceedings of the Tokyo Symposium on Women*. Tokyo: International Group for the Study of Women.

———. 1987. *Urban Japanese Housewives: At Home and in the Community*. Honolulu: University of Hawaii Press.

Inaba, Nanako. 2002. "Kokusai Jinken Kijun to Nihon ni Okeru Ijūsha no Kenri Hoshō no Genjō" (International human rights standards and the status of human rights protection of migrant workers in Japan). In IMADR, ed., *Hanjinshushugi, Sabetsu Teppai Sekaikaigi to Nihon* (World Conference against Racism, Racial Discrimination, Xenophobia, and Related Intolerance and Japan). Tokyo: Kaiho Shuppansha.

Inoue, Mayako. 1998. *Feminusuto Kaunseringu e no Shōtai* (Invitation to feminist counseling). Tokyo: Yukku.

Inoue, Teruko, Chizuko Ueno, and Ehara Yumiko, eds. 1997. *Nihon no Feminizumu* (Japanese feminism), vols. 1–8. Tokyo: Iwaba Shoten.

Inoue, Teruko, Kazuko Tanaka, et al., eds. 1999. "Joseigaku to Jendā Kenkyu: Zadankai" (Women's studies and gender research). Annual Report of the Japanese Association of Women's Studies, Tokyo.

International Human Rights NGO Network. 1999. *Wocchi! Kiyaku Jinken Iinkai: Doko ga Zureteru? Jinken no Kokusai Kijun to Nihon no Genjō* (Watch! Human rights committee: Where is the gap? International human rights standards and the situation in Japan). Tokyo: Nihon Hyōronsha.

Ito, Masako. 1999. *Kokuritsushi Kominkan no Jissen kara Joseimondaigakushū no Shiten*

(The perspectives of women's issues studies from the experiences of public civic centers). Tokyo: Miraisha.

Ito, Shuko. 2002. "Nihon no Mainoriti Josei no Genjō wo Rikai Suru: Jinken Bunya de no Tōkei no Hitsuyosei" (Understanding the situation of minority women in Japan: The need for human rights data). In IMADR, ed., *Hanjinshushugi, Sabetsu Teppai Sekaikaigi to Nihon* (World Conference against Racism, Racial Discrimination, Xenophobia, and Related Intolerance and Japan). Tokyo: Kaiho Shuppansha.

Japan Federation of Bar Associations. 1998. *Kazoku, Bōryoku, Gyakutai no Kōzu* (The structure of family, violence, and abuse). Tokyo: Yoimuri Shimbunsha.

Japan's Network for Women and Health. 1995. *1994 Kairo Kokusai Jinkō Kaihatsu Kaigi: Josei to Kenkō Nettowaaku Hōkokusho.* 1994 Report by Japan's Network for Women and Health on the Cairo Conference on Population and Development.

———. 1999. Voices from Japan NGO Report.

Joachim, Jutta. 1999. "Shaping the Human Rights Agenda: The Case of Violence Against Women." In Mary Meyer and Elisabeth Prugl, eds., *Gender Politics in Global Governance.* Boulder, Colo.: Rowman and Littlefield.

Johnson, Chalmers. 1982. *MITI and the Japanese Miracle.* Stanford, Calif.: Stanford University Press.

Jones, Philip. 1990. "UNESCO and the Politics of Global Literacy." *Comparative Education Review* 34, no. 1: 41–60.

Kajiyama, Sumiko. 1999. *Onna o Naguru Otokotachi: Domesutikku Baiorensu ha Hanzai de aru* (Men who beat women: Domestic violence is a crime). Tokyo: Bungei Shunchu.

Kanai, Yoshiko. 1994. "Issues for Japanese Feminism." In AMPO–Japan Asia Quarterly Review, ed., *Voices from the Japanese Women's Movement.* London: M.E. Sharpe.

———. 1998. "Joseigaku no 'Shuhen' kara no 'Joseigaku' Saikō: Nihon no Joseigaku no Tsuginaru Suteiji e" (A reexamination of "women's studies" from "marginalized" women's studies: Toward a second stage of women's studies in Japan, *Women's Studies*, Vol. 6.

Kanazumi, Fumiko. 1997. "Problematizing Reproductive Technologies." In Sandra Buckley, ed., *Broken Silence: Voices of Japanese Feminism.* Berkeley: University of California Press.

Kano, Ayako. 1997. "Nihon Feminizumu Ronshō Shi" (Japanese feminist debates in the twentieth century). In Ehara Yumiko and Yoshiko Kanai, eds., *Feminizumu* (Feminism). Tokyo: Shinyosha.

Kaplan, Caren. 1994. "The Politics of Location as Transnational Feminist Critical Practice." In Inderpal Grewal and Caren Kaplan, eds., *Scattered Hegemonies: Postmodernity and Transnational Feminist Practices.* Minneapolis: University of Minnesota Press.

Kawamura, Fumi. 1999. *Wagamama na Onna wa Shiawase ni Nareru: Let's Jiko Hyōgen and Jiko Sonchō Toreiningu* (Selfish women can become happy: Let's try self-respect and self-assertion training). Tokyo: Femix.

Kawashima, Yoko. 1999. "Discourse, Power, Sexuality, and Construction of Subjectivity." *Journal of Gender Studies* 2 (Mar.): 3–23.

Keck, Margaret, and Katherine Sikkink. 1998. *Activists Beyond Borders.* Ithaca, N.Y.: Cornell University Press.

Kerr, George. 2000. *Okinawa: The History of an Island People*. Boston: Tuttle.

Kikuzato, Yasuko. 2002. "'Okinawa' wo 'Senjū Minzoku' to iu Gainen de Kangaeru" (Conceptualizing Okinawa from an indigenous peoples' perspective). In IMADR, ed., *Hanjinshushugi, Sabetsu Teppai Sekaikaigi to Nihon* (World Conference against Racism, Racial Discrimination, Xenophobia, and Related Intolerance and Japan). Tokyo: Kaiho Shuppansha.

Kim, Puja. 1996. "'Jugun Ianfu' Mondai: Undō to sono Imi" (The question of comfort women: The movement and its meaning). In Hiroko Hara, Mari Osawa, Makoto Maruyama, and Yasushi Yamamoto, eds., *Jendā* (Gender). Tokyo: Shinseisha.

Kohno, Masaru. 1997. *Japan's Postwar Party Politics*. Princeton, N.J.: Princeton University Press.

Koyama, Kaoru. 1999. "Gaikokujin Rōdōsha Mondai." In International Human Rights NGO Network, ed., *Wocchi! Kiyaku Jinken Iinkai: Doko ga Zureteru? Jinken no Kokusai Kijun to Nihon no Genjō* (Watch! Human rights committee: Where is the gap? International human rights standards and the situation in Japan). Tokyo: Nihon Hyōronsha.

Kuninobu, Junko, ed. 2000. ASPBAE (Asian South Pacific Bureau of Adult Education) Mid-term Report on Violence Against Women. Mumbai, India.

LeBlanc, Robin. 1999. *Bicycle Citizens: The Political World of the Japanese Housewife*. Berkeley: University of California Press.

Legro, Jeffrey. 1997. "Which Norms Matter?" *International Organizations* 51, no. 1 (Winter).

Lerner, Gerda. 1979. *The Majority Finds Its Past: Placing Women in History*. New York: Oxford University Press.

Lie, John. 2001. *Multiethnic Japan*. Cambridge, Mass.: Harvard University Press.

Linger, Daniel. 2001. *No One Home: Brazilian Selves Remade in Japan*. Stanford, Calif.: Stanford University Press.

Lyotard, Jean François. 1984. *The Postmodern Condition: A Report on Knowledge*. Minneapolis: University of Minnesota Press.

McAdam, Doug. 1982. *Political Process and the Development of Black Insurgency, 1930–1970*. Chicago: University of Chicago Press.

McAdam, Doug, Sidney Tarrow, and Charles Tilly. 1994. "To Map Contentious Politics." *Mobilization: An International Journal*, I Mar. (1): 17–34.

McCarthy, John, and Mayer Zald. 1977. "Resource Mobilization and Social Movements: A Partial Theory." *American Journal of Sociology* 82, no. 6: 1212–41.

McKean, Margaret. 1981. *Environmental Protest and Citizen Politics in Japan*. Berkeley: University of California Press.

Mackie, Vera. 2000. "Sexual Violence, Silence and Human Rights Discourse: The Emergence of the Military Prostitution Issue." In Anne-Marie Hilsdon, Martha Macintyre, Vera Mackie, and Maila Stivens, eds., *Human Rights and Gender Politics: Asia-Pacific Perspectives*. London: Routledge.

———. 2001. "The Language of Globalization, Transnationality and Feminism." *International Feminist Journal of Politics* 3, no. 2: 180–206.

———. 2002. "'Asia' in Everyday Life: Dealing with Difference in Contemporary Japan." In Brenda Yeoh, Peggy Teo, and Shirlena Huang, eds., *Gender Politics in the Asia-Pacific Region*. London: Routledge.

Maeda, Akira. 2002. "Shokuminchi Shihai, Doreisei de Nihon wo Tsuikyū" (Pressing Japan on the issues of colonization and slavery). In IMADR, ed., *Hanjinshushugi, Sabetsu Teppai Sekaikaigi to Nihon* (World Conference against Racism, Racial Discrimination, Xenophobia, and Related Intolerance and Japan). Tokyo: Kaiho Shuppansha.

Martinez, D. P, ed. 1998. *The Worlds of Japanese Popular Culture: Gender, Shifting Boundaries and Global Cultures.* New York: Cambridge University Press.

Matsui, Yayori. 1997. Interview. In Sandra Buckley, ed., *Broken Silence: Voices of Japanese Feminism.* Berkeley: University of California Press.

———. 2000. "The Governor of Tokyo Ishihara Is a Proponent of Ethnic Discrimination (Racism) and an Advocate of Sexism—We Demand His Resignation!" *Women's Asia 21: Voices from Japan*, no. 6 (Autumn).

Matsui, Yayori, Midori Wakakuwa, et al., eds. 1996. *Feminizumu wa Dare no Mono* (Whose feminism). Shizuoka: Z Kai Peburu.

Meyer, John, John Boli, George Thomas, and Francisco Ramirez. 1997. "World Society and the Nation-State." *American Journal of Sociology* 103, no. 1 (July): 144–81.

Miller, Francesca. 1991. *Latin American Women and the Search for Social Justice.* Hanover, N.H.: University Press of New England.

Mitsui, Mariko. 2000. "Women and Politics in Japan." *Women's Asia 21: Voices from Japan*, no. 6 (Autumn).

Miyazaki, Shigeki. 1999. "Kokusai no Shiten kara" (Introduction: From an international perspective). In Shigeki Miyazaki, ed., *Human Rights in an International Era and the Buraku Issue.* Tokyo: Akashi Shoten.

Morita, Yuri. 1999. *Kodomo to Bōryoku* (Children and violence). Tokyo: Iwanami Shoten.

Moriyama, Mayumi. 1999. *Jidō Kaishun, Jidō Poruno Kinshihō* (Child prostitution and child pornography prohibition law). Tokyo: Gyōsei.

Mundy, Karen, and Lynn Murphy. 2001. "Transnational Advocacy, Global Civil Society? Emerging Evidence from the Field of Education." *Comparative Education Review* 45, no. 1 (Feb): 85–126.

Mushakoji, Kinhide. 2002. "Gurobaruka to Han Tero Senso ni Kiin Suru Shosabetsu to no Tatagai" (Combating various forms of discrimination resulting from globalization and the anti-terrorism war). In IMADR, ed., *Hanjinshushugi, Sabetsu Teppai Sekaikaigi to Nihon* (World Conference against Racism, Racial Discrimination, Xenophobia, and Related Intolerance and Japan). Tokyo: Kaiho Shuppansha.

Nagata, Eriko. 1995. "Sei no Shōhinka wa Dotokuteki ka?" In Ehara Yumiko, ed., *Sei no Shōhinka* (The commodification of sex). Tokyo: Keiso Shobo.

Nakajima, Michiko. 2000. "The Problems of the Basic Law on the Cooperative Participation of Men and Women in Society." *Women's Asia 21: Voices from Japan*, no. 6 (Autumn).

Nakamura, Akira. 1998. *Danseigaku no Susume* (Recommending men's studies).Toyama: Toyama Prefecture Women's Community Center "Sun Forte."

Nakane, Chie. 1970. Japanese Society. Berkeley: University of California Press.

Narita, Norihiko. 1999. *About Japan Series: Political Changes in the 1990s.* Tokyo: Foreign Press Center.

National Women's Education Center. 1999. *Joseigaku Kyoiku/Gakushū Handobukku* (Women's studies education and learning handbook). Tokyo: Yuhikaku.

Neary, Ian. 1989. *Political Protest and Social Control in Pre-War Japan: The Origins of Buraku Liberation*. Manchester: Manchester University Press.

———. 1997. "Burakumin in Contemporary Japan." In M. Weiner, ed., *Japan's Minorities: The Illusion of Homogeneity*. London: Routledge.

———. 2002. *The State and Politics in Japan*. Cambridge: Polity Press.

NGO Committee for the Reporting on the ICERD. 2001. Collective Report among Japan-Based NGOs on the International Convention on the Elimination of All Forms of Racial Discrimination.

Nichibenren. 2000. *Domesutikku Baiorensu Bōshi Hōritsu Handobukku* (Domestic violence prevention law handbook). Tokyo: Akashi Shoten.

Norgren, Tiana. "Abortion Before Birth Control: The Interest Groups Politics Behind Postwar Japanese Reproduction Policy." *Journal of Japanese Studies* 24, no. 1 (1998) 59–94.

Ochiai, Emiko. 1988. *Kintai Kazoku to Feminizumu* (Contemporary family and feminism). Tokyo: Keiso Shobō.

Office of the High Commissioner for Human Rights. 1998. *Human Rights Education: Lessons for Life*. Basic Information Kit No. 4.

Ogoshi, Aiko. 1997. *Kindai Nihon no Jendā* (Gender in contemporary Japan). Tokyo: Sanichi Shobo.

Okamoto, Masataka. 1999a. "Jiyūken Kiyaku no Nihon Seifu Hōkokusho no Shinki" (The examination of the Japanese government report on ICCPR). In International Human Rights NGO Network, ed., *Wocchi! Kiyaku Jinken Iinkai: Doko ga Zureteru? Jinken no Kokusai Kijun to Nihon no Genjō* (Watch! Human rights committee: Where is the gap? International human rights standards and the situation in Japan). Tokyo: Nihon Hyōronsha.

———. 1999b. "Zainichi Korean Mainoriti" (Korean Resident Minority). In International Human Rights NGO Network, ed., *Wocchi! Kiyaku Jinken Iinkai: Doko ga Zureteru? Jinken no Kokusai Kijun to Nihon no Genjō* (Watch! Human rights committee: Where is the gap? International human rights standards and the situation in Japan). Tokyo: Nihon Hyōronsha.

Okimoto, Daniel. 1989. *Between MITI and the Market*. Stanford, Calif.: Stanford University Press.

Okuda, Akiko, ed. 1997. *Mainoriti toshite no Joseishi* (Women's history from a minority perspective). Tokyo: Sanichi Shobō.

Okuyama, Akira. 1999. *Shokuba no Sekushyaru Harasumento* (Sexual harassment at the workplace). Tokyo: Yuhikaku.

Onoyama, Ryo. 2002. "Monchi ni Motozuku Sabetsu: Sekaiteki na Kanshin Jiko e" (Discrimination based on descent: Toward a Global Concern). In IMADR, ed., *Hanjinshushugi, Sabetsu Teppai Sekaikaigi to Nihon* (World Conference against Racism, Racial Discrimination, Xenophobia, and Related Intolerance and Japan). Tokyo: Kaiho Shuppansha.

Onuma, Yasuaki. 1997. "In Quest of Intercivilizational Human Rights." In D. Warner, ed., *Human Rights and Humanitarian Law*. London: Kluwer Law International.

Osawa, Mari. 2000. "Government Approaches to Gender Equality in the mid-1990s." *Social Science Japan Journal* 3, no. 1: 3–19.

Otto (Koibito) kara no Bōryoku Chosa Kenkyukai (Domestic violence survey research group). 1999. Tokyo: Yuhikaku.

Owada, Hisashi. 1999. "Japan, International Law and the International Community." In

Nishuko Ando (Japanese association of international law), ed., *Japan and International Law: Past, Present and Future.* The Hague: Kluwer Law International.

Patel, Jayan. 1996. "The Role of the Bureaucracy in the Enforcement of Human Rights." In Roger Goodman and Ian Neary, eds., *Case Studies on Human Rights in Japan.* Surrey: Japan Library.

Peek, John. 1992. "Japan, the United Nations and Human Rights." *Asian Survey* 32, no. 3 (Mar.): 217–29.

Pekkanen, Robert. 2000. "Japan's New Politics: The Case of the NPO Law." *Journal of Japanese Studies* 26, no 1: 111–48.

Pempel, T. J., ed. 1990. *Uncommon Democracies: The One-Party Dominant Regimes.* Ithaca, N.Y.: Cornell University Press.

Pharr, Susan. 1990. *Losing Face: Status Politics in Japan.* Berkeley: University of California Press.

Prime Minister's Commission on Japan's Goals in the 21st Century. 2000. *The Frontier Within: Individual Empowerment and Better Governance in the New Millennium: Overview.* www.kantei.go.jp/jp/21century/report/overview.html.

Prugl, Elisabeth, and Mary Meyer. 1999. "Introduction: Gender Politics in Global Governance." In Mary Meyer and Elisabeth Prugl, eds., *Gender Politics in Global Governance.* Boulder, Colo.: Rowman and Littlefield.

Ramirez, Francisco. 2001. "World Society and the Political Incorporation of Women." In Bettina Heintz, ed., Special Issue on Gender Studies, *Kölner Zeitschrift für Soziologie und Sozialpsychologie* (Oct.): 356–74.

Risse-Kappen, Thomas, ed. 1995. *Bringing Transnational Relations Back in: Nonstate Actors, Domestic Structures and International Institutions.* New York: Cambridge University Press.

Ruggie, John. 1998. *Constructing World Polity: Essays on International Institutionalization.* New York: Routledge.

Rupp, Leila. 1997. *Worlds of Women: The Making of an International Women's Movement.* Princeton, N.J.: Princeton University Press.

Ryang, Sonia, ed. 2001. *Koreans in Japan: Critical Voices from the Margin.* London: Routledge.

Sancho, Nelia, ed. 1998. *War Crimes on Asian Women: Military Sexual Slavery by Japan During World War II.* Manila: Asian Women's Human Rights Council.

Sattler, Cheryl L. 2000. *Teaching to Transcend.* Albany: State University of New York Press.

Schreurs, Miranda. 1997. "Domestic Institutions and International Environmental Agendas in Japan and Germany." In Miranda Schreurs and Elizabeth Economy, eds., *The Internationalization of Environmental Protection.* Cambridge: Cambridge University Press.

Schwartz, Frank and Susan Pharr, ed. 2003. *The State of Civil Society in Japan.* Cambridge: Cambridge University Press.

Scott, Matthew. 2001. "Daner-Landmines! NGO–Government Collaboration in the Ottawa Process." In Michael Edwards and John Gaventa, eds., *Global Citizen Action.* Boulder, Colo.: Lynne Rienner.

Sellek, Yoko. 1997. "Nikkeijin: The Phenomenon of Return Migration." In M. Weiner, ed., *Japan's Minorities: The Illusion of Homogeneity.* London: Routledge.

Sellers, Patricia Viseur. 1999. "The Culture Value of Sexual Violence." *ASIL Proceedings.*

Shiga-Fujime, Yuki. 1993. "The Prostitutes' Union and the Impact of the 1956 Anti-Prostitution Law in Japan." *US-Japan Women's Journal*. English Supplement no. 5.

Shimizu, Tateo. 1999. "Japan, the Ambiguous, and its Flag and Anthem." *Japan Quarterly* (Oct.–Dec.).

Siddle, Richard. 1996. *Race, Resistance and the Ainu of Japan*. London: Routledge.

Snow, David, and Robert Benford. 1988. "Ideology, Frame Resonance, and Participant Mobilization." *International Social Movement Research* 1: 197–217.

Soh, Chung-hee Sarah. 2000. "From Imperial Gifts to Sex Slaves: Theorizing Symbolic Representations of the 'Comfort Women.'" *Social Science Japan Journal* 3, no. 1 (Apr.).

Stevens, Georgina. 2001. "The Ainu and Human Rights: Domestic and International Legal Protections." *Japanese Studies* 21, no. 2: 181–99.

Stromquist, Nelly, and Karen Monkman, eds. 2000. *Globalization and Education: Integration and Contestation Across Cultures.* Boulder, Colo.: Rowman and Littlefield.

Suzuki, Yoko. 1997. *Sensō Sekinin to Jendā* (War responsibility and gender). Tokyo: Miraisha.

Szymkowiak, Kenneth, and Patricia Steinhoff. 1995. "Wrapping Up in Something Long: Intimidation and Violence by Right-Wing Groups in Postwar Japan." *Terrorism and Political Violence* 7, no. 1 (Spring).

Taira, Koji. 1997. "Troubled National Identity: The Ryukyuans/Okinawans." In M. Weiner, ed., *Japan's Minorities: The Illusion of Homogeneity*. London: Routledge.

Takeuchi, Junko. 2002. "Hisabetsu Buraku Shusshin no Josei no Tachiba Kara" (From the standpoint of discriminated women of Buraku origins). In IMADR, ed., *Mainoriti Josei ga Sekai wo Kaeru!* (Minority women change the world!). Tokyo: Kaihō Shuppansha.

Tarrow, Sidney. 1983. *Struggling to Reform: Social Movements and Policy Change during Cycles of Protest.* Ithaca, N.Y.: Western Societies Program, Cornell University.

Tawara, Yoshifumi. 1997. *Kyōkasho Kōgeki no Shinsō* (The depth of curriculum attack). Tokyo: Gakushū no Tomo.

Tinker, Irene. 1999. "NGOs: An Alternative Power Base for Women?" In Mary Meyer and Elisabeth Prugl, eds., *Gender Politics in Global Governance.* Boulder, Colo.: Rowman and Littlefield.

Tokuza, Akiko. 1999. *The Rise of the Feminist Movement in Japan.* Tokyo: Keio University Press.

Tominaga, Kenzo. 1999. "Buraku Mondai" (Buraku issue). In International Human Rights NGO Network, ed., *Wocchi! Kiyaku Jinken Iinkai: Doko ga Zureteru? Jinken no Kokusai Kijun to Nihon no Genjō* (Watch! Human rights committee: Where is the gap? International human rights standards and the situation in Japan). Tokyo: Nihon Hyōronsha.

Tomioka, Akemi. 1997. "Rezubian Feminizumu" (Lesbian feminism). In Ehara Yumiko and Yoshiko Kanai, eds., *Feminizumu* (Feminism). Tokyo: Shinyosha.

Tsunoda, Yukiko. 1993a. "Sexual Harassment in Japan: Recent Legal Decisions." *US-Japan Women's Journal.* English Supplement no. 5.

———. 1993b. *Sei no Horitsugaku* (The legal study of sexuality). Tokyo: Yuhikaku.

Uemura, Hideaki. 1999. "Ainu Mizoku no Kenri to Okinawa no Jinken Joho" (Ainu people's rights and the human rights situation of Okinawa). In International Human Rights NGO Network, ed., *Wocchi! Kiyaku Jinken Iinkai: Doko ga Zureteru? Jinken no Kokusai Kijun to Nihon no Genjō* (Watch! Human rights committee: Where is the gap? International human rights standards and the situation in Japan). Tokyo: Nihon Hyōronsha.

———. 2002. "Dāban e no Nagai Michinori, soshite, Sabetsu Teppai no Mirai e no Shiza" (The long road to Durban and the vision toward elimination of discrimination). In IMADR, ed., *Hanjinshushugi, Sabetsu Teppai Sekaikaigi to Nihon* (World Conference against Racism, Racial Discrimination, Xenophobia, and Related Intolerance and Japan). Tokyo: Kaihō Shuppansha.

———. 1994. *Kintai Kazoku no Seiritsu to Shūen* (The formation and demise of the contemporary family) Tokyo: Iwanami.

———. 1997a. "'Oyaji' ni Naritakunai Kimi no Tame no Menzu Ribu no Susume" (Recommending men's studies to you who don't want to become old men). In Teruko Inoue, Chizuko Ueno, and Ehara Yumiko, eds., *Nihon no Feminizumu: Danseigaku* (Japanese feminism: Men's studies). Tokyo: Iwaba Shoten.

———. 1997b. *Stop the Academic Harassment: Campus Sexual Discrimination.* Tokyo: Sanshodo.

———. 1998. *Nashonarizumu to Jendā* (Nationalism and gender). Tokyo: Seitōsha.

United Nations. 1985. Nairobi Forward-Looking Strategies for the Advancement of Women.

———. 1996. *The Beijing Platform for Action.*

Upham, Frank. 1987. *Law and Social Change in Postwar Japan.* Cambridge, Mass.: Harvard University Press.

Van Wolferen, Karel. 1989. *The Enigma of Japanese Power.* New York: Random House.

Watanabe, Kazuko. 1994. *Josei, Bōryoku, Jinken* (Women, violence, and human rights). Tokyo: Gakuyōshobo.

Weiner, Michel. 1997. "The Invention of Identity: 'Self' and 'Other' in Pre-war Japan." In M. Weiner, ed., *Japan's Minorities: The Illusion of Homogeneity.* London: Routledge.

Wendt, Alexander. 1999. *Social Theory of International Politics.* Cambridge: Cambridge University Press.

West, Lois. 1999. "UN Women's Conferences and Feminist Politics." In Mary Meyer and Elisabeth Prugl, eds., *Gender Politics in Global Governance.* Boulder, Colo.: Rowman and Littlefield.

Wolfrum, Rudiger. 2001. "The Elimination of Racial Discrimination: Achievements and Challenges." In UNESCO, ed., *United to Combat Racism.* Paris: UNESCO.

Yamamoto, Naohide. 1998. *Sei no Jinken Kyoiku Ron* (Human rights education of sexuality). Tokyo: Akashi Shoten.

Yamashita, Yasuko. 1993. "The International Movement Toward Gender Equality and Its Impact on Japan." *US-Japan Women's Journal.* English Supplement no. 5.

Yoshida, Shinichi. 1999. "Rethinking the Public Interest in Japan: Civil Society in the Making." In Tadashi Yamamoto, ed., *Deciding the Public Good.* New York: Japan Center for International Exchange.

Yoshimi, Yoshiaki. 1995. *Jugun Ianfu* (Military comfort women). Tokyo: Iwanami Shoten.

Yui, Masako. 1997. "95–96 Okinawa no Onnatachi" (Okinawan women in 1995–96). In Yuimaru Semina, ed., *Okinawa Onnatachi wa imma* (Okinawan women today). Tokyo: Domesu Shuppan.

Index

Action Network for the Issue of Military Sexual Slavery Japan, 59, 135
Action Women's Group (Japan), 55
Activism: environmental protests, 14–15; influence of international factors, 15–16; institutional opposition to, 14–15; protests against Narita airport, 15; and social change, 18. *See also names of specific activist groups*; Nongovernmental organizations (NGOs)
Additional Protocols, to Geneva Convention (1949), 29
Affirmative action, legislation in Japan, 50–51
Agreed Conclusions on Gender and All Forms of Discrimination, in Particular Racism, Racial Discrimination, Xenophobia and Related Intolerance (2001), 36
AIDS: cited as reason for withholding of birth control pill, 54–55, 122; groups, as NGO representatives at Vienna World Conference on Human Rights, 102; and National Action Plan on human rights, 72, 73; patients and human rights, 70; and recommendation of sexual abstinence by right-wing countries in UN, 34
Ainu Association of Hokkaido, 118
Ainu Culture Promotion Law (1997), 3, 107, 136
Ainu people: alliances with domestic and international indigenous groups, 98; attempted assimilation by Japan, 97; denial of indigenous status by Japanese government, 106–7; domestic pro-rights networks, 118; and ideology of Japanese homogeneity, 149; mention in international human rights instruments and conferences by Japanese government, 117; mobilization leading to change in Japanese government policy, 136; and National Action Plan on human rights, 72, 73; NGO attendance at WCAR, 95, 103, 104, 106–8; population, 96; recognition as ethnic minority, 3, 107; recognition as indigenous people, 107; solidarity with other indigenous people, 106; use of international human rights mechanisms, 98; women, as victims of sexism in their own culture, 115; women, intersectional discrimination against, 116; women, lack of data on, 115. *See also* Ainu Culture Promotion Law (1997)
Amnesty International, 25, 104
Anti-Domestic Violence Law (2001), 85, 137, 148
Anti-Prostitution Law (1956), 41, 46, 66
Anti-Stalking Law (2000), 51, 103, 137
Ashino, Yuriko, 127
Asian Center for Women's Human Rights, 80, 134
Asian People's Friendship Society, 150
Asian Women's Fund: and compensation for comfort women, 8, 76; as controversial, 61; creation of, 121, 132–33, 135, 138; established for compensation for comfort women, 60
Asian Women's Human Rights Council, 116
Asia-Pacific Symposium on Trafficking in Persons, 91
Assertiveness training (AT), 83
Association for Research on the Impact of War and Military Bases on Women's Human Rights, 80, 82

Association for the Day for Respect for Life (Seimei Soncho no Hi Jikko Jinkai), 122, 135
Association of the Bereaved Families of the War Dead, 122, 135
Association on Men and Prostitution, 78, 82

Backlash, *see* Right-wing backlash
Bangladesh, source of illegal male migrant workers, 99
Banton, Michael, 35
Basic Law for a Gender-Equal Society (1999): and advancement of human rights of women in Japan, 2; associated education activities, 88; as evidence of domestic political change, 137; passage of, after Beijing Conference (1995), 103; as result of political pressure, 121; stipulations, 42, 51, 87
Basic Policy Concerning the Measures for Victims of Crime, 48
Battered women, *see* Domestic violence
Baxi, Uprenda, 68
Beijing conference, *see* World Conference on Women (FWCW) (Fourth, Beijing, 1995)
Beijing Japan Accountability Caucus (Beijing JAC), 63, 78
Beijing Platform for Action (1995): on abuse of rights of the girl child, 30; and issue of child prostitution, 9; and national educational efforts, 69, 94. *See also* World Conference on Women (FWCW) (Fourth, Beijing, 1995)
Beijing-Plus-Five Conference on Women (New York, 2000): information on violence against women, 26; right-wing backlash against women's rights, 33–34; workshops, 10, 85–86
Birth control pill: and activities of Women's Online Media, 79; example of domestic mobilization of global norms, 7–8, 135; formerly termed as "a problem of morality," 5; grassroots mobilization for, 53–55, 138; legalization of (1999), 1, 2, 51, 103, 126, 137; opposition to, 122, 135; and public policy paper on gender equality, 40; redefinition as reproductive right, 139
Bright Japan Diet Members Coalition (Akarui Nihon Kokkai Gün Renmei), 60
Bunch, Charlotte, 24
Buraku Liberation League, 70, 97, 118
Burakumin people: connection with UN and international NGOs, 97; denial of minority status by Japanese government, 3, 104; domestic pro-rights networks, 118; education for, 70; internal divisions in liberation movement, 104; mention in international human rights instruments and conferences by Japanese government, 117; and National Action Plan on human rights, 72, 73; NGO attendance at WCAR (2001), 95, 103, 104–6; NGO representatives at Vienna World Conference on Human Rights (1993), 102; as part of global anti-caste discrimination campaign, 105; population, 96; use of international human rights mechanisms, 98; women, in Buraku liberation group as supporters of men, 115; women, intersectional discrimination against, 73, 116; women, lack of data on, 115
Bureaucracy, Japan: departments dealing with women's issues, 41; and international relations, 14; lack of coordination in human rights jurisdictions, 119–20; mediation of social conflicts, 13; and political changes in 1990s, 138; role of, 12–13
Business interest groups, and "Triumvirate" model of Japanese state, 14

Cairo conference, *see* International Conference on Population and Development (Cairo, 1994)
Cairo Declaration on Population and Development (1994), 69, 94
Cairo Programme of Action, 30
Campus Sexual Harassment Network, 3, 57, 135
Caste: excluded as basis for discrimination from WCAR declaration, 37, 106; global anti-caste campaign, 105; and International Convention on the Elimination of All Forms of Racial Discrimination (ICERD) (1965), 34; report on "untouchables" in India by Human Rights Watch, 104; system, abolished in Japan (1871), 96
Catholic Family and Human Rights Institute, 33
CEDAW, *see* Convention on the Elimination of All Forms of Discrimination against Women (1979)
Central Pharmaceutical Advisory Council, 55, 122
Centre for Women's Global Leadership, 24
CERD, *see* International Convention on the Elimination of All Forms of Racial Discrimination (ICERD) (1965)

Child abuse: banning of, 40; police outreach program, 92; prevention, international standards, 77; prevention legislation, 51; related to abuse of mother, 146. *See also* Child Abuse Prevention Law (2000); Child pornography; Child prostitution; Child sexual abuse
Child Abuse Prevention Center, 66
Child Abuse Prevention Law (2000): and human rights of children in Japan, 2; passage, after Beijing Conference (1995), 103; passage, not due to bureaucratic initiative, 120; passage, political efforts for, 67, 137; stipulations of, 51
Child Assault Prevention (CAP) programs, 64; assertiveness training for children, 82; based on similar programs in U.S., 123; as epistemic networks, 135; increasing in schools and communities, 77, 81; and issues of child sexual abuse, prostitution and pornography, 71; proliferation since 1994, 129
Child Family Bureau (Japan), 47
Child pornography: banning of, 40; and CAP programs, 71; issue first raised by NGO groups, 124; Japan as former leading trafficking country of, 128; as part of Japanese culture, 41; redefined as "commercial sexual exploitation," 130; students' views on, 66. *See also* Child Prostitution and Pornography Prohibition Law (1999)
Child prostitution: banning of, 40; and CAP programs, 71; and concept of sexual self-determination, 144; denial of importance by Japanese officials, 9; as difficult area for reform, 7; as example of global norms redefining children's human rights in Japan, 7, 135; formerly termed "assisted entertainment," 5, 9, 66, 135, 144; grassroots mobilization around, 64–67, 123; issue first raised by NGO groups, 124; opposition to legislation against, 135; as part of Japanese culture, 41; redefined as "commercial sexual exploitation," 130, 139; reframing of issue at world conferences led by NGOs, 128; students' views on, 66. *See also* Child Prostitution and Pornography Prohibition Law (1999)
Child Prostitution and Pornography Prohibition Law (1999): associated education activities, 88; and children's human rights, 2; drafting of, 121; and epistemic networks, 135; opposition to, 122–23, 130; passage, not due to bureaucratic initiative, 120; passage of, after Beijing Conference (1995), 103; passage of, as evidence of domestic political change, 9, 137; passage of, political efforts for, 129–30; stipulations of, 51
Child sexual abuse: and activities of Forum on Sex Issues, 78; and CAP programs, 71; congresses and conventions on, 30–31; grassroots mobilization around, 64, 66–67; as issue for overlapping global women's networks, 25; legislation in Japan, 51. *See also* Child pornography; Child prostitution; Child Prostitution and Pornography Prohibition Law (1999)
Children and Textbooks Japan Net 21 (Kodomo to Kyokasho Net 21), 85
Children's Constitution (Kodomo Kensho), 65
Children's human rights: compatibility with women's human rights, 145; contribution of NGO participation in world conferences, 5; disabled children, 64; education regarding, 71; effect of leverage politics in recognition of, 131; expanding list of issues, 73; global norms on, 30–31; illegitimate children, 64; lack of consensus on definition of terms, 143; legal changes to, 1997–2001, 2; minority children, 64; and National Action Plan on human rights, 72, 73; as new concept in Japan, 128; NGO support and education groups, 3, 5; opposition to, 71–72, 145; refugee children, 64; reproductive health, and right-wing opposition, 34; rights of the girl child, 30; and sex education, 77; and sexual violence issues, 73; and trafficking in children, 73. *See also* Child Abuse Prevention Law (2000); Child Prostitution and Pornography Prohibition Law (1999); Law to Promote Human Rights Education (2000); World Congress against Commercial Sexual Exploitation of Children (CSEC) (First, Stockholm, 1996)
Children's rights movement: built on feminist campaign against violence against women, 30; debate over desirability of human rights approach, 145
Children's Rights Network 97 (Kodomo no Kenri Nettwwakingu 97), 64
Children's Rights Sub-Committee, of Japan Federation of Bar Associations (Nichibenren), 146

China: source of comfort women, 124; source of illegal male migrant workers, 99

Christian Temperance Women Union, 22, 40, 59

Citizenship: denied to Korean residents of Japan, 111; and ICERD, 35; national, as core notion in Japanese social organization, 6

Civil Code (Japan), Article 30, on maintenance of public order, 102

CLADEM, *see* Latin American Committee for the Defense of Women's Rights

Colonization: and reparation, mention excluded from WCAR documents, 37; reparation for, not covered in UN conventions, 35; and slavery, in WCAR Declaration and Programme of Action, 112–13

Comfort women: admission of enforced sexual slavery by Japanese government, 40, 59–60; case histories, 57–58; deletion of mention in Japanese school textbooks, 61; and divisions in Japanese feminist movement, 6, 125, 131; as example of domestic mobilization of global norms, 135; as example of intersectional discrimination, 115; as example of racial aspects of gender discrimination, 134–35; grassroots mobilization for compensation, 7, 57–61, 138; and information on women's human rights in Japan in 1990s, 75; issue raised by Korean women's movement, 124; lacking united support of female politicians, 131; media reporting on, 76; mentioned in Vision of Gender Equality policy paper, 42; movement, as representative of paradigm shift in Japanese feminism, 98; nationalities of, 58, 124; opposition to recognition, 122; and Promotion of Resolution for Issues Concerning Victims of Wartime Sexual Coercion (Japan, 2001), 40; redefined as "military sexual slavery," 139; redefinition of issue from bilateral foreign policy to international human rights, 133; right-wing backlash against, 85; and right-wing backlash against, 60. *See also* Military sexual slavery; Promotion of Resolution for Issues Concerning Victims of Wartime Sexual Coercion (Japan, 2001)

Commercial sexual exploitation: previously described as "assisted entertainment," 5, 9, 66, 135, 144; as redefinition of "child prostitution" and "child pornography," 130, 139

Commission on Japan's Goals in the 21st Century, 146–47

Conference on Environment and Development (Rio de Janeiro, 1992): mobilization around issues by women's activists, 25–26; and transnational feminist organizing, 141; Women's Action Agenda 21, 24; Women's Caucus, introduction of, 25

Conference on Human Settlements (Habitat II) (Istanbul, 1996), 141

Congrès international de droit des femmes (Paris, 1878), 21–22

Consciousness raising (CR), 83

Constitution (Japan): Article 9, on use of force in anti-terrorist attacks, 102; and human rights, 69, 70, 102, 111

Constructivist theory of state: activists and social change, 18; as embedded network state, 19; interpretations of social change in Japan, 10; sociological, emphasizing world culture/society, 16. *See also* State, theories of

Convention against Transnational Organized Crime (2000), 30

Convention No. 29 on Forced Labor (1930), 134

Convention on the Elimination of All Forms of Discrimination against Women (CEDAW) (1979): adoption of, 34; equality/equal opportunity approach to women's rights, 23; feminism and issues of minority women, 141; lack of mention of gender-specific violence, 23; monitoring by NGOs, 84; Optional Protocol, allowing individual complaint procedure, 27; translation, into Japanese, 88–89; use in anti-discrimination cases in Japan, 100

Convention on the Elimination of All Forms of Racial Discrimination, *see* International Convention on the Elimination of All Forms of Racial Discrimination (ICERD) (1965)

Convention on the Protection of the Rights of All Migrant Workers and Members of Their Families (1990), 98, 113–14

Convention on the Rights of the Child (CRC) (1990): absence of mention of women's rights, 22; adoption of, 34; advocacy for, in Japan, 65; and establishment of children's human rights education in Japan, 71; as international standard, 77; and Japanese NGOs regarding children's rights, 64; lack

of consensus on interpretation, 145; and Optional Protocol on Sexual Exploitation of Children (2000), 31; provision on sexual abuse, 30; signed by Japan (1994), 9, 102, 128; and World Congress against Commercial Sexual Exploitation of Children (First, Stockholm, 1996), 30–31
Convention on the Status of Refugees (1982), 111
Coomaraswamy, Radhika, 132
Copenhagen conferences, *see* World Conference on Women (Second, Copenhagen, 1980); World Summit for Social Development (Copenhagen, 1995)
Copenhagen Declaration and Programme of Action, at World Summit for Social Development (Copenhagen, 1995), 28
Council on Gender Equality (Japan): address of Prime Minister Hashimoto Ryutaro (1997), 1, 2; as advisory and liaison organization, 119; on Basic Law on Gender Equality, 147–48; as coordinating body, 120; establishment of Subcommittee on Violence against Women (1997), 42; and human rights education in Japan, 87; public policy paper on women and children's issues (1996), 40; report on violence against women (1999), 43
Counseling: for battered women, in Japan, 46–47; feminist, 3, 63; for sexual assault, 89
Covenant on Civil and Political Rights (CCPR), 102–3
Covenant on Economic, Social, and Cultural Rights (CESR), 103
Crenshaw, Kimberlé, 36
CSEC, *see* World Congress against Commercial Sexual Exploitation of Children (First, Stockholm, 1996)
CSW, *see* UN Commission on the Status of Women

Dalit women, intersectional discrimination against, 116
DAW, *see* Division for the Advancement of Women
Dawn Center (Osaka, Japan), 50
Declaration on the Elimination of Violence against Women (1994): adoption of, 27; and human rights education in Japan, 69, 94; mentioned in Vision of Gender Equality policy paper (1996), 42
Declaration on the Rights of Indigenous Peoples (draft, 1995), 108
Democratic Party (Japan), 138
Dentsu (Japanese corporation), 44
Disabled people: children, 64; and human rights education, 70; human rights of, 70; and National Action Plan on human rights, 72, 73
Discrimination: core notions in Japanese political culture, 6; against ethnic, racial and sexual minorities, 149; mobilization for anti-discrimination legislation, 151. *See also* International Convention on the Elimination of All Forms of Racial Discrimination (ICERD) (1965); Intersectional discrimination; Minorities; Racial discrimination; World Conference against Racism, Racial Discrimination, Xenophobia, and Related Intolerance (WCAR) (Durban, 2001)
Division for the Advancement of Women (DAW): and Expert Group Meeting on Race and Gender (Zagreb, 2000), 35; resolutions on violence against women, 23. *See also* UN Commission on the Status of Women (CSW)
Doi, Takako, 121
Domestic social movements: crucial role in human rights legislation, 123–25; results due to mobilization of global norms on human rights, 125–26
Domestic violence: compatibility of women's and children's rights, 145; denial of existence by Japanese officials, 8–9; denounced at World Summit for Social Development (Copenhagen, 1995), 28; as difficult area for reform, 7; early research on spousal violence, 62; effect of Fourth World Conference on Women (1995) on Japanese mobilization against, 9; effect of leverage politics in recognition of, 131; formerly termed "marital dispute," 5, 135; grassroots mobilization against, 3, 61–64, 123, 124, 135, 138; information proliferation on, in Japan in 1990s, 75; initiatives by local Japanese governments, 49–50; as issue for overlapping global women's networks, 25; lack of reporting by non-Japanese women, 115; legal responses to, 92; men's batterer prevention programs, 3, 63; opposition interest groups, 135; and public policy paper on gender equality, 40; redefined as human rights is-

sue, 139; resources for women, 46–47, 62, 78, 80; self-defense as legitimate defense, 62; self-help groups for batterers, 83; surveys of, 26, 43–44, 124, 125; term introduced in Japan, 43; translated as "domesutikku baiorensu (DV)", 64; and U.S. battered women's movement, 9; violence of children against parents, 61–62. *See also* Child abuse; Domestic Violence Prevention Law (2001); DV Survey Research Group; Women's shelters
Domestic Violence Act (Malaysia, 1994), 26
Domestic Violence Legal Manual, 78, 84
Domestic Violence Prevention Law (2001): and advancement of human rights of women in Japan, 2; example of domestic mobilization of global norms, 135; and FWCW, 9; passage of, after Beijing Conference (1995), 103; stipulations of, 51
Domestic Violence Research Project (DV Mondai Kenkyu Project), 50
Domoto, Akiko, 121, 127, 130, 138
Dowa education (Burakamin people): changing to human rights education, 72, 73; Dowa Educators' Associations, 70; as part of Buraku liberation movement, 70
Durban 2001 Japan coalition, 103. *See also* World Conference against Racism, Racial Discrimination, Xenophobia, and Related Intolerance (WCAR) (Durban, 2001)
DV Prevention Project for Batterers, 63
DV Survey Research Group, 3, 50, 124, 135

East Asia, source of illegal female migrant workers, 99
Economic and Social Council for the Asia-Pacific Region (ESCAP), 128
ECPAT, *see* End Child Prostitution in Asian Tourism
Education: changes, for women in Japan, 48–49, 70–71; and diffusion of global norms, 68; empowerment education, 79, 82; equal opportunity for women in universities, 70–71; through transnational social movements, 142–43. *See also* Law to Promote Human Rights Education (2000); Women's studies
Efforts to Eradicate Violence against Women with the Family and Society (Resolution, 1988), 23
Eisaku, Sato, 54
El Taller International, 116
Elderly, and National Action Plan on human rights, 72, 73
Elimination of Violence Against Women Week (Japan), 49
Embedded network state, in global human rights community: as constructivist approach to international relations, 4; and domestic epistemic NGO networks, 12, 19, 138; global human rights norms and Japanese education, 86; view of core notions in Japanese political culture, 6
Emperor Hirohito: accused of crimes against humanity, 134; as symbol of nationalist Japan, 101
End Child Prostitution in Asian Tourism (ECPAT) International (Thailand): founding of, 66; organization of World Congress against Commercial Sexual Exploitation of Children (1996), 30, 128
End Child Prostitution in Asian Tourism (ECPAT) Japan: and domestic mobilization of global norms, 124, 135; founding of, 66, 129; mission statement, 129
English, proposed as second official Japanese language, 150–51
Environmental protests, 14–15, 25–26
Epistemic human rights network: and global human rights community, 12, 19, 138; as influence on Japanese state, 18–19; knowledge production and dissemination by NGOs, 5, 135; organization of international conferences, 21–26
Equal Employment Opportunity Law (1985), 44
Equal Employment Opportunity Law (revised 1997): and advancement of human rights of women in Japan, 2; associated education activities, 88; example of domestic mobilization of global norms, 135; passage, as evidence of domestic political change, 137; revision of, after Beijing Conference (1995), 103; revision of 1985 law, 50, 57; and sexual harassment prevention, 8, 55; stipulations of, 50; training of civil servants in prevention of sexual harassment, 92–93
ESCAP, *see* Economic and Social Council for the Asia-Pacific Region
Eugenics Protection Law, 64
Expert Group Meeting on Race and Gender (Zagreb, 2000), 35–36

Expert Group on Women in Development of the OECD (Organization for Economic Cooperation and development) (1992), inclusion of women's human rights, 24

Family: breakup, and women's independence, 146; and difficulty of mobilizing on domestic violence in Japan, 9; primacy of, in Japan, 147. *See also* Child abuse; Children's human rights; Domestic violence; Women's human rights
Family and Violence Study Group, of Japan Federation of Bar Associations (Nichibenren), 145
Family Planning Federation of Japan, 127
Federation for the Protection of Children's Human Rights Japan (Kodomo no Jinken Ren), 3, 102, 135
Federation of Economic Organizations (Keidanren), 122, 135
Federation of Employers Associations (Nikkeiren), 56, 122, 135
Female genital mutilation: first discussed at Copenhagen conference (1980), 23; as issue for overlapping global women's networks, 25
Femin Net (Japan), survey of initiatives on women's issues by local governments, 49
Feminism: "global," and issues of intersectionality of race and gender, 141–42; and human rights, 144; and information on women's human rights in Japan in 1990s, 75; and male women's studies scholars, 83; transnational feminist organizing, 140–42
Feminism, Japan, *see* Women's movement, Japan
Feminist Therapy Research Association, 79
Filipino people: comfort women, 58, 124; illegal male migrant workers, 99; imported brides in Japan, 99
Forced Labor, Convention No. 29 (ILO, 1930), 134
Foreigners, in Japan: human rights of, 70; and National Action Plan on human rights, 72, 73; population, in Japan, 96. *See also* Japanese returnees from China; Migrant workers; *names of specific nationalities*; Nikkeijin (South American Japanese)
Forum on Sex Issues, 78, 85
Forum Yokohama, 50
Fourth World Conference on Women (FWCW) (Beijing, 1995), *see* World Conference on Women (FWCW) (Fourth, Beijing, 1995)
France: interministerial circular on policies concerning domestic violence (1999), 26; survey on domestic violence (2000), 26
Freedom of expression, and objection to law on child prostitution and pornography, 130
Fujioka, Hidenobu, 60, 61
Fukushima, Mizuho, 138
FWCW, *see* World Conference on Women (Fourth, Beijing, 1995)

Gakko Hōkai (School breakdown), 145
Gay rights movement, 149–50
Gender: and increase in information on women's human rights in Japan in 1990s, 75; introduction to Japanese vocabulary, 74
Gender equality: and activities of Tokyo Women Foundation, 79; introduction of term in Japan, 42; opportunities for, improved by coalition of political parties, 121. *See also* Basic Law for a Gender-Equal Society (1999); Women's human rights; "Vision of Gender Equality"
Gender Equality Sub-Committee, of Japan Federation of Bar Associations (Nichibenren), 146
Gender-Related Dimensions of Racial Discrimination (General Recommendation XXV of CERD Committee) (2000), 35
Geneva Convention, Additional Protocols (1949), 29
Germain, Adrienne, 27
Global Campaign for Women's Human Rights, 24
Global human rights community: global discourse and domestic follow-up on issues, 5; Japanese non-governmental (NGO) organizations within, 1–2, 4–5; and local mobilization of women and children's rights in Japan, 7; rise of global civil society, 141
Global Leadership Institute (1991), 24
Gokan Shien Center (Rape Crisis Center), 123
Goose, Stephen, 143
Government, Japan: bureaucracy, role of, 12–13; Diet (parliament) as key policy decision forum, 13; local government initiatives on women's issues, 49–50. *See also* Bureaucracy, Japan; Japan; *names of specific*

ministries; *names of specific political parties*; Political parties; Prime Minister's Office; State, theories of
Group orientation, as core notion in Japanese political culture, 6
GRULAC group, 108

Hara, Hiroko, 128
Harmony (non-legalism): as core notion in Japanese political culture, 6; debate on necessity for legal solutions, 148; human rights legislation as contrast to traditional social management, 147
Hashimoto, Ryutaro (Prime Minister), 1, 2
Hata, Tsutomu, 101
Headquarters for the Planning and Promotion of Policies Relating to Women, 41
Headquarters for the Promotion of Human Rights Education, 72
Heyzer, Noeleen, 28
Hierarchical social organization: as core notion in Japanese political culture, 6; and new practices of horizontal networking, 148–49
Hiranuma, Takeo, 107
Hiratsuka, Raicho, 40
HIV, *see* AIDS
Hokkaido Development Agency, 97
Hokkaido Former Natives Protection Act (1899), 97, 106
Hokkaido Utari Welfare Policy, 106
Holy See, *see* Vatican
Homogeneity (national citizenship): as core notion in Japanese political culture, 6; and issues of minority groups, 149; pressure for multicultural society, 151
Homosexuality, social movements, 149–50
Honor killings: global campaign against, 26; as issue for overlapping global women's networks, 25; provisions in Hague Convention (1907), 29
hooks, bell, 81
Hosokawa, Morihiro, 120
Hot Line on Violence against Women, 57
Human rights: and feminism, 144; as global issues, 2–3; handled by administrative guidance rather than legal procedures in Japan, 70; individualism, and traditional Japanese culture, 6; and issue of sexuality, 144; and local advocacy education, 4; National Plan of Action, 72. *See also* Children's human rights; Law to Promote Human Rights Education (2000); Women's human rights; World Conference on Human Rights (Vienna, 1993)
Human rights education: as alternative form of politics, 74; and creation of knowledge-based community as resource, 76; and curriculum changes, 83–85; First National Plan of Action for Human Rights Education, 68–73; foreign terms introduced to Japanese language, 86; Japan national plan of action for human rights education, 91; legislation in Japan, 51; participatory, introduction of, 83; policy, 70; reframing of human rights issues at world conferences, 4; translation of foreign documents, 84–85; and UNESCO, 31; in universities, 70
Human Rights Forum 21, 73
Human Rights Subcommission on the Prevention of Discrimination and the Protection of Minorities, 131
Human Rights Watch, 25, 104, 105

ICC, *see* International Criminal Court
ICERD, *see* International Convention on the Elimination of All Forms of Racial Discrimination (1965)
Ichikawa, Fusae, 40
ICTR, *see* International Criminal Tribunal for Rwanda (1995)
ICTY, *see* International Criminal Tribunal for the Former Yugoslavia (1993)
Ienaga, Saburo, 85
Illegitimate children, in Japan, 64
IMADR, *see* International Movement against All Forms of Discrimination and Racism
Immigration Control Act (1990), 99
India: caste, and racial discrimination, 34; objection to "descent" in WCAR Programme of Action, 105–6; report on "untouchables" by Human Rights Watch, 104
Indigenous people: lack of protection under ICERD and ICCPR, 35; mention excluded from WCAR documents, 37. *See also* Ainu people; Burakumin people; Okinawan people
Indigenous Peoples' Caucus, 108
Individualism: at odds with traditional Japanese culture, 6; shift towards, in Japan, 147
Inter-American Convention on the Preven-

tion, Punishment and Eradication of Violence against Women (1994), 27
Inter-American Institute for Human Rights, 24
Interest groups: influence on bureaucracy and political parties, 14; opposition to political change, 121–22; and political changes in 1990s, 138. *See also* Activism; Nongovernmental organizations (NGOs); Women's groups
International Bureau for the Suppression of Traffic in Women and Children (1899), 22
International Confederation of Trade Unions, 55
International Conference on Population and Development (Cairo, 1994): effect on mobilization for birth control pill in Japan, 8, 139; emphasis on right to sexual self-determination, as influence on view of child prostitution in Japan, 144; emphasis on rights of girl child, 30; impact of, 5; introduction of concept of violence as form of control of women's health and sexuality, 27; link between violence against women and population and development, 26; and mobilization of global norms on human rights in Japan, 126; Program of Action, defining reproductive health as women's human rights issue, 27; and transnational feminist organizing, 141
International Covenant on Civil and Political Rights (ICCPR) (1966): lack of protection of indigenous people, 35; and Law for the Promotion of Ainu Culture (1997), 107
International Convention on the Elimination of All Forms of Racial Discrimination (ICERD) (1965): absence of mention of women's rights, 22; and acknowledgment of Japan's discrimination against Burakumin people, 105; adoption of, 34; on lack of distinction between citizens and noncitizens, 35; lack of protection of indigenous people, 35; ratification in Japan (1995), 98; ratified by Japanese in 1995, with little effect on minority group rights, 9; and role of International Human Rights NGO Network, 102, 103; statement on gender and discrimination, 35; and status of migrant workers, 114
International Convention on the Protection of the Rights of All Migrant Workers and Members of Their Families (1990), 9–10, 35
International Council for Women Peace Committee (1913), 22
International Criminal Court (ICC), 29
International Criminal Police Organization, 91
International Criminal Tribunal for Rwanda (ICTR) (1995), 29
International Criminal Tribunal for the Former Yugoslavia (ICTY) (1993), 29
International Dalit Solidarity Network, 104, 105
International Family Planning Association world congress (Tokyo, 1955), 7
International Gay and Lesbian Human Rights Commission, 150
International Human Rights NGO Network, 102
International Labor Organization Committee of Experts, on military sexual slavery as forced labor, 134
International Labor Organization (ILO) Convention 169, 108
International Military Tribunal for Nuremberg, 29
International Movement against All Forms of Discrimination and Racism (IMADR), 104, 106, 118
International Women's Health Coalition, 27
International Women's Rights Action Watch (IWRAW), 84
International Women's Year (1975), 71
International Year of the World's Indigenous Peoples (1993), 108
Intersectional discrimination: definition, 36; of female migrant workers, 114; and human rights education, 73; of minority women, 98, 116; race and gender discrimination, 134–35, 141. *See also* Comfort women; Migrant women; Minority women
Iran, source of illegal male migrant workers, 99
Ishihara, Shintaro, 101
ISIS International, 23
Islamic countries: opposition to children's sex education, 34; opposition to women's rights, 33

JAIWR, *see* Japanese Association of International Women's Rights
Japan: acceptance of global human rights norms and domestic political change, 137–40; accountability politics, and interna-

tional opinion, 139–40; constructivist view of, and international relations, 4, 6, 12; core notions in political culture, 6; culture, as slow to change, 7; economic success, and bureaucratic role, 12–13; English proposed as second official language, 150–51; ethnic populations, 96; institutional changes and women's issues, 44–50, 52; international relations, 14; low birth rate, 55; nationalist legacy of, 101; party politics, 120–21; policy changes on women's rights, 41–44; social change, constructivist interpretations of, 10; state as educator of global human rights norms, 88–94; susceptibility to foreign pressure in trade and economics, 7. *See also* Embedded network state, in global human rights community; Government, Japan; State, theories of

Japan Anti-Prostitution Association (JAPA), 59

Japan Association for Maternal Welfare (Nihon Bosei Hogo I Kyokai), 122

Japan Association for the Lesbian and Gay Movement (OCCUR), 150

Japan Association of Obstetrics and Gynecology for Maternal Protection, 54

Japan Association of the Bereaved Families of the War Dead, 122, 135

Japan Association of Women's Human Rights, 148

Japan Civil Liberties Union, 63, 78, 147

Japan Domestic Violence Prevention and Information Center, 63, 78, 82, 84–85

Japan Federation of Bar Associations (Nichibenren): Children's Rights Sub-Committee, 146; Family and Violence Study Group, 145; Gender Equality Sub-Committee, 146; hotline for battered women, 62

Japan-Korea Summit, and apology to Korea for military sexual slavery of comfort women, 59

Japan Midwives Association, 122

Japan New Party, 120

Japan Pacific Information Network, 56

Japan Renewal Party, 120

Japan Society of Obstetrics and Gynecology, 54

Japan Youth Research Institute, 66

Japanese Association of International Women's Rights (JAIWR), 84

Japanese returnees from China, 95

Japanese Society for History Textbook Reform (Atarashii Rekishi Kyokasho wo Tsukuru Kai), 60, 85, 101–2

Japanese Society for the Protection of Children, 64

Japanese Teachers' Union (Nikkyoso), 65, 102

Japanese Women's Studies Association, 57, 82

Japan's Federation of Employers Associations, 56, 122, 135

Japan's Network for Women and Health: Cairo, 94; and issue of "reproductive health," 126–27; and lobby for the birth control pill, 55, 127, 128, 135

Kansai Counseling Center, 89

Kawahashi, Yukiko, 138

Keidanren (Federation of Economic Organizations), 122

Kim Hak Shun, 59–60

Kobe earthquake, 76

Kobe Lawyers Association, Gender Equality Committee, 63

Kodomo no Jinken Ren (Federation for the Protection of Children's Human Rights Japan), 65

Kodomo no Kenri Nettwwakingu 97 (Children's Rights Network 97), 64

Komeito (political party), 121, 138

Komiyama, Yoko, 138

Korea, as colony of Japan, 97

Korea Church Women United, 59

Korean Council for the Women Drafted for Sexual Slavery by Japan, 59, 80, 124, 134

Korean Democratic Women's Club, 125

Korean residents, in Japan: advancement of rights, due to ratification of Refugee Convention, 136; assimilative education policy, 111; denial of Japanese citizenship, 111; denial of racial minority status, 111–12; domestic pro-rights networks, 118; foreigner status, and struggle for rights, 98; and human rights education, 70; and ideology of Japanese homogeneity, 149; imposition of South Korean citizenship, 97; Japanese policy towards, 110; as laborers in Japan, 97; lack of social security and voting rights, 111; mention in international human rights instruments and conferences by Japanese government, 117; NGO representatives at Vienna World Conference on Human Rights, 102; NGO representatives at WCAR

(2001), 95, 103, 112; population, 96, 111; pressure to change name to Japanese form, 111; as "special permanent residents," 3, 111; use of international human rights mechanisms, 98. *See also* Comfort women
Korean women, in Japan: grassroots mobilization for compensation for comfort women, 58–59; as imported brides in Japan, 99; intersectional discrimination against, 115, 116; lack of data on, 115; as majority of "comfort women," 58. *See also* Comfort women; Korean residents, in Japan

La Nuestra (satellite conference, Vienna, 1993), 24
Landmines, banning of, 140, 143
Latin American Committee for the Defense of Women's Rights (CLADEM), 23
Latin American women, and transnational women's movement, 22
Law for the Promotion of Ainu Culture (1997), 107
Law to Promote Human Rights Education (2000): and advancement of human rights of women and children in Japan, 2; enactment, as evidence of domestic political change, 137; inclusion of women's human rights, 51; stipulations of, 72, 87
Lawyers Network against Violence against Women, 3, 89, 135
Legalism: bureaucratic mediation preferred to litigation, 13; at odds with traditional Japanese culture, 6
Lesbian rights movement, 149–50
Leverage politics, through alliance with target domestic politicians, 5
Liaison Group of International Women's Year, 59
Liberal Democratic Party (LDP): Bright Japan Diet Members Coalition (Akarui Nihon Kokkai Gün Renmei), 60; changes and coalition politics in 1990s, 138; demise of dominance of, 120–21; durability of, 13; and issue of child prostitution and pornography, 129; and one-party rule in Japan, 101
Liberal Party, 121, 138
Liberal Revisionist Research Institute (Jiyushugishikan Kenkyukai), 60
Lifelong education, of women, 48, 71
Local governments (Japan), initiatives on women's issues, 49–50. *See also names of specific local governments*
Lyotard, Jean Francois, 52

Malaysia, Domestic Violence Act (1994), 26
Manchuria, as Japanese puppet state, 97
Martinez, D. P., 12
Matsushima women's clinic, 89
McDougall, Gay, 134
Media reports, of women's human rights issues, 76
Medical Institute on School Refusal Culture, 64
Men's festival, 83
Men's groups, 3, 63, 82–83
Men's Lib Kanagawa, 63
Men's Lib Tokyo, 3, 63
Men's Liberation Festival, 63
Men's Liberation Research Association, 83
Men's studies, 83
Mexico conference, *see* World Conference on Women (First, Mexico, 1975)
Migrant Rights Group, 104
Migrant women: intersectional discrimination against, 115, 116; and prostitution in Japan, 41; status of, debates at WCAR, 114; trafficking of, 73; violence against, as issue for overlapping global women's networks, 25. *See also* Migrant workers
Migrant workers: and assumption of homogeneity in Japanese society, 149, 150; current immigration policy based on descent, 113; denial of national insurance, public assistance and voting rights, 3; domestic pro-rights networks, 118; government attitude towards, 101; illegal, population increase in, 99; inability of Japanese NGOs to obtain political support for, 136; ineligible for social services, 3, 113; international convention on, 35; mention excluded from WCAR documents, 37; mention in international human rights instruments and conferences by Japanese government, 117; NGO attendance at WCAR (2001), 95; NGOs in Durban 2001 Japan coalition, 103, 113–14; as "overstayers," 113; as permanent residents of Japan, 99; population, 113; three stages of migration to Japan, 99. *See also* Migrant women
Migration and Refugees NGO Caucus, 113–14
Military comfort women (Jugun Ianfu), 58

Military sexual slavery: and activities of Asian Center for Women's Human Rights, 80; and activities of Association for Research on the Impact of War and Military Bases on Women's Human Rights, 80; and activities of Korean Council for the Military Sexual Slavery by Japan, 80; and activities of Violence against Women-Net Japan, 80; and activities of Women's Caucus for Gender Justice, 80; admission by Japanese government, 59–60; case histories, 57–58; as combination of gender and racial politics, 8; complicity of Japanese women, 8; denial of legal responsibility by Japanese government, 8; as difficult area for reform, 7; as divisive issue in Japanese women's movement, 8, 136; as example of domestic mobilization of global norms, 135; grassroots mobilization against, 57–61; history of, 131–36; and ideology of Japanese homogeneity, 149; ignored by post-war military treaties, 58; and mobilization by Korean women's groups, 8; opposition to mention in history textbooks, 60, 135; previously described as "comfort women," 5, 135; recognition of, and crucial role of domestic social movements, 123; as violation of international humanitarian law, 132. *See also* Comfort women; Women's International War Crimes Tribunal on Japan's Military Sexual Slavery (2002)

Ministry of Education: approval of elimination of war clauses in history textbooks, 101–2; and changes in women's education, 48–49; guidelines on sexual harassment, 46, 125; Lifelong Learning Bureau, Gender Equality Education Division, 49; responsibility for equal-gender education, 120; and slow introduction of children's human rights, 71–72

Ministry of Finance, studies of, 119

Ministry of Foreign Affairs: Asia-Pacific Symposium on Trafficking in Persons, 91; Human Rights and Refugee Section, 90; Multilateral Cooperation Department, 90; as traditional agency for handling relationship with UN, 90; workshop on human rights education, 90

Ministry of Health and Welfare: acknowledgement of AIDS in Japan, 54–55; Central Pharmaceutical Advisory Council, 122; investigation of pill by Oral Contraception Committee, 54; lack of initiative in children's sexuality issues, 120; on lack of social services to migrant workers, 113; quick approval of Viagra, 128; violence against women as political concern, 46

Ministry of International Trade and Industry (MITI): and formulation of industrial policy, 14; studies of, 119

Ministry of Justice: Civil Liberties Bureau, and human rights protection, 69; proposal to eliminate time limit on reporting rape, 48

Ministry of Labor: and change in handling of sexual harassment, 44–46; increase of reporting of sexual harassment, 44; responsibility for sexual harassment prevention, 120; sexual harassment study group, 57; survey on sexual harassment (1993), 44

Minorities: attitude towards, 96; limited impact of global minority rights norms on, 3, 9–10; mention in international human rights instruments and conferences by Japanese government, 117; NGO mobilization for, 95–118; population count, 96. *See also* Ainu people; Burakumin people; Korean residents, in Japan; Migrant workers; Minority children; Minority rights; Minority women; Okinawan people

Minority children, 64

Minority rights: absence of world conferences on, 5; development of, within United Nations, 34–38; and Japanese ideology as homogenous race, 95

Minority Rights Group, 97

Minority women: domestic pro-rights networks, 118; inability of Japanese NGOs to obtain political support for, 136; mention in international human rights instruments and conferences by Japanese government, 117; multiple discrimination against, 73, 115, 151; NGOs in Durban 2001 Japan coalition, 103, 115–18; not specifically covered by UN convention, 35; violence against, as issue for overlapping global women's networks, 25

MITI, *see* Ministry of International Trade and Industry

Miyazawa, Kiichi, 59–60

Mori, Arinori, 151

Mori, Yoshiro, 101

Moriyama, Mayumi, 130, 138

Murayama, Tomiichi, 121, 138

Mushakoji, Kinhide, 105–6
Muslim countries, *see* Islamic countries

Nagano, Shigeto, 60, 101
Nairobi conference, *see* World Conference on Women (Third, Nairobi, 1985)
Nakasone, Yasuhiro, 101
Narita, Tokuhei, 98
National citizenship (homogeneity), as core notion in Japanese political culture, 6
National Committee on Violence against Women (Australia), 26
National Convention on Family Planning and Maternal and Child Health (1972), 54
National Dalit Human Rights Campaign, 104
National Federation of UNESCO Association in Japan, 64
National Institute for Japanese Language, 151
National Network in Solidarity with Migrant Workers, 113, 118
National Plan of Action for Human Rights Education (1997), 72, 73, 77, 87
National Plan of Action for the Promotion of a Gender-Equal Society by Year 2000 (Japan, 1996), 42, 86–87, 149
National Police Agency (NPA): anti-stalking task force, 51; and guidelines on sexual harassment, 125; handling of sex crimes in Japan, 47–48; International Criminal Affairs Division, 91; Police Policy Research Center, 92; responsible for measures for victims of sex crimes, 120
National Report of the Government of Japan for the Fourth World Conference on Women (1994), 44
National Shelter Network, 135
National Women Counselors Network, 63
National Women's Education Center (NWEC), 49, 74, 79, 82
National Women's Shelters Network, 3, 80
Native people, *see* Indigenous people
Network to Fight against Sexual Violence, 62
Network to Study Sexual Harassment in the Workplace, 56
Networking ("nettowakingu"), among NGOs, 149
New History Teaching Diet Members Coalition (Atarashii Rekishi wo Tsutaeru Kokkai Giin Renmei), 60
New Japan Party (Shinshinto), 60
New Women Association (Shin Jujin Kyokai), 40
NGO Global Tribunal on Violations of Women's Human Rights (Geneva, 1993), 24
NGO Group for the Convention of the Rights of the Child, 30
NGO Liaison Group for the World Conference on Human Rights, 102
Nibutani Dam case, 107
Nichibenren (Japan Federation of Bar Associations), 62, 145, 146
Nichibo (Japan Association for Maternal Welfare), 122
Nihon Bosei Hogo I Kyokai (Japan Association for Maternal Welfare), 122
Nikkei Shimbun (Japanese corporation), 44–45
Nikkei Woman, 56
Nikkeijin (South American Japanese), 99, 113
Nikkeiren (Federation of Employers Associations), 56, 122, 135
Nikkyoso (Japanese Teachers' Union), 65
Nishimura, Shingo, 39
No! Sexual Harassment, 57
Noda, Seiko, 129
Nogata Police Station (Tokyo), 89
Non-governmental organizations (NGOs): ambivalence about working with Japanese government, 149; attendance at world human rights conferences, 139; on children's rights, 30–31, 64–67; embedded in global human rights community, 4, 6, 86, 138–39; and information on women's human rights in Japan in 1990s, 75, 76; and Japanese government emphasis on networking, 149; mobilization for anti-discrimination legislation, 151; networking ("nettowakingu") among, 149; push for education in human rights, 31–32, 84–85; role in implementation of laws, 148; special rapporteur system, 140; successful campaigns, 140; working relationships with female politicians, 5, 139. *See also names of specific groups; titles of conferences*
Non-legalism, *see* Harmony (non-legalism)

OCCUR, *see* Japan Association for the Lesbian and Gay Movement
Office for Gender Equality, 47
Office for Women's Affairs, 41

Office of High Commissioner for Human Rights, 35, 90
Ogata, Sadako, 150
Ohio State Rape Crisis Center, 82
Okayama Prefectural Assembly, 61
Okinawa, annexation by Japan, 97
Okinawa, rape incident involving U.S. military personnel, 115
Okinawa Development Agency, 109
Okinawan Citizen Info Center, 118
Okinawan people: denial of status as ethnic or indigenous people of Ryukyu Islands, 3, 109–10; domestic pro-rights networks, 118; and ideology of Japanese homogeneity, 149; inability of Japanese NGOs to obtain political support for, 136; independence movement associated with anti-militarism movement, 109; mention in international human rights instruments and conferences by Japanese government, 117; NGO attendance at WCAR (2001), 95; NGOs in Durban 2001 Japan coalition, 103, 109–10; objection to Ryukyu Islands as military bases, 110; population, 96; use of international human rights mechanisms, 98; women, intersectional discrimination against, 116; women, lack of data on, 115
Optional Protocol on Sexual Exploitation of Children to the Convention on the Rights of the Child (2000), 130–31
Organization of African Unity (OAU), 37
Organization of Islamic Countries (OIC), 33, 37
Ota, Masahide, 110
Otto (koibito) kara no Boryoku (Violence from Husbands or Partners Survey Research Group), 62
Owaki, Masako, 127, 129, 138

Pakistan, source of illegal male migrant workers, 99
Personnel Authority: and Rule 10–10, 45; sexual harassment guidelines for civil servants, 45, 125
Philippines: comfort women, 58, 124; source of illegal male migrant workers, 99; source of imported brides, 99
"Pill." *See* Birth control pill
Police Policy Research Center, 92
Political parties: and bureaucracy, 12; female politicians, support for women and children's human rights, 138; female politicians, working relationships with NGOs, 139; and international relations, 14; party politics, history of, 120–21
Population, of minorities in Japan, 96, 99, 113. *See also* International Conference on Population and Development (Cairo, 1994)
Pornography, child, *see* Child pornography; World Congress against Commercial Sexual Exploitation of Children (CSEC) (First, Stockholm, 1996)
Prime Minister's Office: Advisory Council on Women's Affairs, 41; Commission Report on Japan's Goals in the 21st Century, 146–47, 150; Office for Gender Equality, 88–89, 90, 119
Prisoners, released, and National Plan of Action Plan on Human Rights Education, 72, 73
Pro-life groups, 122
Promotion of Resolution for Issues concerning Victims of Wartime Sexual Coercion (Japan, 2001), 2, 40
Prostitution: and Association on Men and Prostitution, 78; illegal female migrants as sex workers in Japan, 99; and information on women's human rights in Japan in 1990's, 75; as issue for overlapping global women's networks, 25; issue raised by international women's groups in 1891 and 1899, 22; as part of Japanese culture, 40–41; shelters and counseling for women, in Japan, 46–47. *See also* Child pornography; Child prostitution
Prostitution, child, *see* Child prostitution; World Congress against Commercial Sexual Exploitation of Children (CSEC) (First, Stockholm, 1996)
Protocol to Prevent, Suppress and Punish Trafficking in Persons, Especially Women and Children (2000), 30
Purification of Social Moral Environment Campaign (Japan), 49

Racial discrimination: draft bill against (2002), 2; history of minorities in Japan, 96–99; and ideology of homogeneity in Japan, 95; and International Covenant on Civil and Political Rights (ICCPR), 34; intersection with gender, 8, 35–36; laws, lobbying for, 5; right-wing support for racial purity in Japan, 101;

use of international conventions in anti-discrimination cases in Japan, 100; xenophobia as source of, 114. *See also* International Convention on the Elimination of All Forms of Racial Discrimination (ICERD) (1965); Intersectional discrimination; Minorities; World Conference against Racism, Racial Discrimination, Xenophobia, and Related Intolerance (WCAR) (Durban, 2001)
Rape, in war, *see* War, and violence against women
Rape Crisis Center (Gokan Shien Center), 123
REAL Women of Canada, 33
Reform Forum 21, 120
Refugee children, 64
Regulatory Law on Adult Entertainment Business, 41
Report by the Council for Gender Equality to the Prime Minister: "Towards a Society without Violence against Women" (1999), 44, 87
Report on Comfort Women, by UN Permanent Court of Arbitration, 132
Report on Japan's Goals in the 21st Century, 146–47
Report on the Mission to the Democratic People's Republic of Korea, the Republic of Korea, and Japan on the issue of Military Sexual Slavery in Wartime, 133–34
Reproductive health: children's, right-wing backlash against, 34; as example of domestic mobilization of global norms, 135; and information proliferation on women's human rights in Japan in 1990s, 75; as reframing of issue of birth control, 126–27; translated as "repurodakutibu herusu/raitsu," 127. *See also* Birth control pill; Reproductive rights
Reproductive rights: as example of domestic mobilization of global norms, 135; and information on women's human rights in Japan in 1990s, 75; introduction to Japanese vocabulary, 74; as issue for overlapping global women's networks, 25; as women's human rights issue, 27. *See also* Birth control pill; Reproductive health
Research Action Institute for the Koreans in Japan (RAIK), 112, 118
Research Group on Multiple Discrimination against Minority Women, of IMADR, 115, 118
Right-wing backlash: against children's human rights, 145; against foreign workers in Japan, 99; against recognition of comfort women in Japan, 60–61; against women's rights, 33–34; in Japan, issues of, 101
Rio de Janeiro Conference, *see* Conference on Environment and Development (Rio de Janeiro, 1992)
Robinson, Mary, 104
Role of the United Nations Development Fund for Women in Eliminating Violence against Women (Japan, 1995), 52
Roman Catholic backlash, against women's rights, 33
Rule 10–10: on prevention of sexual harassment in Japanese bureaucracy, 45; on prevention of sexual harassment in Japanese schools, 46
Ryukyu Islands: denial of Okinawans' status as ethnic or indigenous people of, 3, 109–10; as U.S. military base, 110

Sakai, Mitsuru, 100
Sakigake (political party), 121, 128, 138
San Francisco Peace Treaty, 110
Sanger, Margaret, 53
Sankei Shimbun (newspaper), 60
Santama Group Concerned with Work and Sexual Discrimination: publication of "Stopping Sexual Harassment," 55–56, 124; sexual harassment survey, 56
Sapporo city government: initiatives on women's issues, 50; Women's Planning Section, and prevention of violence against women, 89–90
School Breakdown (Gakko Hokai), 145
School refusal, 64
Schools: alternative, 64, 65; assimilation policy, 111, 112; Japan, sexual harassment in, 45–46; school refusal, 64
SDP, *see* Social Democratic Party
Second Tokyo Lawyers Association: Commission on Children's Rights, 65; draft sexual harassment legislation, 56; hotline on sexual harassment, 56
Seimei Soncho no Hi Jikko Jinkai (Association for the Day for Respect for Life), 122, 135
Senda, Kako, 58
Sex crimes, handling of, 47–48, 89

Sex education: advances in, 77; based on human rights, 144; survey on sexual activity of adolescents, 81
Sex tours, Asian, 41. *See also* End Child Prostitution in Asian Tourism (ECPAT)
Sexual assault: forced sex in marriage, 62; and information proliferation on women's human rights in Japan in 1990s, 75. *See also* Military sexual slavery; Sex crimes, handling of
Sexual harassment: and activities of Feminist Therapy Research Association, 79; and activities of Japan Civil Liberties Union, 78; and activities of National Women's Education Center, 79; cases, in Japan, 56–57; concept of "favorable working environment," 56; as difficult area for reform, 7; as example of domestic mobilization of global norms, 8, 135; as former taboo subject, 39; grassroots mobilization against, 55–57, 138; hotline, 56; and information proliferation on women's human rights in Japan in 1990s, 75; institutional changes, in Japan, 44–46; Japan, and public policy paper on gender equality, 40; legislation, in Japan, 50; NGO support and education groups, 3; opposition to legislation against, 122, 135; policies, in Japanese companies, 44–45; prevention training, for civil servants, 92–93; prevention training, in Japanese universities and schools, 45–46; previously described as "unpleasant sexual experiences," 5, 135; prominence as issue due to NGO support of court cases, 124; redefined as human rights issue, 125, 139; role of domestic social movements in mobilizing against, 123; survey, Japan (1993), 44; translated as "seku hara," 39. *See also* Equal Employment Opportunity Law (revised 1997)
Sexual Harassment Summit (Japan), 56
Sexual orientation: draft bill against discrimination (2002), 2; gay, lesbian, transgender and transsexual movement, 149–50; as tightly monitored issue in United Nations by Asian, African, Islamic states and Vatican, 37
Sexual self-determination, and view of child prostitution, 144
Shelters, *see* Women's shelters
Shimin Gaiko Centre, 118
Shimizu, Sumiko, 66, 127, 129, 130, 138
Shin Jujin Kyokai (New Women Association), 40
Sixteen Days of Activism (1991), 24
Slavery: recognition as crime in WCAR Declaration and Programme of Action, 112–13; reparation for, not covered in UN conventions, 35, 112. *See also* Military sexual slavery
Social Democratic Party (SDP), 63, 121, 129, 138
Social education, of women, 71
South American Japanese (Nikkeijin), 99
South East Asia, source of illegal female migrant workers, 99
Special Law on the Immigration Control of Those Who Have Lost Japanese Nationality and Others on the Basis of the Treaty of Peace with Japan (1991), 111
Special Measures Regarding the U.S. Military Use and Expropriation of Land (Japan, 1997), 110
Special rapporteur system, of United Nations, *see* UN Special Rapporteur System
Sri Lankan women, as imported brides in Japan, 99
Stalking: legislation against, in Japan, 51; and public policy paper on gender equality, 40. *See also* Anti-Stalking Law (2000)
State, theories of: bureaucratic dominance, 12–13; constructivist, 16–19; interest groups theory of state, 15–16; network state/triumvirate of bureaucracy-LDP-business, 14; party politics, 12–14. *See also* Constructivist theory of state; Government, Japan
Status and Policy Concerning Women (Fujin no Genjo to Seisaku) (1990), 44
Status and Policy Concerning Women (Josei no Genjo to Seisaku) (1993), 41
"Status of women," introduced to Japan by World Conference of the International Year of the Woman (1975), 41
Stockholm conference, *see* World Congress against Commercial Sexual Exploitation of Children (CSEC) (First, Stockholm, 1996)
Stop Children's Sexual Abuse, 66, 124
Stop the Academic Harassment, 93
"Stopping Sexual Harassment" (booklet), 55–56, 124
Students: awareness of domestic violence, 63; views on child prostitution and pornography, 66. *See also* Child pornography; Child

prostitution; Children's human rights; Education; Sex education
Subcommission on the Promotion and Protection of Human Rights, 105
Subcommittee on Violence against Women, 42
Suihesha (Buraka NGO group), 70
Suzuki, Muneo, 107
Sweden, as co-organizer of World Congress against Commercial Sexual Exploitation of Children (1996), 128
Symposium on Violence against Women, 89

Taiwan, as Japanese colony, 97
Tamura, Tajiro, 58
Tanaka, Kakuei, 54
Tanigaki, Shinichi, 66
"Testimony on Sexual Harassment" (booklet), 56
Toitsu Kyokai (United Church), 145
Tokuoka, Takao, 151
Tokyo Buraku Liberation League, 73
Tokyo metropolitan government: child abuse prevention department, 51; founded Tokyo Human Rights Education Center, 72; inclusion of sexual orientation in human rights program, 150; Labor Economics Bureau, publication of sexual harassment statistics, 56; publication of sexual harassment manual, 57; survey on domestic violence, 63
Tokyo War Crimes Tribunal, 29
Tokyo Women Foundation, 79, 148
"Towards a Society without Violence against Women" (Japan, 1999), 44, 87
Trafficking in women: and human rights education, 73; as issue for overlapping global women's networks, 25. *See also* Comfort women
Transgender rights movement, 150
Translation, of human rights publications, 124
Transnational social movements, as educational process, 142–43
Transsexual and Transgender Support Group, 150
Transsexual rights movement, 150
Tsujimoto, Kiyomi, 138
Turkey, on definition of racism, 37

Ueno, Chizuko, 93
UN Children's Fund (UNICEF): campaign on violence against women, 26; involvement in World Congress against Commercial Sexual Exploitation of Children (1996), 128
UN Commission for Trade and Development (UNCTAD), 26
UN Commission on Human Rights: and issue of violence against women, 26, 132; meetings attended by Buraku Liberation League, 97; Subcommission on the Prevention of Discrimination and Protection of Minorities, 107
UN Commission on the Status of Women (CSW): Agreed Conclusions on Gender and All Forms of Discrimination, 36; and issue of violence against women, 23, 26; mandate, 22; as marginalized within UN system, 22. *See also* Division for the Advancement of Women (DAW)
UN Committee against Torture, absence of mention of women's rights, 22
UN Committee on Economic and Social Rights, absence of mention of women's rights, 22
UN Committee on the Elimination of All Forms of Discrimination against Women (CEDAW), 10
UN Decade for Human Rights Education (1995–2004), 32, 69, 72, 94, 108
UN Development Fund for Women (UNIFEM): campaign on violence against women, 26; dissemination of information at Geneva World Conference on Human Rights (1993), 24–25; and Expert Group Meeting on Race and Gender (Zagreb, 2000), 35; on forms of violence against women, 28
UN Development Program (UNDP), 26
UN Fund for Children (UNICEF): and Asia-Pacific Symposium on Trafficking in Persons, 91–92; and First World Congress against Commercial Sexual Exploitation of Children (Stockholm, 1996), 30–31; UN General Assembly Special Session on Children (2000), 34
UN High Commissioner for Human Rights, 32
UN High Commissioner for Refugees (UNHCR), 26, 150
UN Human Rights Committee, 10, 22
UN Permanent Court of Arbitration, Report on Comfort Women, 132
UN Population Fund (UNFPA), 26
UN Special Rapporteur on Systematic Rape,

Sexual Slavery and Slavery-like Practices during Armed Conflict: report on wartime sexual slavery, 134. *See also* UN Special Rapporteur on Violence against Women
UN Special Rapporteur on Violence against Women: redefinition of "comfort system" as "military sexual slavery," 139; report on comfort women, 132, 133; report on domestic violence, 77, 78. *See also* UN Special Rapporteur on Systematic Rape, Sexual Slavery and Slavery-like Practices during Armed Conflict
UN Special Rapporteur System, 140
UN Voluntary Fund for Indigenous Populations, 107
UN Working Group on Indigenous Populations, 107
UNCTAD, *see* UN Commission for Trade and Development
UNDP, *see* UN Development Program
UNESCO: and human rights education, 31; and lifelong education for women, 48
UNFPA, *see* UN Population Fund
UNHCR, *see* UN High Commissioner for Refugees
UNICEF, *see* UN Fund for Children
UNIFEM, *see* UN Development Fund for Women
United Church (Toitsu Kyokai), 145
United Nations: change in attitude to women and children's rights, 20; separation of women's and human rights, 22. *See also names beginning with UN*
Universal Declaration of Human Rights (1948), 69
Universities: equal access for women, 70–71; human rights departments and programs, 70; Japan, sexual harassment in, 45–46, 56–57
"Untouchables," *see* Caste
Utari people, 106

Vatican: monitoring of issue of sexual orientation, 37; opposition to children's sex education, 34
Viagra, approval in Japan, 55, 128
Vienna conference, *see* World Conference on Human Rights (Vienna, 1993)
Vienna Declaration and Platform for Action (1993), 25, 69, 94
Violence against women: and activities of Beijing Japan Accountability Caucus (JAC), 78; and activities of National Women's Shelters Network, 80; change in attitude towards, in Japan, 39–52; denounced at World Summit for Social development (Copenhagen, 1995), 28; denounced in Programme for Action of Fourth World Conference on Women (Beijing, 1995), 28; emergence as issue at UN conferences, 23; as human rights issue, 25, 28, 41; increase of discourse on, 4; term introduced to Japan, 41; treated as foreign issue in Japan, 41–42. *See also* Domestic violence; Female genital mutilation; Military sexual slavery; Sexual harassment; War, and violence against women
Violence against Women in All Its Forms (NGO experts meeting, 1991), 23
Violence against Women in War-Net Japan, 3, 134, 135
Violence against Women-Net Japan, 80
Violence from Husbands or Partners Survey Research Group (Otto (koibito) kara no Boryoku), 62
Violence within the Family with Special Emphasis on Women (NGO experts meeting, 1986), 23
"Vision of Gender Equality: Creating New Values for the 21st Century" (Japan, 1996): address of Prime Minister Hashimoto Ryutaro (1997), 1, 2; on human rights of women and children in Japan, 2; incorporation of domestic violence issue, 63; and issue of violence against women, 42; legislative changes as result of, 40; as major policy document, 44, 146–47, 150; on need to educate public and civil servants, 86, 87

War, and violence against women: as issue for overlapping global women's networks, 25; issue raised by international women's groups in 1913, 22; recognized by international tribunals, 29. *See also* Military sexual slavery
Waseda University: committees on sexual harassment prevention, 93–94; Women and Human Rights student group, 63
WCAR, *see* World Conference against Racism, Racial Discrimination, Xenophobia, and Related Intolerance (Durban, 2001)
WHO, World Health Organization
Williams, Jody, 143

Women and Tourism conference (1988), 59
Women Democratic Congress, 63
"Women Employment Management and the Communication Gap" (1993), 44
Women in Law and Development in Africa, 25
"Women's Action Agenda 21" (1992), 24
Women's Assistance Unit (Japan), 47
Women's Career Foundation, 56
Women's Caucus for Gender Justice, 80
Women's centers: and grassroots education of women, 49, 74, 85; initiatives on domestic violence, 50; programs on domestic violence, 50, 62–63. *See also* Women's shelters
Women's Christian Temperance Union (Japan), 59
Women's Coalition for Abortion Rights and Contraceptive Pills (Chupiren) (Japan), 54
Women's groups: as nonparty grassroots organizations, 15; as political interest group, 14. *See also* Feminism; Women's movement, Japan; Women's movement, U.S.
Women's human rights: and activities of Association for Research on the Impact of War and Military Bases on Women's Human Rights, 80; affirmed at World Human Rights Conference in Vienna (1993), 139; contribution of NGO participation in world conferences to, 5; effect of leverage politics in recognition of, 131; issue of compatibility with children's human rights, 145; and issue of violence against women, 41; lack of consensus on definition of terms, 143; legislative changes in Japan, 1997–2001, 2; ministerial responsibility for, 70; and National Action Plan on human rights, 72, 73; NGO representatives at Vienna World Conference on Human Rights, 102. *See also* Anti-Stalking Law (2000); Basic Law for a Gender-Equal Society (1999); Birth control pill; Domestic Violence Prevention Law (2001); Equal Employment Opportunity Law (revised 1997); Law to Promote Human Rights Education (2000); Promotion of Resolution for Issues concerning Victims of Wartime Sexual Coercion (Japan, 2001); Women's rights
Women's International War Crimes Tribunal on Japan's Military Sexual Slavery (2002), 10, 134
Women's movement: international, history of, 21–22; Korea, role in recognition of comfort women, 124
Women's movement, Japan: avoidance of issue of race, 98–99; as divided on issue of military sexual slavery, 8, 136; divisions in, 6, 8; and grassroots education of women, 74; introduction of term to Japanese vocabulary, 74; mainstream, and ethnicity, race and sexual issues, 142; scholars, and relationships with NGOs, 139
Women's movement, U.S.: impact on development of sexual violence issues in Japan, 123. *See also* Women's movement, Japan
Women's Online Media, 79, 86
Women's rights: absence of mention in human rights treaties and committee agendas, 22; backlash against, 33–34; equality/equal opportunity approach at early international women's conferences and conventions, 22–23; global epistemic network and international conferences on, 21–26; as human rights, 20–21, 27–30; and intersectionality of multiple forms of discrimination, 36. *See also* Women's human rights
Women's shelters: and information on women's human rights in Japan in 1990's, 75; modeled after U.S.'s, 123–24; as NGO effort, 124; and Symposium on Violence against Women, 89
Women's studies: establishment of, 71; and non-governmental organizations, 85; provided at women's centers, 49. *See also* Education
Working Group on Contemporary Forms of Slavery: and issue of Japanese comfort women, 131, 132; on redefinition of comfort women as military sexual slavery, 134
Workplace discrimination legislation, Japan, 50
World Conference against Racism, Racial Discrimination, Xenophobia, and Related Intolerance (WCAR) (Durban, 2001): and CERD statement on gender and racial discrimination, 35; and framing of minority rights in Japan, 5; intersectional discrimination addressed in Programme of Action, 116–17, 141; Japanese NGO mobilization around, 95, 103–18; official themes, 36–37; reports, 10
World Conference of Indigenous People (1981), 98

World Conference of the International Year of the Woman (1975), 41
World Conference on Children (First, 1990), 141
World Conference on Human Rights (Vienna, 1993): and human rights education, 32; impact of, 5; mobilization around issues by women's activists, 26; and mobilization of global norms on human rights in Japan, 126; preparation by international women's NGOs, 24; statement on military sexual slavery, 131–32; and transnational feminist organization, 139, 141; Vienna Declaration and Platform for Action (1993), 25; Women's Caucus, importance of, 25; on women's rights as human rights, 20
World Conference on Women (First, Mexico, 1975), 22
World Conference on Women (FWCW) (Fourth, Beijing, 1995): effect on domestic social movements in Japan, 138; effect on Japanese mobilization against sexual harassment, 8; and establishment of women's studies in Japan, 71; impact of, 5; influence on Japanese women's human rights, 103; and Japanese mobilization against domestic violence, 9; and mobilization of global norms on human rights in Japan, 126; Platform for Action, redefinition of forms of violence against women as international human rights issues, 28; Programme of Action, 28; and transnational feminist organization, 139, 141; and women's human rights norms in Japan, 88. *See also* Beijing-Plus-Five Conference on Women (New York, 2000)
World Conference on Women (Second, Copenhagen, 1980): first appearance of issue of violence against women, 23
World Conference on Women (Third, Nairobi, 1985): equality/equal opportunity approach to women's rights, 22; inclusion of issue of violence against women in Forward-Looking Strategies, 23
World Congress against Commercial Sexual Exploitation of Children (CSEC) (First, Stockholm, 1996): Declaration and Agenda for Action, 30–31; and domestic mobilization of global norms, 126; and impact of global norms on Japanese government, 5, 128; Japanese delegation, 66–67; and transnational feminist organization, 139, 141
World Congress against Commercial Sexual Exploitation of Children (CSEC) (Second, Yokohama, 2001): as follow-up to successful first conference, 10; hosted by Japanese government, 131; reiteration of efforts against sexual exploitation of children, 31
World Congress of the International Family Planning Association (Tokyo, 1955), 7
World Constitution for Women, *see* Convention on the Elimination of All Forms of Discrimination Against Women (CEDAW) (1979)
World Health Organization (WHO): report on health and violence (2001), 26; on the safety of the birth control pill, 54
World Organization of the Billings Ovulation Method, 33
World Report on Health and Violence (2001), 26
World Summit for Social Development (Copenhagen, 1995): Declaration and Program of Action, linking of violence against women and social issues, 28; and transnational feminist organization, 141
World Trade Organization, mobilization against by NGOs, 140, 143
World's Women's Christian Temperance Union (1891), 22

Xenophobia, as source of racism, 114

Yasukuni Shrine, 101
Yokoyama, Knock, 57
Yoshimi, Yoshiaki, 59, 61
Youth Policy Headquarters (Japan), 62
Yun Chung-Ok, 59